CakePHP Application Development

Step-by-step introduction to rapid web development using the open-source MVC CakePHP framework

Ahsanul Bari

Anupom Syam

PUBLISHING

BIRMINGHAM - MUMBAI

CakePHP Application Development

Step-by-step introduction to rapid web development using the open-source MVC CakePHP framework

First published: July 2008

Production Reference: 1080708

Published by Packt Publishing Ltd.
32 Lincoln Road
Olton
Birmingham, B27 6PA, UK.

ISBN 978-1-847193-89-6

www.packtpub.com

Cover Image by Michelle O'Kane (michelle@kofe.ie)

Credits

Authors

Ahsanul Bari

Anupom Syam

Reviewers

John Mark Diaz

Junal Rahman

Senior Acquisition Editor

David Barnes

Development Editor

Nikhil Bangera

Technical Editors

Ajay Shanker

Rasika Ramesh Sathe

Editorial Team Leader

Mithil Kulkarni

Project Manager

Abhijeet Deobhakta

Project Coordinator

Lata Basantani

Indexer

Rekha Nair

Proofreader

Camille Guy

Production Coordinator

Aparna Bhagat

Cover Work

Aparna Bhagat

About the Authors

Ahsanul Bari is a web application developer from Dhaka, Bangladesh. After graduating from North South University with a bachelor's degree in Computer Science, he has been involved in developing various web applications for local businesses. At a very early stage of his career, he felt the need for tools and techniques to build structured and maintainable web applications. That is when he found out about CakePHP. It was love at first sight and he decided to use CakePHP for his future projects. He never had to look back, and from then on, he has been heavily using CakePHP for all kinds of projects. Most notably, using CakePHP, he developed an ERP solution for companies involved in urban and land development.

Apart from that, he has also 'irregularly' contributed to the CakePHP Documentation Team. He is also an 'irregular' blogger (`http://ahsanity.com` and `http://ahsanity.wordpress.com`). Just when people start to think that he has given up blogging, he is known to write a post from nowhere! Among his friends and colleagues, he is known as a fanboy for CakePHP.

Currently, he is working at Trippert Labs, where he has been involved in making a travel-based blogging system, `http://www.trippert.com`.

This book could not have been possible without the help and support of many people. I would like to thank Hasin Hyder for encouraging us to write this book. Thanks go to David Barnes, our acquisition editor, for always being the best critic, and giving us the push when we needed one. A special thanks to the hardworking people of PacktPub who made this book a reality. Thanks go to all my colleagues at TrippertLabs, who are eagerly waiting for a treat when the book is out. I would also like to thank all my friends for always encouraging me to carry on writing. I would also like to thank the CakePHP community for developing and maintaining such a wonderful framework. But, I will not thank Anupom, the co-author of this book, because I never thank him for anything.

Lastly, I would like to apologize to the three most dearest persons in my life: my mom, my sister, and my jaan Simin. I have written this book during the time that I was supposed to spend with them.

Anupom Syam is a web application developer from Dhaka, Bangladesh. He started programming back in 1998 in C when he was a high school kid. In his early university years, he met Java and fell in love immediately. Through the years, he has become proficient in various aspects of Java (ME, SE, and EE). Early in his career, he was engaged mainly in building localized mobile applications. Over time, his interest in web technologies grew and he did not hesitate to jump onto the Web 2.0 bandwagon. Over the last five years, he has been working with different startups and building web/mobile applications. He currently works as a Development Engineer at Trippert, Inc. where he has been involved in developing a travel-based blogging system http://www.trippert.com (which is developed using CakePHP) as the lead back-end programmer.

He loves to build rich-client web apps with JavaScript/AJAX in the front end and CakePHP/RoR/MySQL in the back end. He still uses Java heavily for his personal fun-time projects. He also maintains blogs: http://anupom.wordpress.com and http://syamantics.com. Besides programming, he is interested in many things, ranging from the most recent scientific discoveries to ancient Vedic philosophies.

First of all, thanks to my parents and my sweet little sister Antara, who stood by patiently while my weekends were occupied with writing inexplicable technical minutiae! A very special thanks to Hasin Hayder, without his inspiration and encouragement I would never find myself writing a book! Thanks to my colleagues, coworkers, and friends— your endless support kept me going. David Barnes, our acquisition editor at Packt, has my deepest respect and gratitude for his patience, understanding, perseverance and suggestions that had really taught me how to write computer books! Not to mention, the heart and soul effort from people of Packt Publication—Abhijeet Deobhakta, Lata Basantani and Nikhil Bangera who made this book (at last) a reality. Also, thanks to our vigorous and veteran technical editors and reviewers: Rasika, Felix, and Junal, without whom this book would be much less accurate.

And finally, I wish to give my sincerest thanks to the developers of the brilliant PHP framework—CakePHP.

About the Reviewer

Junal Rahman is a Computer Science graduate from Independent University of Bangladesh. His areas of expertise include programming with PHP framework and Facebook applications. He has worked for several software companies as a Web Application Developer. During his undergraduate studies, Junal fell in love with .NET programming, but as soon as he started his internship, he fell in love with PHP. He currently works as a Development Engineer at Trippert Labs. At Trippert, Junal collaboratively works to create Facebook applications. He also maintains a blog that can be found at http://junal.wordpress.com. Apart from keeping up with the ever changing field of information technology, he spends much of his private life pursing his interests in screenplay and script writing. In the future, Junal hopes to create films and short dramas, and eventually make his very own movies.

Four years ago, I met a fairy. Since then she has been with me as a shadow. I would like to thank her.

*We dedicate this book to all the amazing people of the vibrant CakePHP community,
who are working selflessly for other's betterment*

Table of Contents

Preface

Cake is a rapid development framework for PHP that uses well-known design patterns and provides a structured framework that enables PHP users at all levels to rapidly develop robust web applications, without any loss of flexibility. It means you can code faster, your code is better, and it makes writing Web 2.0-style apps a snap.

This book builds on your knowledge as a PHP developer to provide a fast-paced, step-by-step tutorial in building CakePHP applications. The book is packed with example code and demo applications, so that you can see techniques in action.

What This Book Covers

Chapter 1 will take a look at: what CakePHP is, how CakePHP helps in structuring and maintaining the code, how CakePHP helps in reducing the development time and effort, and which version of Cake should be used.

Chapter 2 will take a quick look at setting up Cake in our local machine.

Chapter 3 will cover how to develop a small application that we'll call the "CakeTooDoo". It will be a simple to-do-list application, which will keep record of the things that we need to do—a shopping list, chapters to study for an exam, etc.

Chapter 4 will cover the nuts and bolts of the CakePHP controller.

Chapter 5 will be a thorough experience of some of the model basics.

Chapter 6 will take an in-depth look at various types of associations and their uses.

Chapter 7 will closely look at the different view components in CakePHP.

Chapter 8 will cover one of the shell scripts called bake. We will build a simple blog using this tool where a user can post articles and comments.

Chapter 9 will look at creating a new web application called 'Quickwall'.

Chapter 10 will cover adding user authentication to our web application — Quickwall.

Chapter 11 will take a look at how to use JavaScript and AJAX with CakePHP.

Chapter 12 will take a look at adding more features to the Quickwall application.

Who is This Book for

If you already know PHP and want to develop cutting-edge Web 2.0 applications, or see how to write code in a faster, more productive way, then this book is ideal for you.

Conventions

In this book, you will find a number of styles of text that distinguish between different kinds of information. Here are some examples of these styles, and an explanation of their meaning.

There are three styles for code. Code words in text are shown as follows: "We can include other contexts through the use of the `include` directive."

A block of code will be set as follows:

```php
<?php else: ?>
  <dl>
  <?php foreach($question['Answer'] as $answer) : ?>
    <dt><span><?php e($answer['User']['username']); ?></span></dt>
    <dd>
```

When we wish to draw your attention to a particular part of a code block, the relevant lines or items will be made bold:

```php
<?php if($loggedIn): ?>
        <?php e($html->link('Your Questions', array('controller'
            => 'users', 'action' => 'show', $loggedIn))); ?>|
        <?php e($html->link('Search', array('controller' =>
```

Any command-line input and output is written as follows:

```
# cp /usr/src/asterisk-addons/configs/cdr_mysql.conf.sample
   /etc/asterisk/cdr_mysql.conf
```

New terms and important words are introduced in a bold-type font. Words that you see on the screen, in menus or dialog boxes for example, appear in our text like this: "clicking the **Next** button moves you to the next screen".

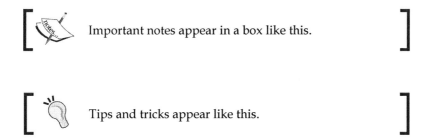

Important notes appear in a box like this.

Tips and tricks appear like this.

Reader Feedback

Feedback from our readers is always welcome. Let us know what you think about this book, what you liked or may have disliked. Reader feedback is important for us to develop titles that you really get the most out of.

To send us general feedback, simply drop an email to `feedback@packtpub.com`, making sure to mention the book title in the subject of your message.

If there is a book that you need and would like to see us publish, please send us a note in the **SUGGEST A TITLE** form on `www.packtpub.com` or email `suggest@packtpub.com`.

If there is a topic that you have expertise in and you are interested in either writing or contributing to a book, see our author guide on `www.packtpub.com/authors`.

Customer Support

Now that you are the proud owner of a Packt book, we have a number of things to help you to get the most from your purchase.

Downloading the Example Code for the Book

Visit `http://www.packtpub.com/files/code/3896_Code.zip` to directly download the example code.

The downloadable files contain instructions on how to use them.

Errata

Although we have taken every care to ensure the accuracy of our contents, mistakes do happen. If you find a mistake in one of our books—maybe a mistake in text or code—we would be grateful if you would report this to us. By doing this you can save other readers from frustration, and help to improve subsequent versions of this book. If you find any errata, report them by visiting http://www.packtpub.com/support, selecting your book, clicking on the **Submit Errata** link, and entering the details of your errata. Once your errata are verified, your submission will be accepted and the errata are added to the list of existing errata. The existing errata can be viewed by selecting your title from http://www.packtpub.com/support.

Questions

You can contact us at questions@packtpub.com if you are having a problem with some aspect of the book, and we will do our best to address it.

1
Introduction to CakePHP

Most technical books start by outlining the good features of the concerned technology, so that the reader is convinced that the technology is worth learning, and the book is worth reading. But unlike those books, this one starts with a warning:

> "Once readers have gone through the book, there will be no turning back! Web development will never be the same again. Developing a web application will become so easy, that it might make the readers very lazy. As a matter of fact, readers might even forget the basic syntaxes of PHP! And the word Cake will have a completely new meaning to them"

If you are still determined to read along, you are welcome! But do not blame us later; you have been warned!

We are going to start our journey into CakePHP by trying to understand what CakePHP is and how it will help us develop web applications faster, that are also easy to manage and maintain. To be more specific, in this chapter, we are going to see:

- What is CakePHP?
- How CakePHP helps in structuring and maintaining the code?
- How CakePHP helps in reducing the development time and effort?
- And, which version of Cake should be used?

What is CakePHP?

According to the official CakePHP website (`http://cakephp.org`):

> "Cake is a rapid development framework for PHP which uses commonly known design patterns like Active Record, Association Data Mapping, Front Controller and MVC. Our primary goal is to provide a structured framework that enables PHP users at all levels to rapidly develop robust web applications, without any loss to flexibility."

Someone who is new to frameworks might not understand parts of the definition. But understanding a few key terms will make the job much easier.

A PHP Framework

A PHP framework is a collection of code, libraries, classes, and run-time environment that helps developers build web applications faster. The main idea behind using frameworks is to provide the developers with commonly used functionalities and a basic structure that they can build their application on. Most PHP developers, who have some experience, have their own set of libraries and structure to help them develop faster, as they can use their code base (and experience) from one project to another. But, building a web application on an open-source framework like CakePHP has its obvious benefits. By doing so, the developers not only use their own experience, but also the experiences of many other developers who have used and developed the framework. Also, the framework is much more reliable as it is used and tested by many application developers. Besides, using a framework like CakePHP has the advantage that all the developers involved in a project have to follow the same conventions and rules to structure the application. It makes it very easy for new developers to settle down if they are familiar with the conventions of the framework.

Common Design Patterns

A design pattern is a general solution to a commonly occurring problem in web development. A design pattern is not a complete code, rather it is a description for how to solve a problem that can be used in many different situations. In web development, there are many common design patterns that are used to solve repeating and common problems. CakePHP has many of these design patterns integrated into it. Some of them are mentioned in the above definition: Active Record, Association Data Mapping, Front Controller and MVC. Among them, MVC, which stands for Model View Controller, is at the core of CakePHP. We will soon discuss MVC, and other important design patterns, in this chapter. The other design patterns will be discussed throughout the book.

Rapid Web Development

The integration of common design patterns into CakePHP means that developers need not waste time in trying to solve problems that are commonly present in almost all web projects. These are already solved in CakePHP! As a result, the developer can focus on the specific business logic of the application, rather than being busy in trying to reinvent the wheel. This results in much faster and rapid application development.

Works with PHP4 and PHP5

Though it is not mentioned in the definition, CakePHP works out of the box with both PHP4 and PHP5. So, as long the developer follows the CakePHP convention, their application will be easily portable between the two versions of PHP. Unlike many PHP frameworks, the developer need not worry about compatibility issues. Web servers with either PHP4 or PHP5 will gladly run CakePHP-based applications. But having said that, it is always a better idea to use PHP5 if compatibility is not an issue for the project. Since most CakePHP apps are custom applications, PHP4 compatibility is normally not an important factor. So, using PHP5 for CakePHP application is definitely recommended.

CakePHP is Free and Open Source

Yes, that is right: CakePHP is an open-source project and it is free for anyone who wants to use it. It is distributed under the MIT License. That means that not only will people be able to use it free of charge, but they will also be able to look at the source code of CakePHP, and find out how the magic works.

Now, that we have a better understanding of the main concepts behind CakePHP, do have a second look at the definition! It should be much easier to understand. More importantly, we now have a good understanding of what to expect from CakePHP, as we now know what it is!

Improved Code Structure

PHP is a wonderful programming language for server-side web development. One of its benefits is that PHP is very easy to learn. Any person with some basic programming skills (even without it) can start making dynamic web pages. PHP gives developers a lot of flexibility in the way that they code. In other words, it does not restrict the developer to follow a certain structure. This is also one of its major drawbacks. As inexperienced programmers start to built bigger applications, most of the time, the code becomes so unstructured that it becomes very hard to debug or modify even a small change. The same situation also occurs with experienced PHP developers, when the application becomes complex. The situation gets even worse, when multiple developers work in a single project, each following their own way of coding. The main reason for this problem is that PHP does not restrict the developers to follow a certain structure.

CakePHP helps to solve this problem by restricting the developers to follow a strict structure. By doing so, it makes sure that the overall code of the project has a structure that is easy to manage and maintain.

The most important design pattern that CakePHP uses to maintain a structured code is the MVC (Model View Controller) pattern

Understanding the MVC Pattern

The MVC (Model View Controller) pattern is a commonly used design pattern in software development, where the code is separated into three major parts: models, views, and controllers. The exact purpose of each part depends on the implementation, as it may vary from one framework to another. Here, we are going to describe the way CakePHP implements the MVC pattern. So, this is not a general discussion on MVC pattern, rather we are only going to see Cake's own MVC implementation. As we have already mentioned, CakePHP separates the code into three separate parts: models, views, and controllers.

Models

In CakePHP, a model represents a particular database table. Each database table should have a model representing it. So, in CakePHP, every database table has its own model. All PHP code related to accessing, adding, modifying or deleting records from the table are situated in the model. The model also contains code that defines its relationship with other models. Other than that, the model also defines the data validation rules when adding or updating data for that model. Model can be thought of as the data layer of the application. The model is also the place where the business logic related to the model should be defined. For example, if we have a model to represent cars, all actions related to it like buy car, sell car etc. should be defined in the model. Models should be the place where the core business logic of an application are defined.

Controllers

Controllers, in CakePHP, control the application flow or logic of the application. Each web request is directed to a particular controller where the user input (POST or GET data) is accepted. The controller logic then decides what response is generated. The controller logic normally contains calls to models to access data, and also other functionalities like access control check etc. Lastly, the controller passes the response (output) to the view (discussed next). Controller can be thought as the control logic layer of the application. As mentioned above, the model should have all the business logic of an application. The controllers should just delegate the actions to the model, and be light. This design philosophy is sometimes referred to as the "fat models and thin controllers".

Views

Views are the outputs or responses that are sent back to the user once a request is processed. They basically consists of markup (like HTML) code with embedded PHP code, but they can also be other forms of output like XML, PDF document etc. depending on the situation. Views can be thought as the presentation layer of the application.

How It Works

So now that we have a better understanding of all the three components of CakePHP MVC, let's see how these three components work together to handle a request.

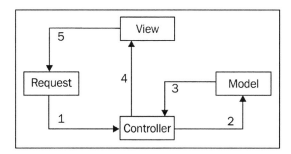

The diagram above shows how it all works together:

1. The request is dispatched to the controller, with user data (POST and GET data).
2. The controller processes the request, and calls the model to access the data.
3. The model responses to the controller's call, by sending or storing data.
4. The controller then sends the output data to the view.
5. The view outputs the data in the proper format.

As we have already seen earlier, using the MVC pattern helps to structure the code into modular segments. This allows the developer to quickly make any changes if required and as a result, debugging and modification becomes a much easier job. Using MVC also has the added benefit of reusing code. For example, a single model code can be used in any controller that needs to access the data in that model.

Another benefit of MVC is that it results in a shorter development time. But MVC is not the only tool that CakePHP has to quicken the development time. There are many more as we discuss next.

Faster Development

One of the main reasons that most of the modern web applications are built on a framework is for faster development. Using frameworks, like CakePHP, it is possible to develop web applications much faster than it would have been possible using raw PHP. Other than the MVC pattern, CakePHP comes with many other tricks and magic that aids in faster web development.

Less Configuration, More Convention

One of the main philosophies of the CakePHP design is to have minimum number of configurations. Configurations are normally required to make sure that the system is properly set up, and behaving the way we want it. But with CakePHP, these configurations are kept to minimum. In fact, the only thing that we need to get CakePHP running is to let it know the name of the database to use, and nothing else need to be specified!

CakePHP was designed in a way that it relied more on conventions than on configurations. Conventions are stuffs like the name of the database fields, name and locations of models, controllers and views. If these are named and placed according to the CakePHP conventions, Cake will automatically find and use them properly. That is why it is important to understand the naming conventions that CakePHP uses. Once we are familiar with that, we will never have to worry about configuration again.

Auto Code Generation

Just imagine how much easier it would be if we have a working code base that is specific to the application we want to develop, even before we have started to write a single line of code. Well, with CakePHP, we do not need to imagine anymore, because it is a reality. CakePHP built-in code generator is more commonly known as the baking script. All we need to do is to specify the database tables for the project, and start baking! It will automatically create the models, controllers, and views that we need. Using this generated code, we will have a running application that can insert, edit, list, and delete data from all the database tables.

Quick Access to Related Data

CakePHP has useful design patterns integrated that makes it very easy to access and modify data from the database. It has a very neat data abstraction layer, and also has support for association data mapping.

With Cake's data abstraction layer,, we will never need to write SQL queries again, to retrieve or modify data. By calling appropriate model functions, we will be able to access the data very easily. All data will be returned in nicely formatted associated arrays without any hassle.

Association data mapping is a technique by which CakePHP is able to fetch data from not only a single table, but if necessary, all (or selected) related data from other database tables as well. For example, suppose we have a posts table that contains blog posts, and another table named comments that contain all the comments. Now, if we want to fetch a single post along with all the comments of that post, all we need to do is to call a single model function that will not only return the post, but also all the related comments. CakePHP will automatically fetch all the related data from other tables, and send them along with the desired data. We no longer need to write complex or multiple SQL statements to do it.

Built-in Commonly Used Functionalities

Other than the above mentioned features, CakePHP has loads of other functionalities so that the developers do not have to waste time coding solutions to commonly found features in web applications. Some of them are mentioned below:

- **Built-in Data Validation**: CakePHP has a very extensive data validation mechanism, where we just need to specify the valid data type, and CakePHP will handle the rest.

- **Custom Page Layout**: Most of the time, an application has a common look-and-feel for all the pages. Using CakePHP's layout functionality, we just need to put the layout file in the proper location, and all the pages will use it.

- **Access Control**: If we are building an application where we need to control the access of different parts of the application, depending on the user type, we can easily accomplish this by using the Access Control List.

- **AJAX Helper**: Adding AJAX functionalities using the built-in AJAX helper (that uses Prototype and Scriptaculous) is very easy. This can be accomplished without writing a single line of JavaScript.

Other than these, there are other many useful features that help in developing an application in record time, using CakePHP.

Versions of CakePHP: 1.1 and 1.2

Now that we know all the exciting features of CakePHP, the next thing is to decide on which CakePHP version to use. There are two major versions present at the moment: the more stable 1.1, and the exciting new 1.2. Though 1.2 has been around for quite sometime, it is still in beta stage. But having said that, the Cake community is very confident of this version, and proudly declares that 1.2 is one of the most stable beta software out there. There are many production quality web applications that are running on 1.2. And, the new features and enhancements made to this version are too good to not use it. As a result, we will be using the 1.2 version in this book. Hopefully, by the time this book is out, the stable version of 1.2 will be out too. So, without any delay, download the latest CakePHP 1.2, and move to the next chapter to find out how to install it.

Summary

In this chapter, we saw what CakePHP is, and how it can help us to develop web applications that are well structured, and that are also fast to develop. We also discussed what we understand by a PHP framework and what design patterns are. We looked closely into the MVC pattern, which is an important part of CakePHP and helps to organize the code neatly. Then, we discussed the features of CakePHP that helps in developing applications faster. Lastly, we saw why we will be using CakePHP 1.2 for all the chapters in this book.

2
A Quick Installation

In the first chapter, we learned how CakePHP can help us build web applications that are well structured, and that can be developed rapidly. The next logical step for us is to install Cake, so that we can start baking delicious and yummy Cake applications.

In this chapter, we take a quick look at setting up Cake in our local machine. As we will see, installing and setting up Cake in the local machine is not a very difficult task. If we are already familiar with developing web applications in Apache, MySQL, and PHP-based environments, this chapter should be a simple walk through.

In this chapter, we will:

- Download the latest version of CakePHP 1.2
- Other software that we need to run Cake
- Configure Apache to run Cake
- Place Cake in the web root of Apache
- Run Cake for the first time

Downloading CakePHP

In this section, we will see how to download the latest version of CakePHP 1.2. Though this is a simple task, this section has another objective. You will see that this section is divided into two parts: *Time for Action* and *What Just Happened*. Throughout the rest of the book, we will be using this format to accomplish different tasks. In the *Time for Action* segment, we will show the steps involved in completing the task. In other words, the *Time for Action* segment will take you through the step-by-step process of what needs to be done. In the *What Just Happened* segment, we are going to discuss in detail about why we did take the steps. So, without any delay, here is the first of many *Time for Actions* to come:

Time for Action

1. Open up a web browser, and point to `http://cakephp.org/`. We will land in the homepage of CakePHP:

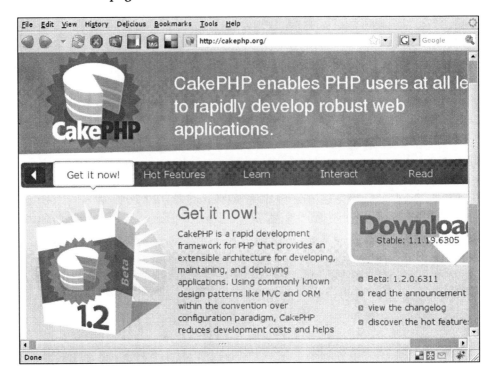

   In the **Get it now!** tab, click on the 1.2.x.xxx link (x's will be numbers, depending on the latest 1.2 release). This link is located just below the **Download** button, on the right of the page.

2. This will take you to a page that will have a list of links, as shown in the following screenshot. The latest version of CakePHP 1.2 will be highlighted. From the list, click on the compressed file type (`.zip`, `.tar.bz2` and `.tar.gz`) of your choice, to download.

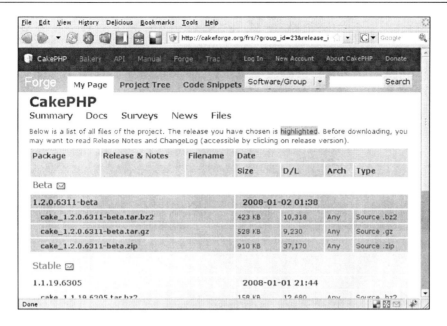

3. Once you click on it, you will be taken to the donation page, shown in the following screenshot. You have the choice to donate some money to the Cake Software Foundation. This money will be used in the betterment of CakePHP. So, if you think you can help, do not hesitate to. Or, else you can choose the **No Thanks** option.

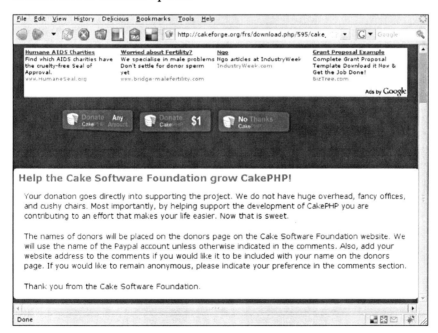

4. This will finally take you to the download page (shown in the following screenshot), that will have a link at the bottom **Download Latest Release**. Clicking on the link will open up a dialog box that will ask you to either save it or open it. Choose to save, and point to a suitable location to save the file. Lastly, press **OK**. Your cake should be on its way!

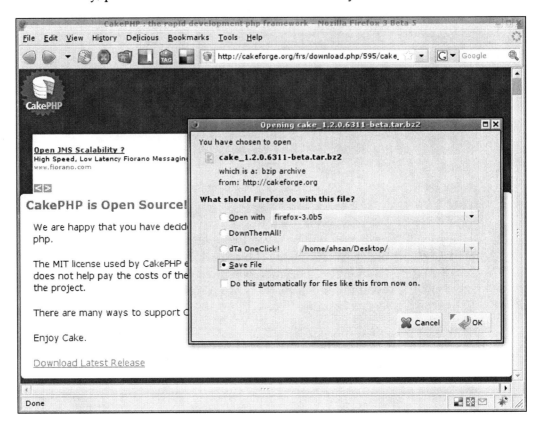

What Just Happened?

In this section, we saw the steps needed to download Cake from the official CakePHP site. The steps are all self explained. So, we do not need to really describe anything more here.

But, in later *What Just Happened* segments, we will be giving insights to why we took the actions in the corresponding *Time for Action*.

Platform Requirements

In this quick installation, it will be assumed that we are using Apache as our web server, MySQL as our database server, and of course PHP. To run Cake, the minimum version of PHP that we will need is PHP 4.3.2. All later versions of PHP, including 4.3.2, should work fine with CakePHP. CakePHP is also known to work with other web servers and database servers as well. Before you proceed further, please make sure that your local machine fulfils the requirements.

Configuring Apache

There is some tweaking that we need to perform in order to make sure that Apache runs CakePHP applications smoothly. Many Apache installations may not require the following tweaking, as they might be set as default, but it is always a good idea to check if the following settings are present.

AllowOverwrite is Set to All

We need to make sure that the web root directory, or the directory in which we plan to keep CakePHP has `AllowOverwrite` set to `all`. We can do this by checking Apache's main configuration file `http.conf`. This file should be located in the directory called `conf`, where we have installed Apache. In this file, there should be `<Directory>` option for the web root directory. As the following configuration shows, the web root (which is `L:/wamp/www` for this particular installation) has a Directory entry in which the `AllowOverwrite` option is set to `all`. If the directory under web root, in which we plan to keep Cake, has a directory entry, we need to check that one too.

```
<Directory "L:/wamp/www">

    Options Indexes FollowSymLinks
    AllowOverride all
    Order Deny,Allow
    Deny from all
    Allow from 127.0.0.1

</Directory>
```

Mod_rewrite Module is Loaded

We also need to make sure that the Apache is loading the `mod_rewrite` module. To do this, we again have to check the `http.conf` file. There should be a section in the `http.conf` file named `Dynamic Shared Object (DSO) Support`, where all the different modules that are loaded by Apache are listed. The modules that are not being loaded are commented out with # in the beginning of the line. So, we need to make sure that the `mod_rewrite` module line is not commented out. If it is, we just need to remove the # from the beginning of the line:

```
LoadModule rewrite_module modules/mod_rewrite.so
```

Make sure to restart Apache once you have made the above changes.

As long as the above configurations are set accordingly, Apache should be running CakePHP applications without any issues at all.

Setting Up Cake in Web Root

In this section, we will be placing the cake files into our web server. This is again a very easy process, if you are already familiar with Apache, PHP, extracting compressed files, and renaming directories.

Time for Action

1. Copy the newly downloaded compressed file to the web root of Apache.

2. Extract the compressed file using your favorite tool in the web root directory.

3. This will create a new directory inside the web root directory. The directory will have a name similar to **cake_1.2.x.xxxx** (depending on the latest version). Rename this directory to `myfirstcake`.

4. If we go into the `myfirstcake` directory, we should see a directory structure similar to the one shown in the following screenshot:

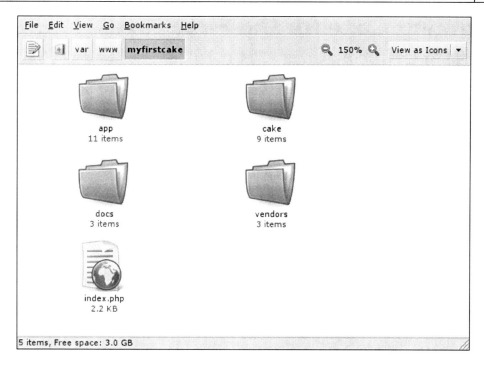

What Just Happened?

In this section, we extracted the compressed Cake file, and placed it in the web root of the Apache.

In the first step, we copied the compressed file into the web root. If you are not sure where your web root is located, you can take a look in the `http.conf` file. It should have an entry, called `DocumentRoot` that should point to the Web Root. It should be noted that `http.conf` has another entry named ServerRoot, which should not be confused with the Web Root.

In step 2, we extracted the file. There are many different extracting/decompressing software out there. I am sure we all are familiar with some. I do not want to underestimate your intelligence by describing how to use it! Once the file is extracted, we will get a new directory in the web root.

The next step, we renamed the extracted directory. By default, it will have the name similar to **cake_1.2.x.xxxx**. We named it to `myfirstcake`. Of course, we can name it to anything we want. It is a good practice to name it similar to the name of the project we are using it for.

Lastly, we had a look at the directory structure. Later in the book, we will get familiar with some of them, and know what lies inside them.

Running Cake for the First Time

Now, we are ready to check if Cake is running properly in our localhost. Let us open our web browser and point it to `http://localhost/myfirstcake/`. We should get a screen like the following:

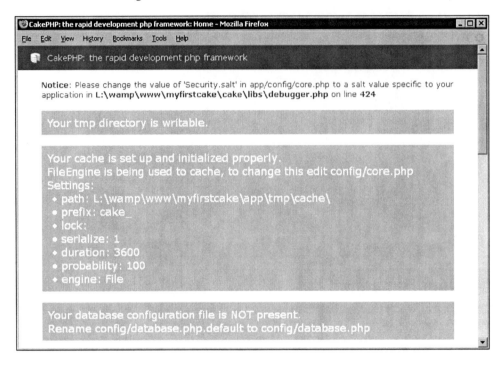

If you have got the above screen, you have successfully installed CakePHP. The important thing to notice in the above screen is to see whether the `tmp` directory is writable. This is important if you are on a UNIX-based system. Make sure Apache has write access to the `tmp` directory found inside the location .../`myfirstcake/app`.

If everything is all right, and you followed the instructions in this chapter correctly, you should have a CakePHP installation that is ready to bake some fresh cakes! And, that is exactly what we are going to do in the next chapter.

Summary

In this chapter, we saw how to install CakePHP in a local machine. We started by discussing how to download the correct version of CakePHP, and what are the other software that we will need to run Cake. We also discussed how to configure Apache for CakePHP. Lastly, we showed how to extract Cake into the Web Root, and run Cake for the first time.

3
A Quick App

The ingredients are fresh, sliced up, and in place. The oven is switched on, heated, and burning red. It is time for us to put on the cooking hat, and start making some delicious cake recipes. So, are you ready, baker?

In the first chapter, we understood the CakePHP basics, and learnt how it can make our life easier. Then, in the second chapter, we installed CakePHP in our local machine, and configured Apache to handle the heat. Now, it's time for some real action!

In this chapter, we are going to develop a small application that we'll call the "CakeTooDoo". It will be a simple to-do-list application, which will keep record of the things that we need to do. A shopping list, chapters to study for an exam, list of people you hate, and list of girls you had a crush on are all examples of lists. CakeTooDoo will allow us to keep an updated list. We will be able to view all the tasks, add new tasks, and tick the tasks that are done and much more. Here's another example of a to-do list, things that we are going to cover in this chapter:

- Make sure Cake is properly installed for CakeTooDoo
- Understand the features of CakeTooDoo
- Create and configure the CakeTooDoo database
- Write our first Cake model
- Write our first Cake controller
- Build a list that shows all the tasks in CakeTooDoo
- Create a form to add new tasks to CakeTooDoo
- Create another form to edit tasks in the to-do list
- Have a data validation rule to make sure users do not enter empty task title
- Add functionality to delete a task from the list
- Make separate lists for completed and pending Tasks
- Make the creation and modification time of a task look nicer
- Create a homepage for CakeTooDoo

Making Sure the Oven is Ready

Before we start with CakeTooDoo, let's make sure that our oven is ready. If we have followed the instructions in chapter 2, we should have everything in place. But just to make sure that we do not run into any problem later, here is a check list of things that should already be in place:

1. Apache is properly installed and running in the local machine.
2. MySQL database server is installed and running in the local machine.
3. PHP, version 4.3.2 or higher, is installed and working with Apache.
4. The latest 1.2 version of CakePHP is being used.
5. Apache `mod_rewrite` module is switched on.
6. `AllowOverride` is set to `all` for the web root directory in the Apache configuration file `httpd.conf`.
7. CakePHP is extracted and placed in the web root directory of Apache.
8. Apache has write access for the `tmp` directory of CakePHP.

If anything is not as mentioned above, please read chapter 2 to find out how to get them in place. Also, in chapter 2, we renamed the Cake directory to `myfirstcake`. In this case, we are going to name it `CakeTooDoo`.

CakeTooDoo: a Simple To-do List Application

As we already know, CakeTooDoo will be a simple to-do list. The list will consist of many tasks that we want to do. Each task will consist of a title and a status. The title will indicate the thing that we need to do, and the status will keep record of whether the task has been completed or not. Along with the title and the status, each task will also record the time when the task has been created and last modified.

Using CakeTooDoo, we will be able to add new tasks, change the status of a task, delete a task, and view all the tasks. Specifically, CakeTooDoo will allow us to do the following things:

1. View all tasks in the list
2. Add a new task to the list
3. Edit a task to change its status
4. View all completed tasks
5. View all pending or not done tasks

6. Delete a task

7. A homepage that will allow access to all the features.

You may think that there is a huge gap between knowing what to make and actually making it. But wait! With Cake, that's not true at all! We are just 10 minutes away from the fully functional and working CakeTooDoo. Don't believe me? Just keep reading and you will find it out yourself.

Configuring Cake to Work with a Database

The first thing we need to do is to create the database that our application will use. Creating database for Cake applications are no different than any other database that you may have created before. But, we just need to follow a few simple naming rules or conventions while creating tables for our database. Once the database is in place, the next step is to tell Cake to use the database.

Time for Action: Creating and Configuring the Database

1. Create a database named `caketoodoo` in the local machine's MySQL server. In your favourite MySQL client, execute the following code:

   ```
   CREATE DATABASE caketoodoo;
   ```

2. In our newly created database, create a table named `tasks`, by running the following code in your MySQL client:

   ```
   USE caketoodoo;
   CREATE TABLE tasks (
      id int(10) unsigned NOT NULL auto_increment,
      title varchar(255) NOT NULL,
      done tinyint(1) default NULL,
      created datetime default NULL,
      modified datetime default NULL,
      PRIMARY KEY (id)
   );
   ```

3. Rename the main cake directory to `CakeTooDoo`, if you haven't done that yet.

4. Move inside the directory `CakeTooDoo/app/config`. In the `config` directory, there is a file named `database.php.default`. Rename this file to `database.php`.

5. Open the `database.php` file with your favourite editor, and move to line number 73, where we will find an array named `$default`. This array contains database connection options. Assign `login` to the database user you will be using and `password` to the password of that user. Assign `database` to `caketoodoo`. If we are using the database user `ahsan` with password `sims`, the configuration will look like this:

```
var $default = array(
    'driver' => 'mysql',
    'persistent' => false,
    'host' => 'localhost',
    'port' => '',
    'login' => 'ahsan',
    'password' => 'sims',
    'database' => 'caketoodoo',
    'schema' => '',
    'prefix' => '',
    'encoding' => ''
);
```

6. Now, let us check if Cake is being able to connect to the database. Fire up a browser, and point to `http://localhost/CakeTooDoo/`. We should get the default Cake page that will have the following two lines: **Your database configuration file is present** and **Cake is able to connect to the database**, as shown in the following screen shot. If you get the lines, we have successfully configured Cake to use the `caketoodoo` database.

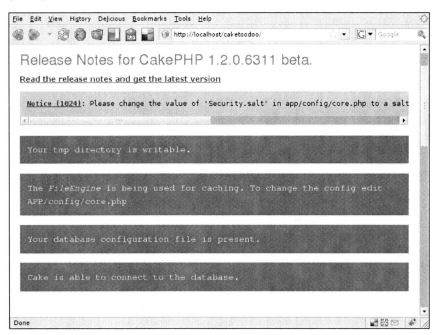

What Just Happened?

We just created our first database, following Cake convention, and configured Cake to use that database.

Our database, which we named `caketoodoo`, has only one table named `task`. It is a convention in Cake to have plural words for table names. Tasks, users, posts, and comments are all valid names for database tables in Cake. Our table `tasks` has a primary key named `id`. All tables in Cake applications' database must have `id` as the primary key for the table.

> **Conventions in CakePHP**
> Database tables used with CakePHP should have plural names.
> All database tables should have a field named `id` as the primary key of the table.

We then configured Cake to use the `caketoodoo` database. This was achieved by having a file named `database.php` in the configuration directory of the application. In `database.php`, we set the default database to `caketoodoo`. We also set the database username and password that Cake will use to connect to the database server.

Lastly, we made sure that Cake was able to connect to our database, by checking the default Cake page.

> Conventions in Cake are what make the magic happen. By favoring convention over configuration, Cake makes productivity increase to a scary level without any loss to flexibility. We do not need to spend hours setting configuration values to just make the application run. Setting the database name is the only configuration that we will need, everything else will be figured out "automagically" by Cake. Throughout this chapter, we will get to know more conventions that Cake follows.

Writing our First Model

Now that Cake is configured to work with the `caketoodoo` database, it's time to write our first model. In Cake, each database table should have a corresponding model. The model will be responsible for accessing and modifying data in the table. As we know, our database has only one table named `tasks`. So, we will need to define only one model. Here is how we will be doing it:

Time for Action: Creating the Task Model

1. Move into the directory CakeTooDoo/app/models. Here, create a file named task.php.

2. In the file task.php, write the following code:

```php
<?php
class Task extends AppModel {

    var $name = 'Task';

}
?>
```

3. Make sure there are no white spaces or tabs before the <?php tag and after the ?> tag. Then save the file.

What Just Happened?

We just created our first Cake model for the database table tasks. All the models in a CakePHP application are placed in the directory named models in the app directory.

> **Conventions in CakePHP:**
> All model files are kept in the directory named models under the app directory.

Normally, each database table will have a corresponding file (model) in this directory. The file name for a model has to be singular of the corresponding database table name followed by the .php extension. The model file for the tasks database table is therefore named task.php.

> **Conventions in CakePHP:**
> The model filename should be singular of the corresponding database table name.

Models basically contain a PHP class. The name of the class is also singular of the database table name, but this time it is CamelCased. The name of our model is therefore Task.

> **Conventions in CakePHP:**
> A model class name is also singular of the name of the database table that it represents.

You will notice that this class inherits another class named AppModel. All models in CakePHP must inherit this class.

The AppModel class inherits another class called Model. Model is a core CakePHP class that has all the basic functions to add, modify, delete, and access data from the database. By inheriting this class, all the models will also be able to call these functions, thus we do not need to define them separately each time we have a new model. All we need to do is to inherit the AppModel class for all our models.

We then defined a variable named $name in the Task'model, and assigned the name of the model to it. This is not mandatory, as Cake can figure out the name of the model automatically. But, it is a good practice to name it manually.

Writing our First Controller

With our Task Model in place, it is time to write our first controller. When a request is made to the web application, the controllers are where it is decided what should be done. In other words, controllers are where the application flow is controlled. If data needs to be accessed, the controller calls the models and fetches the data. The controller then sends the output to the views to be displayed. For CakeTooDoo, we will only need one controller called the Tasks Controller.

Time for Action: Creating the Tasks Controller

1. Move into the directory CakeTooDoo/app/controllers. Create a file named tasks_controller.php.

2. In the file tasks_controller.php, write the following code:

```php
<?php
class TasksController extends AppController {

    var $name = 'Tasks';

}
?>
```

3. Make sure there are no white spaces or tabs before the <?php tag and after the ?> tag. Then, save the file.

What Just Happened?

Like models, controllers in Cake are placed in a separate directory called controllers in the app directory. All the controllers in a Cake application must be placed in this directory.

Conventions in CakePHP:

All controller class files are kept in the directory name `controllers` under the app directory.

Each model in the application has a corresponding controller in Cake. So, for our `Task` model, the corresponding controller is `Tasks` Controller.

It is not a must that all models have a corresponding controller, or vice versa. When we make more complicated applications in later chapters, we will see that a controller may use more than one model if required.

The file name of the tasks controller is `tasks_controller.php`. It is a convention in Cake that controller file names are the plural of the model name followed by an underscore and the word controller, with `.php` extension.

Conventions in CakePHP:

Controller filenames are plural of their model names, followed by an underscore and the word `controller`.

Like the `model` class, the controller class name is also CamelCased. In this case it is `TasksController`. Notice that 'Tasks' is plural for the controller class name as in the controller file name. All Cake controllers must inherit from the `AppController` class.

Conventions in CakePHP:

Controller class names should be CamelCased and plural.

`AppController` inherits the `Controller` class, which is a core class of CakePHP. The `Controller` class has all the basic functionalities that a controller needs to perform. As a result, by extending the `AppController` class, all controllers will have these functionalities and we do not need to define them again in our controllers.

Lastly, we defined the variable `$name` in the `Tasks` controller and assigned the name of the controller to it. Again, like models, Cake will be able to identify the name of the controller automatically, but it is always a good practice to add the `$name` variable in controllers.

Conventions in CakePHP:

Model names are always singular, whereas controller names are always plural.

Viewing All Tasks in CakeTooDoo

Now that the `Task` model and the `Tasks` controller are in place, let us add some functionality to our application. The first thing that we would like to do is to view a list of all the tasks. To do this, we will need to add a function to the `Tasks` controller, and also add a view to show us the list of tasks.

Time for Action: Viewing All Tasks

1. Open the file `tasks_controller.php` and add a method named `index` to the `TasksController` class with the following code. Any public functions inside controller classes are called actions. So, after adding the index action code to the `TasksController` class, our `tasks_controller.php` file will look like this:

    ```php
    <?php
    class TasksController extends AppController {
        var $name = 'Tasks';
        function index() {
            $this->set('tasks', $this->Task->find('all'));
        }
    }
    ?>
    ```

2. Move into the directory `CakeTooDoo/app/views`. Create a directory named `tasks` inside the `view` directory.

3. Inside the `tasks` directory that we just created, create a new file named `index.ctp` and add the following code to it:

    ```php
    <h2>Tasks</h2>
    <?php if(empty($tasks)): ?>
        There are no tasks in this list
    <?php else: ?>
        <table>
            <tr>
                <th>Title</th>
                <th>Status</th>
                <th>Created</th>
                <th>Modified</th>
                <th>Actions</th>
            </tr>
            <?php foreach ($tasks as $task): ?>
                <tr>
                    <td>
                        <?php echo $task['Task']['title'] ?>
                    </td>
    ```

```
<td>
  <?php
    if($task['Task']['done']) echo "Done";
    else echo "Pending";
  ?>
</td>
<td>
  <?php echo $task['Task']['created'] ?>
</td>
<td>
  <?php echo $task['Task']['modified'] ?>
</td>
<td>
  <!-- actions on tasks will be added later -->
</td>
</tr>
<?php endforeach; ?>
</table>
<?php endif; ?>
```

4. Now point the browser to `http://localhost/CakeTooDoo/tasks/index` to view the list of all the tasks. Since we have not added any task, we should be getting a **There are no tasks in this list** message, as shown in the following screenshot:

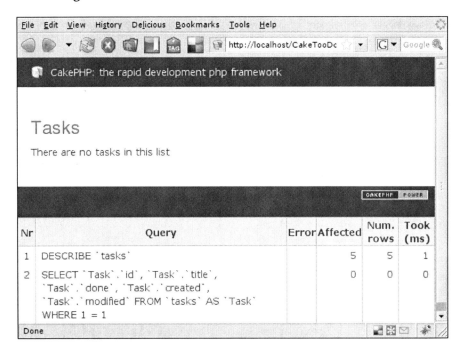

What Just Happened?

We created a controller method named `index`. Methods in controllers are called 'actions'. The `index` action, that we just added, handles a request whenever a request is made with the URL `http://localhost/CakeTooDoo/tasks/index`.

 All Cake URLs have the following form: `http://domainName/cakeApplicationFolder/controllerName/actionName`

When a request is made to the index action, the following line is executed: `$this->set('tasks', $this->Task->find('all'));`. This line calls the function `find()` of the `Task` model that returns all the tasks stored in the tasks table.

 All models in CakePHP have the `find()` function. It is actually defined in the `Model` Class. This function is used to fetch records from the table of the model. By passing parameters to this function, we can control which records we want to fetch. In the above code, `all` was passed to fetch all the records in the task table.

Then, using the `set()` function of the `Tasks` controller, it sends this data to the view in an array named tasks. We can access this array in the view through the `$tasks` variable.

 The `set()` function is used to pass data from the controller action to the view. Two parameters are normally passed to it. The first is the name of the variable that the data will have in the view, and the second is the actual data that needs to be passed. The `set()` function is actually defined in the `Controller` class that is inherited by `AppController`, which again is inherited by all CakePHP controllers.

Like models and controllers, Cake also has a separate directory to place views. In the `views` directory, we created a directory named `tasks` that will hold all the views of the `Tasks` controller. As a controller can have many actions, and each action can have a view, a controller can have many views. Cake keeps all the views of a controller in its separate directory (with the same name as the controller) inside the views directory.

 Conventions in CakePHP:

All view files in Cake are kept in the `views` directory under the `app` directory. Inside this directory, all the views of a single controller are kept under a subdirectory with the same name as the controller.

Inside the `tasks` directory in views, we created a file named `index.ctp`. This is the view file of the index action of our `Tasks` controller. The action name and its corresponding view file name are always the same. Views always have the `.ctp` extension, which stands for Cake Template Pages.

Conventions in CakePHP

The controller action and its corresponding view file have the same name.

In the `index.ctp` file, we placed the HTML code with embedded PHP code as well. Here, we have a HTML table to display all the tasks present in CakeTooDoo. Remember, that we sent an array named tasks to the view using the `set()` function in the index action? This array is accessible from the view, and using simple PHP codes, we display all the tasks that CakeTooDoo stored.

Adding a New Task

With the help of the `index` action and its view, we were able to display all the tasks in CakeTooDoo. But, because we did not add any task yet, the list displayed no tasks at all. So, let us add a form that will allow us to add tasks to CakeTooDoo. For this, we will need another action in our tasks controller and its corresponding view.

Time for Action: Creating the Add Task Form

1. Open the file `tasks_controller.php` and add a new action named `add` as shown in the following code:

```
function add() {
if (!empty($this->data)) {
    $this->Task->create();
    if ($this->Task->save($this->data)) {
        $this->Session->setFlash('The Task has been saved');
        $this->redirect(array('action'=>'index'), null, true);
    } else {
        $this->Session->setFlash('Task not saved. Try again.');
    }
}
}
```

2. In the same file(`tasks_controller.php`) add an array `$helpers` with the values as shown below:

```
<?php
class TasksController extends AppController {
    var $name = 'Tasks';
    var $helpers = array('Html', 'Form');
```

```
function index() {
    ...
}
function add() {
    ...
}
}
?>
```

3. Inside the directory `/CakeTooDoo/app/views/tasks`, create a new file named `add.ctp` and add the following code to it:

```
<?php echo $form->create('Task');?>
    <fieldset>
        <legend>Add New Task</legend>
        <?php
            echo $form->input('title');
            echo $form->input('done');
        ?>
    </fieldset>
<?php echo $form->end('Add Task');?>
```

4. Now point the browser to `http://localhost/CakeTooDoo/tasks/add` to view the add task form. We should see a form as shown in the following screenshot:

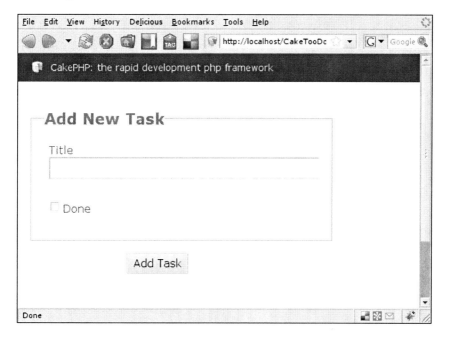

5. Use the form to add the first task to CakeTooDoo and click on the submit button. This will redirect to the list all tasks page where you can view the added task.

6. Now let us link the Task List and the Add Task Page. In the `index.ctp` file in `/CakeTooDoo/app/views`, add the following line at the end of the file:

```php
<?php echo $html->link('Add Task', array('action'=>'add')); ?>
```

7. To link the Add Task page to the View All Task page, add the following at the end of `add.ctp` file, found in `/CakeTooDoo/app/views/`:

```php
<?php
echo $html->link('List All Tasks', array('action'=>'index')); ?>
```

8. Now, go on to add more tasks to the list using the Add Task form we just created.

What Just Happened?

We added another action to the `Tasks` controller named `add`. This action can be accessed by pointing to the URL: `http://localhost/tasks/add`.

When a request is made to this action, it first checks whether any data has been sent via the POST method. Any data sent by POST method is automatically stored by Cake in the array `$this->data` of the controller. If no POST data is present, the `add` action does nothing, and the view is rendered showing the empty 'Add Task' form.

 The view is automatically rendered when the action has finished executing.

When a filled up form is submitted, the submitted data is sent via POST, and stored in `$this->data`..When this happens, it calls the `create()` function of the `Task` model in the line: `$this->Task->create();`. The `create()` function prepares the `Task` model to add or edit data. Then, it calls the `save()` function of the `Task` model to save the data into our database using the code: `$this->Task->save($this->data)`.

 The functions `create()` and `save()` are two very useful model functions that are used frequently.

If the data is successfully saved, a success message is stored in the session and the page is redirected to the `index` action. The `index` action shows the newly added task, along with the success message stored in the session. If for some reason, the data was not saved in the database, an error message is stored in the session, and the add form is displayed again along with the error message.

We also added the HTML and Form helpers to the `Tasks` controller by adding the following line: `var $helpers = array('Html', 'Form');`.

 Helpers are special modules of CakePHP that provide functions that are commonly needed in views to format and present data in useful ways.

Next, we create the view for the `add` action by adding the file `add.ctp` in the `/CakeTooDoo/apps/views/tasks` directory. In `add.ctp`, we first use the CakePHP Form helper to create a HTML form to accept data for the `Tasks` model using the code:

```
echo $form->create('Task');
```

 The Form Helper has useful functions that help in creating HTML forms that can easily show or insert data using a Cake Model.

The HTML Input tags for entering the Title and Status of a task is created using `echo $form->input('title');` and `echo $form->input('done');`. Lastly, we add `echo $form->end('Add Task');` to close the form and add the submit button with the label 'Add Task'.

 You will notice that the creation and modification times are not sent by the add form. This is because CakePHP automatically adds the time to fields that are of the type datetime and are named 'created' or 'modified'. Each time a task is added, Cake saves the time to the field 'created'. And whenever, a task is edited, it saves the time to the field 'modified'.

Lastly, we link the index (List All Tasks) and the add page (Add New Task) by using the HTML helper. Adding `$html->link('Add Task', array('action'=>'add'));` to `index.ctp` creates a hyperlink to the Add Task page. And adding `$html->link('List All Tasks', array('action'=>'index'));` to `add.ctp` adds a HTML hyperlink to the List All Task page.

 There are many useful functions in the HTML helper that can make writing long HTML tags history. Here, we used the function `link()` that created HTML anchor tags. The first parameter passed to this function is the label of the link, and the second parameter is an array that points to the action to be linked to.

Editing a Task

Now that we can add tasks to CakeTooDoo, the next thing that we will be doing is to have the ability to edit tasks. This is necessary because the users should be able to tick on a task when it has been completed. Also, if the users are not happy with the title of the task, they can change it. To have these features in CakeTooDoo, we will need to add another action to our `Tasks` Controller and also add a view for this action.

Time for Action: Creating the Edit Task Form

1. Open the file `tasks_controller.php` and add a new action named `edit` as shown in the following code:

```php
function edit($id = null) {
    if (!$id) {
        $this->Session->setFlash('Invalid Task');
        $this->redirect(array('action'=>'index'), null, true);
    }
    if (empty($this->data)) {
        $this->data = $this->Task->find(array('id' => $id));
    } else {
        if ($this->Task->save($this->data)) {
            $this->Session->setFlash('The Task has been saved');
            $this->redirect(array('action'=>'index'), null, true);
        } else {
            $this->Session->setFlash('The Task could not be saved.
                                        Please, try again.');
        }
    }
}
```

2. Inside the directory /CakeTooDoo/app/views/tasks, create a new file named "edit.ctp" and add the following code to it:

```php
<?php echo $form->create('Task');?>
    <fieldset>
        <legend>Edit Task</legend>
        <?php
            echo $form->hidden('id');
            echo $form->input('title');
            echo $form->input('done');
        ?>
    </fieldset>
<?php echo $form->end('Save');?>
```

3. We will be accessing the Task Edit Form from the **List All Task** page. So, let's add a link from the **List All Tasks** page to the **Edit Task** page. Open the index.ctp file in /CakeTooDoo/app/views directory, and replace the HTML comment `<!-- different actions on tasks will be added here later -->` with the following code:

```
<?php echo $html->link('Edit', array('action'=>'edit',
$task['Task']['id'])); ?>
```

4. Now open the **List All Tasks** page in the browser by pointing it to `http://localhost/CakeTooDoo/tasks/index` and we will see an **edit** link beside all the tasks. Click on the **edit** link of the task you want to edit, and this will take you to do the **Edit Task** form, as shown below:

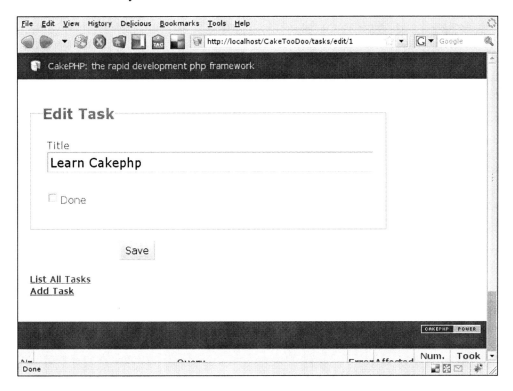

5. Now let us add links in the **Edit Task** Form page to the **List All Tasks** and **Add New Task** page. Add the following code to the end of edit.ctp in /CakeTooDoo/app/views:

```
<?php echo $html->link('List All Tasks', array('action'=>'
                                                index')); ?><br />
<?php echo $html->link('Add Task', array('action'=>'add')); ?>
```

What Just Happened?

We added a new action named `edit` in the `Tasks` controller. Then we went on to add the view file `edit.ctp` for this action. Lastly, we linked the other pages to the **Edit Task** page using the HTML helper.

When accessing this page, we need to tell the action which task we are interested to edit. This is done by passing the task id in the URL. So, if we want to edit the task with the id of 2, we need to point our browser to `http://localhost/CakeTooDoo/tasks/edit/2`. When such a request is made, Cake forwards this request to the `Tasks` controller's `edit` action, and passes the value of the id to the first parameter of the `edit` action. If we check the `edit` action, we will notice that it accepts a parameter named `$id`. The task id passed in the URL is stored in this parameter.

When a request is made to the `edit` action, the first thing that it does is to check if any id has been supplied or not. To let users edit a task, it needs to know which task the user wants to edit. It cannot continue if there is no id supplied. So, if `$id` is undefined, it stores an error message to the session and redirects to the `index` action that will show the list of current tasks along with the error message.

If `$id` is defined, the `edit` action then checks whether there is any data stored in `$this->data`. If no data is stored in `$this->data`, it means that the user has not yet edited. And so, the desired task is fetched from the `Task` model, and stored in `$this->data` in the line: `$this->data = $this->Task->find(array('id' => $id))`;. Once that is done, the view of the edit action is then rendered, displaying the task information. The view fetches the task information to be displayed from `$this->data`.

The view of the `edit` action is very similar to that of the `add` action with a single difference. It has an extra line with `echo $form->hidden('id');`. This creates an HTML hidden input with the value of the task id that is being edited.

Once the user edits the task and clicks on the **Save** button, the edited data is resent to the `edit` action and saved in `$this->data`. Having data in `$this->data` confirms that the user has edited and submitted the changed data. Thus, if `$this->data` is not empty, the `edit` action then tries to save the data by calling the `Task` Model's `save()` function: `$this->Task->save($this->data)`. This is the same function that we used to add a new task in the `add` action.

You may ask how does the `save()` function of model knows when to add a new record and when to edit an existing one? If the form data has a hidden id field, the function knows that it needs to edit an existing record with that id. If no id field is found, the function adds a new record.

Once the data has been successfully updated, a success message is stored in the session and it redirects to the `index` action. Of course the index page will show the success message.

Adding Data Validation

If you have come this far, by now you should have a working CakeTooDoo. It has the ability to add a task, list all the tasks with their statuses, and edit a task to change its status and title. But, we are still not happy with it. We want the CakeTooDoo to be a quality application, and making a quality application with CakePHP is as easy as eating a cake.

A very important aspect of any web application (or software in general), is to make sure that the users do not enter inputs that are invalid. For example, suppose a user mistakenly adds a task with an empty title, this is not desirable because without a title we cannot identify a task. We would want our application to check whether the user enters title. If they do not enter a title, CakeTooDoo should not allow the user to add or edit a task, and should show the user a message stating the problem. Adding these checks is what we call Data Validation. No matter how big or small our applications are, it is very important that we have proper data validation in place. But adding data validation can be a painful and time consuming task. This is especially true, if we have a complex application with lots of forms.

Thankfully, CakePHP comes with a built-in data validation feature that can really make our lives much easier.

Time for Action: Adding Data Validation to Check for Empty Title

1. In the `Task` model that we created in `/CakeTooDoo/app/models`, add the following code inside the `Task Model` class. The `Task Model` will look like this:

```php
<?php
class Task extends AppModel {
    var $name = 'Task';
    var $validate = array(
        'title' => array(
            'rule' => VALID_NOT_EMPTY,
            'message' => 'Title of a task cannot be empty'
        )
    );
}
?>
```

2. Now open the `Add Task` form in the browser by pointing it to `http://localhost/CakeTooDoo/tasks/add`, and try to add a task with an empty title. It will show the following error message:

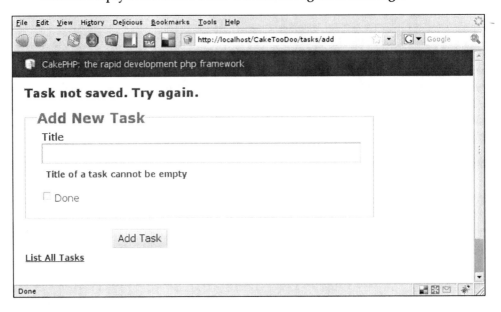

What Just Happened?

We added an array named $value in the `Task Model` class. All validation related to the data in a model should be defined in this array. We then defined an index named `title`. Every database field that we want to validate should have an index defined in $value. As we want to validate the `title` field of the `tasks` table, we declared an index with the same name.

The `title` index also points to an array that contains two more indices named `rule` and `message`. The `rule` index should point to a built-in validation rule. In this case, we do not want the title to be empty, so the rule that checks this is `VALID_NOT_EMPTY`. There are many more useful built-in rules defined in CakePHP. The `message` index should point to the error message that we want to show when users fail to follow the defined rule.

Now, whenever a user adds or edits the title of a task, CakePHP will check the defined rules.

Deleting a Task from CakeTooDoo

CakeTooDoo can now list all tasks, add new tasks, and edit tasks as well. The only thing that is remaining is the ability to delete a task.

As usual, we will need to add an action to the `Task` controller. But, unlike other actions, the `delete` action will not require a view. We will just add a link to the task actions named delete. When clicked it will show a JavaScript confirm dialogue. And once we confirm, the selected task will be deleted.

Time for Action: Adding Data Validation

1. Open the file `tasks_controller.php` and add a new action named `delete` as shown in the following code:

```
function delete($id = null) {
    if (!$id) {
        $this->Session->setFlash('Invalid id for Task');
        $this->redirect(array('action'=>'index'), null, true);
    }
    if ($this->Task->del($id)) {
        $this->Session->setFlash('Task #'.$id.' deleted');
        $this->redirect(array('action'=>'index'), null, true);
    }
}
```

2. We will be deleting task from the List All Task page. So, let's add a link from the List All Tasks page to delete a task. Open the `index.ctp` file in `/CakeTooDoo/app/views` directory, and place the following code below the Edit link we placed earlier:

```
<?php echo $html->link('Delete', array('action'=>'delete',
$task['Task']['id']), null, 'Are you sure you want to delete this
task?'); ?>
```

3. Open the View All Tasks page from the browser by pointing it to `http://localhost/CakeTooDoo/tasks/index`. We will notice a **Delete** link beside all the tasks. Try deleting a task by clicking on this link.

What Just Happened?

As already mentioned, the `delete` action will be accessed through the link in the task actions in the list page. For that we added a HTML link using the HTML helper's `link()` function. The argument passed to the `link()` function is the title of the link, in this case, it is `Delete`. The second argument is an array that declares the action we want to point. In this case, it is the `delete` action that we just created. Since the `delete` action needs to know the task that we want to delete, we also sent the task id in this array. The third argument is null and does not need to be used for the time being. In the fourth argument, we pass the message that should be shown in the JavaScript confirmation dialogue. In this case, we would like to ask the user whether they are sure that they want to delete this task.

Once the user confirms that they want to delete the task, a request is made to the `delete` action of the `task` controller. The id of the task that we want to delete is stored in the first parameter of the delete action that we named `$id`.

If `$id` is empty, the `delete` action does not know which task to delete. So, an error message is stored in the session and the page is redirected to the `index` action.

If an id is present, the `del()` function of the `Task` model is called, which actually deletes the task. After successfully deleting the task, the `delete` action stores a success message into the session and redirects to the index page. Once in the index page, the success message is displayed along with the list of tasks.

Viewing Completed Tasks and Pending Tasks

CakeTooDoo can already list all the tasks that are stored in its database. But as we use it, there will be some tasks that are completed, and some that are still pending. We would like CakeTooDoo to have the ability to list the completed and pending tasks separately. This will allow us to see more clearly which tasks are completed and which are still hanging around.

As you will see, we will not add separate actions for these lists. In fact, we will just modify the `index` action so that it displays different lists. This will be achieved by passing a parameter to the `index` action that will tell what list the user wants to see.

Time for Action: Viewing Completed and Pending Tasks

1. Open the file `tasks_controller.php` and replace the code of the `index` action with this one:

```
function index($status=null) {
    if($status == 'done')
        $tasks = $this->Task->find('all', array('conditions' =>
                                    array('Task.done' => '1')));
    else if($status == 'pending')
        $tasks = $this->Task->find('all', array('conditions' =>
                                    array('Task.done' => '0')));
    else
        $tasks = $this->Task->find('all');
    $this->set('tasks', $tasks);
    $this->set('status', $status);
}
```

2. To access the Completed and Pending Task Lists from the **List All Tasks Page**, add the following code to the end of `index.ctp` file in the `/CakeTooDoo/apps/views` directory:

```php
<?php if($status): ?>
    <?php echo $html->link('List All Tasks', array('action'=>
                                            'index')); ?><br />
<?php endif;?>
<?php if($status != 'done'): ?>
    <?php echo $html->link('List Done Tasks', array('action'=>
                                    'index', 'done')); ?><br />
<?php endif;?>
<?php if($status != 'pending'): ?>
    <?php echo $html->link('List Pending Tasks', array('action'=>
                                    'index', 'pending')); ?><br />
<?php endif;?>
```

3. To access the Completed and Pending Task Lists from the **Add New Task** and the **Edit Task** pages, add the following code to the end of the files `add.ctp` and `edit.ctp` in `/CakeTooDoo/apps/views` directory:

```php
<?php echo $html->link('List Done Tasks', array('action'=>
                                    'index', 'done')); ?><br />
<?php echo $html->link('List Pending Tasks', array('action'=>
                                    'index', 'pending')); ?><br />
```

What Just Happened?

We modified the `index` action by adding some new codes. The first thing that we did is to add a parameter named `$status` to the `index` action. If `$status = 'done'`, then it calls the `find()` function of the `Task` model with a condition: `$this->Task->find('all', array('conditions' => array('Task.done' => '1')))`. Here, we tell the `Task` model to return only those tasks that have the field done equal to 1. Any task that has been completed will have done equal to 1. Or if it is still pending, it will have a done field with the value of 0. If `$status = 'pending'`, then it will return only those tasks that have a done field value of 0. Lastly, if `$status` is undefined, it will return all the tasks present in the tasks table.

All the tasks data returned from either of the three `find()` calls are stored in a local variable named `$tasks`. This is sent to the view by calling the `set()` function of the controller. The status of the tasks sent to the view is also sent to the view.

In the view, we then added separate links to completed tasks and pending tasks. We do not want to show the link to the current page. For example, if we are in the list of all completed tasks, we do not want this page to have a link to the completed tasks. For this, we did a simple check using the `$status` variable sent to the view.

Formatting Date and Time

When we list tasks, you may have noticed that the time of task creation and modification are quite unreadable for a normal user. We would like this to be in a nicer format, so that the user can quickly understand when the task was added or last modified. For this, we will be using another built-in Helper of CakePHP: the Time Helper.

Time for Action: Formatting the Created and Modified Time

1. Add the Time Helper to the `tasks` controller, by adding `Time` at the end of the `$helper` array in `tasks_controller.php`:

```
var $helpers = array('Html', 'Form', 'Time');
```

2. Open the file `index.ctp` in `/CakeTooDoo/app/views/tasks` and replace the code `<?php echo $task['Task']['created'] ?>` with the following:

```
<?php echo $time->niceShort($task['Task']['created']) ?>
```

3. In the same file, replace the code `<?php echo $task['Task']['modified']` `?>` with the following:

```
<?php echo $time->niceShort($task['Task']['modified']) ?>
```

What Just Happened?

Here, we just added another helper to the `Tasks` controller called the Time Helper. The Time Helper is a built-in helper of CakePHP that has functions to help display time and date related data. We then used a function named `niceShort()` of the Time Helper and passed it the creation and modification times to display them in a nicer format. Check the following screenshot:

Creating the CakeTooDoo Homepage

We are almost done. Just to make the features of CakeTooDoo more accessible and easier to follow, we will be creating a homepage. This homepage will introduce the users to all the features of CakeTooDoo, and allow them to access all the other pages quickly.

The homepage does not need any logic, as it is only a static page. So far, all the pages that we created had a corresponding action and a view. As the homepage does not need any control logic, it does not make sense to have a controller action for it.

For pages that do not need any controller action, Cake has a controller called pages. We simply need to add a view for the page, and the page will be viewed. There is no need to add any controller action.

Time for Action: CakeTooDoo Homepage

1. Move into the directory `/CakeTooDoo/app/views/pages` directory, and create a file named `home.ctp`.

2. In the file `home.ctp`, we just created, write the following code:

```
<h1>Welcome to CakeTooDoo</h1>
<p>CakeTooDoo is a simple but useful application to keep a record
        of all the things that you need to do. Using CakeTooDoo,
        you can:</p>
<ul>
    <li><?php echo $html->link('List all your tasks',
       array('controller' => 'tasks', 'action'=>'index')); ?></li>
    <li><?php echo $html->link('List your completed tasks',
       array('controller' => 'tasks', 'action'=>'index','done'));
       ?></li>
    <li><?php echo $html->link('List your pending tasks',
       array('controller' => 'tasks', 'action'=>'index',
             'pending')); ?></li>
    <li><?php echo $html->link('Add new Tasks', array('controller'
                      => 'tasks', 'action'=>'add')); ?></li>
    <li>Edit tasks</li>
    <li>Delete tasks</li>
</ul>
```

3. Now point the browser to `http://localhost/CakeTooDoo/` to view the CakeTooDoo homepage.

What Just Happened?

We created a view file named home.ctp that highlights the features of CakeTooDoo and links to all the pages in CakeTooDoo. As we do not need any controller for this page, we placed the file in the pages directory found in the views directory.

Any page that does not have any controller action should be placed in the pages directory. To access these pages, we have to point the browser to a URL like this: http://localhost/CakeTooDoo/pages/<view file name>. For the homepage, we just created, the URL that we need to call is: http://localhost/CakeTooDoo/pages/home.

But you will have noticed that when we open the URL: http://localhost/CakeTooDoo/, it shows the homepage. This is because Cake makes the home.ctp view in the pages directory the default page of the application. So whenever the application is called without any controller and action name, Cake directs the browser to the default homepage (/views/pages/home.ctp). Here's how the new homepage of CakeTooDoo will look:

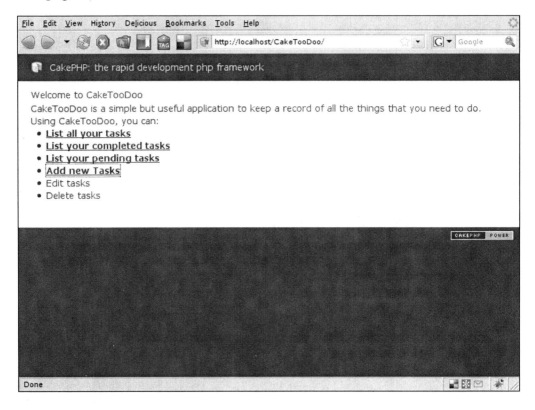

Summary

This chapter was a quick roller coaster ride through the important aspects of CakePHP. We saw how we can create an application that we called CakeTooDoo. It can manage to-do lists, list all the tasks, add tasks, edit tasks, and delete tasks. And it can also do a few more cool stuffs.

This chapter showed how we can create a database that follows the Cake convention, and to configure Cake to use it. It also discussed how to create a model, a controller, and views, and the conventions that we need to follow to make them work together.

In this chapter, we learned a few important model functions like `find()`, `create()`, `save()`, and `del()`. We also saw the use of controller functions like `set()` and `redirect()`. The HTML Form and the Time Helper was also introduced, and we saw how the functions of these helpers can make it easier to display views.

Then, we briefly saw the use of the built-in data validation of Cake. Lastly, we also saw the use of the pages controller that allows the creation of views without controller actions.

Most importantly, this chapter showed us that making a quality and structured web application with Cake is truly a "piece of cake"! But, this was just a preview of some of the goodies that CakePHP comes with. Keep reading, and you will become an expert baker in no time!

4

Controllers: Programming Application Logic

Controller, the name suggests its job—it controls, supervises, and manages. In CakePHP, controllers are the classes that handle browser requests and facilitate communication between models and views. It is the central hub where application logics are defined to control program flows of browser requests.

In CakePHP, every public method of a controller is called 'action'. Each action represents a URL. When a URL is requested from browser, the respective controller action is invoked. A controller generally uses a model class to manipulate and process the user data. Once the data is processed, controller takes it from the model and forwards it to the appropriate view file. The view file is then sent back as the response and displayed in the user's browser. In such a way, controller coordinates between the user, the model, and the views.

In this chapter, we will learn the nuts and bolts of CakePHP controller. We will particularly find out:

1. How to interact with model classes from controllers
2. How to pass controller data to the view
3. How to create a controller action and use action parameters
4. How to get form data from view
5. How to redirect to another action
6. How to add common functionalities to all controllers
7. How to create reusable components that can be used to add functionalities to controllers

Interacting with Model

Most commonly, one single controller manages the logic for one single model. In chapter 3, we already saw how CakePHP automatically finds out that relevant model's class name from a controller's name. The related model class is automatically associated and can be accessed from the controller—we don't need to configure it in the controller class explicitly. In the previous chapter, we also saw an example of this automatic binding. We created a `TasksController` class and CakePHP automatically found out and attached the related model `Task` (through its naming convention) with the controller. We were able to access the `Task` model from the `TasksController` as if that model class is a controller attribute (`$this->Task`).

Attaching Models and Controllers

In CakePHP, generally, every controller has one dependent model class. That's the way Cake is designed to be used. CakePHP will always look for a related model class for a controller through its naming convention unless a controller-model attachment is explicitly defined in that controller. Now, in some unusual situations, we may need a controller that does not have any dependency on any model class. In that case, we have to configure our controller to handle this scenario. Let's see how such a model-less controller can be created.

Time for Action: Controller without a Model

1. Put a fresh copy of CakePHP inside your web root folder. Rename the folder to `applogic`.

2. Inside the `/app/controllers/` directory, create a new PHP file `books_controller.php` and write the following code inside it.

```php
<?php
class BooksController extends AppController {
    var $name = 'Books';
    var $uses = array();
    function index() {
        //nothing's here
    }
}
?>
```

3. Inside the `/app/views/` directory, create a new folder `books`. Create a new view file named `index.ctp` there (`/app/views/books/index.ctp`), with the following code:

```html
<h2>Packt Book Store</h2>
<p>Coming Soon!</p>
```

4. Now, visit the following URL and see what shows up in the browser:

```
http://localhost/applogic/books/
```

What Just Happened?

At first, we have created a new CakePHP project. We already know how to create and configure a new Cake project from Chapter 2. In this case, as we don't need any database, we did not set up the database configuration file (/app/config/database. php). Cake will not find any database configuration file but it will work.

We then created a controller class named BooksController. Inside the controller, we defined an attribute named $uses. The $uses attribute is a special controller attribute that is used to explicitly define the relevant model class name of a controller. If $uses is not defined, Cake tries to find out the relevant model name through its naming convention. We assigned an empty array to this $uses attribute in BooksController. It means that BooksController does not use any model class. We could also assign $uses to null like the following, which would also do the same:

```
var $uses = array();
```

We then wrote an action named index() inside the BooksController. And, we also created the corresponding view file (app/books/index.ctp) for this particular action.

The index() action contains no code. And hence, when this action will be requested, Cake will just render its related view file.

When someone visits the URL http://localhost/applogic/books/, the default action (that is index()) of the BooksController is invoked, and the related view file is rendered. It displays something like the following in the browser:

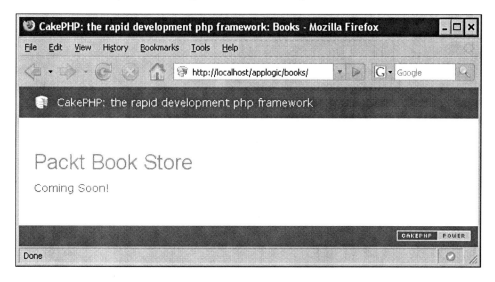

In CakePHP, we can associate models with controllers in 2 ways:

1. **Automatic binding**: CakePHP automatically binds a model with a controller through its naming convention. Like a controller named `BooksController` will be tied with a model named `Book` automatically (unless something else is manually defined).

2. **Manual binding**: If we want to override the automatic binding, we can assign `$uses` controller attribute to an array of models. Those models will be available to the controller.

 'Convention over configuration' is one of the principal philosophies of CakePHP framework. It is recommended to follow the naming conventions of controllers and models and let Cake attach related controllers and models automatically. It would simplify things.

We have already seen how the second method (Manual binding) works. We assigned an empty array to `$uses` attribute of `BooksController` to tell Cake that this controller has no dependency on any model class. We could also manually attach more than one model(s) to a controller using the `$uses` attribute. In that case, we just have to put all the model names in the `$uses` attribute, like this:

```
$uses = array ( 'ModelName1', 'ModelName2' ) ;
```

We just learnt how controllers can be tied up with models. Now, we will see how they can interact with the presentation files, a.k.a views.

Action, Parameters, and Views

In CakePHP, actions are public methods of controllers that represent URLs. A general Cake URL contains suffixes like `/controller_name/action_name` and from this pattern Cake automatically maps the URL with a controller's action. Again, every such controller action can automatically call a view file that contains the display logic for that particular action. The appropriate view file is determined from the controller and action names. As an example, if the `index()` action of the `BooksController` is requested, the view file in `/app/views/books/index.ctp` will be rendered. We very often need to supply processed data to those view files from controllers, so that we can present the data in a suitable format to the user.

Interacting with View

CakePHP determines the appropriate view file for a controller's action by its naming convention. Controller can also supply processed data to those view files. To do that we can use the controller method set(). In chapter 3, we saw some uses of this set() method. In this section, we will learn some more on how we can interact with view files from controllers.

Time for Action: Passing Variables to a View

1. Change the index() action of the BooksController (/app/controllers/ books_controller.php).

```php
<?php
class BooksController extends AppController {

    var $name = 'Books';
    var $uses = array();

    function index() {
        $this->set('page_heading', 'Packt Book Store');

        $book  = array (
                'book_title'    => 'Object Oriented Programming
                                                with PHP5',
                'author'        => 'Hasin Hayder',
                'isbn'            => '1847192564',
                'release_date' => 'December 2007'
            );
        $this->set($book);

        $this->pageTitle = 'Welcome to the Packt Book Store!';
    }
}
?>
```

underscore

2. Change view file index.ctp (/app/views/books/index.ctp) with the following code:

```php
<h2><?php echo $page_heading; ?></h2>
<dl>
<lh><?php echo $bookTitle; ?></lh>
<dt>Author:</dt><dd><?php echo $author; ?></dd>
<dt>ISBN:</dt><dd><?php echo $isbn; ?></dd>
<dt>Release Date:</dt><dd><?php echo $releaseDate; ?></dd>
</dl>
```

CAMEL CASE HERE

3. Now enter the following URL in your browser.

```
http://localhost/applogic/books/.
```

What Just Happened?

In the `index()` action, we first used the `set()` method to set a view variable named `page_heading`.

```
$this->set('page_heading', 'Packt Book Store');
```

The first parameter of `set()` specifies the view variable's name and the second parameter defines its value. In the view file, in the first line, we simply printed out the `$page_heading` variable that displays the text `Packt Book Store` (that was set in the controller).

In the `index()` action, we then created an associative array named `$book`.

```
$book    = array (
            'book_title'   => 'Object Oriented Programming with
PHP5',
            'author'   => 'Hasin Hayder',
            'isbn'         => '1847192564',
            'release_date' => 'December 2007'
          );
```

And then passed this array to the view files using the `set()` method like this:

```
$this->set($book);
```

As we can see, the `set()` method can take a single parameter as well. We can create an associative array (as we created the `$book` array) and pass that array to the `set()` method. It will automatically set all these `key=>value` pairs of the associative array respectively, as view variables and their values. This method can be pretty handy if we want to assign a set of variables to the view quickly. One thing to be noted, in this case, all the underscored array keys will become CamelCased view variables. Like, in our case, the `book_title` and `release_date` keys set in the controller became `$bookTitle` and `$releaseDate` variables in the correspondent view. Inside the view file, we then printed out all those variables set through the associative array `$book`.

Lastly, in the controller action, we defined a controller attribute named `$pageTitle`.

```
$this->pageTitle = 'Welcome to the Packt Book Store!';
```

`$pageTitle` is a special attribute that sets the title of the rendered page. Now, if we visit this page it would look something like the following:

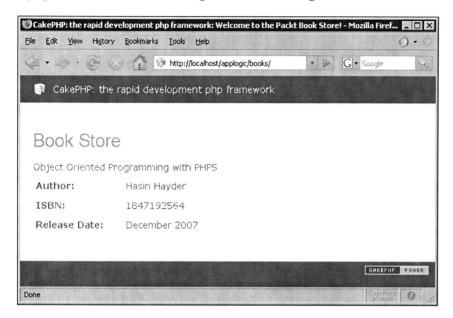

Actions and Parameters

In chapter 3, we already learned how parameters can be passed to a controller action by adding suffixes to the URL. A typical Cake URL looks like this: `http://yourhost/controller/[/action][/parameters]`. The elements in the URL that are appended to the hostname and separated by / are known as request parameters. We will now see more closely how these request parameters are handled by controller actions.

Time for Action: Understanding Actions and Parameters

1. Change the `index()` action of the `BooksController` like the following:

```php
<?php
class BooksController extends AppController {

    var $name = 'Books';
    var $uses = array();

    function index( $id = 0 ) {
        $books = array (
                    '0' => array (
                            'book_title' => 'Object Oriented
                                            Programming with PHP5',
```

```
                                'author'         => 'Hasin Hayder',
                                'isbn'                  => '1847192564',
                                'release_date' => 'December 2007'
                        ),
                '1' => array (
                        'book_title'     => 'Building Websites
                                            with Joomla! v1.0',
                        'author'         => 'Hagen Graf',
                        'isbn'                  => '1904811949',
                        'release_date' => 'March 2006'
                )
            );

        $id = intval($id);
    if( $id < 0 || $id >= count($books) ) {
        $id = 0;
    }

    $this->set($books[$id] );
    $this->set('page_heading', 'Book Store');
    $this->pageTitle = 'Welcome to the Packt Book Store!';
    }
}
?>
```

2. Now visit the following links and see what shows up in the browser:

   http://localhost/applogic/books/index/0

   http://localhost/applogic/books/index/1

   http://localhost/applogic/books/index/xyz

What Just Happened?

We first recreated the BooksController's action index().The index() action can take a parameter named $id:

```
function index( $id = 0 ) {
```

That means, if someone requests the URL http://localhost/applogic/books/index/1, the $id parameter of the index() action will be set to 1. The default value of the parameter $id is 0. So, if no request parameter is provided through URL (like http://localhost/applogic/books/index/), the parameter $id will have the value 0.

We also defined an array named `$books` inside the `index()` action. The `$books` array has two elements containing information about two different books.

```
$books    = array (
                 '0' => array (
                        'book_title' => 'Object Oriented
Programming with PHP5',
                        'author'     => 'Hasin Hayder',
                        'isbn'          => '1847192564',
                        'release_date' => 'December 2007'
                 ),
                 '1' => array (
                        'book_title'    => 'Building Websites with
Joomla! v1.0',
                        'author'     => 'Hagen Graf',
                        'isbn'          => '1904811949',
                        'release_date' => 'March 2006'
                 )
             );
```

Now, we want to show the appropriate book information depending on the request parameter. That is if 0 is supplied as the request parameter, we will show information of the 0th book. We can get the request parameter's value through `$id`. We just passed the `$id`th element of the `$books` array to the view file:

```
$this->set($books[$id] );
```

The view file (`/app/views/books/index.ctp`) that we created in the previous *Time for Action* will work for this one too, without any change. Now, if someone visits the URL `http://localhost/applogic/books/index/0`, the `index()` action will show the information of the first book. If 1 is supplied as parameter `$id`, the second book's information will be displayed.

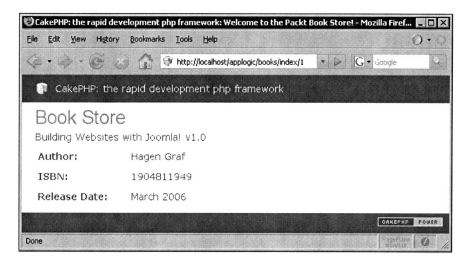

But what if the parameter supplied has got a value that is unacceptable parameter —
like a non integer, or an integer that is less than 0 or greater than 1 (the highest index
of the $books array). In those cases, our code would just throw errors. To handle
these exceptional cases, we added an if condition in the action. If any of those
exception happens, we made $id = 0, so that we can bypass the errors gracefully.

```
$id = intval($id);
if( $id < 0 || $id >= count($books) ) {
$id = 0;
}
```

Now if we go to the URL http://localhost/applogic/books/index/xyz, it
would just show the information of the first book.

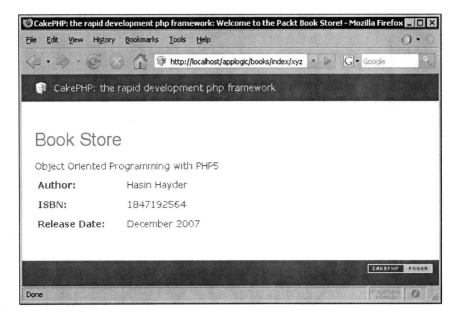

Following the same technique, we can have more than one parameter for a particular
action. In the next *Time for Action*, we will see an example of such a controller action.

Time for Action: Handling more than One Request Parameter

1. Create a new controller MathsController with the following code:

    ```php
    <?php
    class MathsController extends AppController {

        var $name = 'Maths';
        var $uses = array();
    ```

```
function add_digits( $digit1 = 0, $digit2 = 0, $digit3 = 0 ) {
    $sum = intval($digit1) + intval($digit2) + intval($digit3);
    $this->set('sum', $sum);
}
}
?>
```

2. Create its corresponding view file add_digits.ctp (/app/views/maths/add_digits.ctp) using the following code:

```
<h2>The sum is equal to <?php echo $sum; ?></h2>
```

3. Now visit the following links and see what shows up in the browser:

```
http://localhost/applogic/maths/add_digit/1/2/3
http://localhost/applogic/books/index/1/2
```

What Just Happened?

We first created a new controller named MathsController. Inside the controller, we wrote an action called add_digits(). The add_digits() action takes 3 parameters. Each having a default value 0. When this action is requested through URL, it would sum up the digits and pass the result to its view file. We created a very simple view file to display the sum supplied from the controller action. Now, if we visit the URL http://localhost/applogic/maths/add_digits/1/2/3 it should display the sum of the three numbers 1, 2 and 3, like the following:

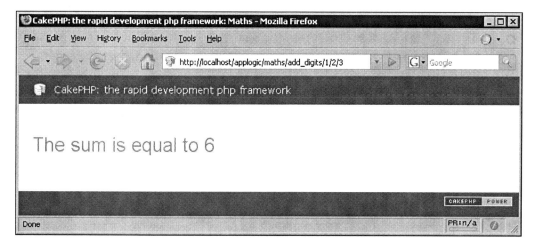

How Cake Handles an Incoming Request?

Cake automatically routes to the appropriate controller and action. It also loads the appropriate model class and displays the correct view file. If all the conventions are followed correctly, it always does the right thing for us without any extra configuration. We will now skim through the whole process to have a clearer understanding of how Cake handles incoming requests. Let's take the BooksController example and assume a request has arrived in the URL http://localhost/applogic/books/index/123. Now, let's see what Cake will basically do with this request:

1. Cake accepts an incoming request from a browser. It determines the target controller's name that should handle this particular request from the first request parameter. In this case, the target controller is the BooksController.

2. It instantiates an object of class BooksController found in the file books_controller.php in the directory /app/controllers/.

3. It loads the related model class Books from the file books.php found in the directory /app/models/. In our case, the target controller is 'configured' to use no model and hence actually it does not load or look for any related model class.

4. The next request parameter suggests the action to be invoked in the target controller. If no second request parameter is provided, it routes to the default action that is index(). In this case, there is a second parameter and it suggests the target action is index().

5. Cake invokes that target action of the target controller, that is the index() action of our BooksController. If some additional parameters are supplied with the request, Cake passes them as parameters while calling the target action. In our case, one additional request parameter is provided with value 123. So, 123 is passed to the index() method of BooksController as parameter.

6. It locates the appropriate view file from the target controller and target action's names that is the file index.ctp inside the directory /app/views/books/. It passes view variables that were set in the controller action to that file. It then renders that view file and the rendered view is sent to browser as a response.

So, this is how an incoming request is generally handled by Cake. We can, though, override the default behavior by configuring our controllers, models or routes. We will learn about them all through this book. So keep reading...

Getting Post Data from the View

HTML forms are the most common way of taking user inputs in web applications. In chapter 3, we already saw how to create simple HTML forms using CakePHP's `FormHelper`. In this section, we will see how to access the submitted form data from a controller action. Let's dive into it...

Time for Action: Getting Post Data from the View

1. Create a controller class `UsersController` using the following code and save it as `users_controller.php` inside the `/app/controllers/` directory.

```php
<?php
class UsersController extends AppController {

    var $name = 'Users';
    var $uses = array();

    function index() {
        if (!empty($this->data)) {
            //data posted
            echo $this->data['name'];
            $this->autoRender = false;    Do not render view
        }
    }
}
?>
```

2. Create a view file named `index.ctp` inside the `/app/views/users/` with the following code:

```php
<?php echo $form->create(null, array('action' => 'index'));?>
<fieldset>
<legend>Enter Your Name</legend>
<?php echo $form->input('name'); ?>
</fieldset>
<?php echo $form->end('Go');?> .
```

3. Now visit the following links and see what shows up in the browser:

```
http://localhost/applogic/users/.
```

What Just Happened?

Before going through the code, let's first learn about a special controller attribute `$data`. This attribute is used to store the POST data sent from HTML forms to the controller. When some data is submitted from an HTML form, Cake automatically fills up the attribute `$data` with the posted data. That's all we need to know. Now, we are ready to step forward and check out what the above piece of code is actually doing.

In the first line of the `index()` action, we checked if `$this->data` attribute is empty. If `$this->data` is not empty, this means some data is submitted from an HTML form. In that case, we will execute the codes inside the `if{}` block. Let's ignore what's going on inside this block for now and check out what's going to happen if no data is submitted. In that case, we will skip the `if{}` block and directly render the corresponding view file (`/apps/views/users/index.ctp`).

Inside the view, we created a simple form using CakePHP's built-in `FormHelper`. We will learn more about the `FormHelper` in Chapter 7. For now, just understand that we can define the model name through the first parameter of the `FormHelper`'s `create()` method. In our case, we defined it as `null`, which means the form fields do not belong to any model. And in the second parameter, we specified that the form is to be submitted to the `index()` action of the current controller.

```php
<?php echo $form->create(null, array('action' => 'index'));?>
```

We then created a text input field using the `input()` method of the `FormHelper`. As we want to take user's name using this field, we supplied `name` as a parameter to this `input()` method.

```php
<?php echo $form->input('name'); ?>
```

This `input()` method will generate an HTML input element like this:

```html
<input type="text" id="Name" value="" name="data[name]"/>
```

At the end of this view file, we ended the form with a submit button called **Go** created using the `FormHelper`'s `end()` method. Now, if we visit the page `http://localhost/applogic/users/` it will display a form like the following:

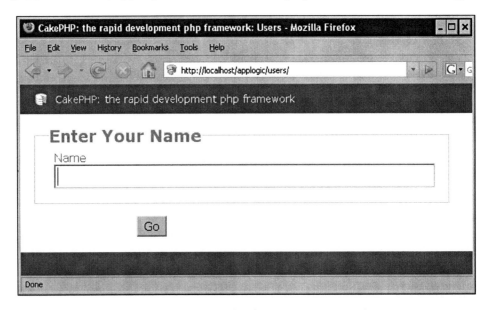

Now, if a name is entered in the input field and the form is submitted, the controller attribute `$data` will be filled up with the submitted POST data. The condition `if (!empty($this->data))` will return a `true`. And the codes inside the `if{}` block will get executed. Inside the block, we directly printed out the value entered in the input field:

```
echo $this->data['name'];
```

Notice how we accessed the value entered in the input field through the `$data` attribute. The key `name` of the `$data` array simply returns the value entered in the field named `name`.

The next line sets the `$autoRender` attribute of the controller to `false`:

```
$this->autoRender = false;
```

It tells the controller that it does not have to render any view. One important thing to be noted: generally, it is not possible to print outputs from a controller action. To do that we have to set the `$autoRender` attribute to `false`. It is not recommended to generate output from controller either, but it sometimes helps for quick debugging.

Redirecting

In dynamic web applications, redirects are often used to control the flow of the application and move the user from one page to another. Without redirects, web applications would be scattered pages without any real flow. In usual PHP-based web applications, the PHP function `header()` is very commonly used to redirect the user from one page to another. Whereas, CakePHP offers a built-in controller method `redirect()` that is used to direct the user from one action to another. Now, without further ado, let's see how to redirect in CakePHP!

Time for Action: Redirecting from One Action to Another

1. Modify the `UsersController` (/app/controllers/users_controller.php).

```
class UsersController extends AppController {
    var $name = 'Users';
    var $uses = array();
    function index() {
        if (!empty($this->data)) {
            $this->redirect(array('controller'=>'users',
              'action'=>'welcome', urlencode($this->data['name'])));
        }
    }
    function welcome( $name = null ) {
        if(empty($name)) {
```

```
            $this->Session->setFlash('Please provide your name!',
                                                        true);
            $this->redirect(array('controller'=>'users',
                                   'action'=>'index'));
        }
        $this->set('name', urldecode($name));
    }
}
```

2. Create a view file named `welcome.ctp` inside the directory `/app/views/users/` with the following code:

   ```
   <h2>Welcome, <?php echo $name; ?></h2>
   ```

3. Now enter the following URL in your browser:

   ```
   http://localhost/applogic/users/
   ```

What Just Happened?

In the `index()` action of the `UsersController`, we changed the code inside the `if{}` block. Instead of printing out the name submitted from the form, we redirected the user to another action using the following line of code:

```
$this->redirect(array('controller'=>'users', 'action'=>'welcome',
urlencode($this->data['name'])));
```

The `redirect()` method is pretty easy to use. The first parameter is an associative array. We specified the controller and action name (where we want to redirect) there through `controller` and `action` keys. Also, additional request parameters can be supplied by appending new elements in this array. When the form is submitted, we redirected the user to the `UsersController`'s `welcome()` action. We also appended the user's name in the URL as a request parameter. We got the name from the `$data` controller attribute and used the PHP function `urlencode()` to make that input URL-friendly.

 `redirect()` by default exits just after the execution. So, codes after the `redirect()` call do not execute, we can though set the third parameter to true while calling the `redirect()` method to avoid the force exit.

Now, let's have a look at the `welcome()` action. This action takes an optional parameter `$name`. Inside this action, we first checked if any request parameter is supplied. If no parameter is specified, we set a flash message and then sent back the user to the `index()` action of the `UsersController` using the `redirect()` method.

```
if(empty($name)) {
    $this->Session->setFlash('Please provide your name!');
    $this->redirect(array('action'=>'index'));
}
```

See, this time while calling the `redirect()` method, we only set the `action` key in the parameter. When the `controller` key is not set, the `redirect()` method redirects to the current controller's action.

If the request parameter `$name` is provided, it will ignore the `if{}` block and pass the URL-decoded name to the view as `$name` variable.

```
$this->set('name', urldecode($name));
```

In the view file, we simply welcomed the user by displaying a 'Welcome,' text before the user's name.

Now, if we visit the URL `http://localhost/applogic/users/` and enter a name there, it should redirect us to the `welcome` action and show us a greeting message.

AppController: The Parent Controller

From Object Oriented perspective, every CakePHP controller is a subclass of the `AppController` class. Recall how we start the class definition of a controller — look at the following line of code as an example:

```
class BooksController extends AppController {
```

Our controllers extend the `AppController` class — this means we set the `AppController` class as the parent class of all of our controllers. As of now, it seems alright. But the next question that quickly pops up in our mind is: where is that `AppController` class located? Well, it can be found inside the `app_controller.php` file under the `/cake/libs/controller/` directory. This `app_controller.php` is actually a placeholder file and can be overridden by our own one.

The main benefit of having our own `AppController` class is we can put in common application-wide methods inside this class and all of our controllers will just inherit them. We can use attributes and methods defined inside the `AppController` from any of our controller class. We will now see how to create our own `AppController` class and how we can make use of the methods written inside the `AppController` from a controller class.

Time for Action: Adding Common Functionalities to all Controllers

1. Create a new file named `app_controller.php` just inside the `/app/` folder with the following code,

```
<?php
class AppController extends Controller {
    function strip_and_clean ( $id, $array) {
```

```
        $id = intval($id);
        if( $id < 0 || $id >= count($array) ) {
            $id = 0;
        }
        return $id;
    }
}
?>
```

2. Modify the `BooksController`'s (`/app/controllers/books_controller.php`) code, replace the `if{}` block with the controller method `strip_and_clean()`,

```php
<?php
class BooksController extends AppController {
    var $name = 'Books';
    var $uses = array();

    function index( $id = 0 ) {
        $books = array (
                    '0' => array (
                        'book_title' => 'Object Oriented
                                          Programming with PHP5',
                        'author'      => 'Hasin Hayder',
                        'isbn'        => '1847192564',
                        'release_date' => 'December 2007'
                    ),
                    '1' => array (
                        'book_title'   => 'Building Websites
                                            with Joomla! v1.0',
                        'author'       => 'Hagen Graf',
                        'isbn'          => '1904811949',
                        'release_date' => 'March 2006'
                    )
                );

        $id = $this->strip_and_clean( $id, $books);

        $this->set($books[$id] );
        $this->set('page_header', 'Book Store');
        $this->pageTitle = 'Welcome to the Packt Book Store!';
    }
}
?>
```

3. Now visit the following links and see what shows up in the browser:

    ```
    http://localhost/applogic/books/index/0
    http://localhost/applogic/books/index/1
    http://localhost/applogic/books/index/xyz
    ```

What Just Happened?

We first wrote a class named AppController and saved it as app_controller.php inside the /app/ folder.

```php
<?php
class AppController extends Controller {
```

Inside this class, we wrote a method named strip_and_clean(). This method takes two parameters - $id and $array.

```php
function strip_and_clean ( $id, $array) {
        if( !is_int($id) || $id < 0 || $id >= count($array) ) {
            $id = 0;
        }
        return $id;
}
```

The strip_and_clean() method simply returns $id, if $id is a non-negative integer and $id is less than the length of $array. Otherwise it returns a 0.

Previously, we did this checking inside the BooksController. And now we have moved this particular code to the AppController method strip_and_clean(). As all of our controllers inherit the AppController class, we can now use this particular routine from any of them.

In BooksController, we replaced the if{} block with the strip_and_clean() method.

```php
$id = $this->strip_and_clean( $id, $books);
```

$id and $books variables are passed to this method as parameters. And the returned result of the method is then stored back to $id. Now, if the request parameter $id is invalid, it will make it to 0. And the /books/index/ action will show us the information about the first book defined in $array.

The new approach is better only when we have some common application wide methods. In those cases, we can just write them inside the AppController class and call them from any of our controllers. But we also have to remember that writing methods inside the AppController is not always the best way. There may be other controllers that do not require those methods (like we have UsersController, which does not need the strip_and_clean() method) but still will inherit them.

The better approach is to load codes on demand, load the methods only where it is required. Moreover, writing methods inside the `AppController` does not increase reusability outside the application—it just increases application-specific and application-wide reusability. We just cannot reuse the methods written inside the `AppController` for one application in any other application directly. If we want to write reusable codes and follow the DRY (Don't Repeat Yourself) principle, it is always better to write our methods in separate classes and load them only from the controllers that require those methods.

CakePHP also provides a way for writing and using reusable classes. In CakePHP, they are called components. In the next section, we will work with CakePHP components and see how it can increase reusability.

Working with Components

Components are reusable classes that can be used from any controller in CakePHP applications. By definition, components are only limited to be used from and inside controllers and its other components. They are used to help controllers with a goal of reusability—we can just port the component classes to any of our Cake applications and use them in those applications. CakePHP ships with some useful components, like `AuthComponent`, `SessionCompoenent`, etc. We will learn about them in Chapter 10. Now, let's see how to create our own custom component and use them from a controller.

Time for action: Creating and Using Reusable Components

1. Create a component class `UtilComponent` using the following code and save it in a file named `util.php` under `/app/controllers/components/` directory.

```php
<?php
class UtilComponent extends Object
{
    function strip_and_clean ( $id, $array) {
        $id = intval($id);
        if( $id < 0 || $id >= count($array) ) {
            $id = 0;
        }
        return $id;
    }
}
?>
```

2. Remove the `strip_and_clean()` method from the `AppController` (`/app/app_controller.php`) class.

```php
<?php
class AppController extends Controller {

}
?>
```

3. Modify the `BooksController` class (`/app/controllers/books_controller.php`),

```php
<?php
class BooksController extends AppController {
    var $name = 'Books';
    var $uses = array();
    var $components = array('Util');
    function index( $id = 0 ) {
        $books = array (
                    '0' => array (
                            'book_title'   => 'Object Oriented
                                               Programming with PHP5',
                            'author'       => 'Hasin Hayder',
                            'isbn'         => '1847192564',
                            'release_date' => 'December 2007'
                        ),
                    '1' => array (
                            'book_title'   => 'Building Websites
                                               with Joomla! v1.0',
                            'author'       => 'Hagen Graf',
                            'isbn'         => '1904811949',
                            'release_date' => 'March 2006'
                        )
                    );

        $id = $this->Util->strip_and_clean($id);

        $this->set('book', $books[$id] );

        $this->pageTitle = 'Welcome to the Packt Book Store!';
    }
}
?>
```

4. Now visit the following links and see what shows up in the browser

   http://localhost/applogic/books/index/0

   http://localhost/applogic/books/index/1

   http://localhost/applogic/books/index/xyz

What Just Happened?

At first, we created a component class named `UtilComponent` and saved it in a file named `util.php` under the `/app/controllers/components/` folder. We then moved (cut-pasted) the `strip_and_clean()` method from the `AppController` to the `UtilComponent`.

 The class name of a component should always have a `Component` postfix. Every component class file should be placed under the `/app/controllers/components/` directory. The filenames should be named after the lowercased classname of the component (without the Component postfix).

Now, to use this `UtilComponent` from our `BooksController`, we have to add this component to the controller. It can be done through the controller attribute `$components`. `$components` holds an array of all the component names that we want to make available inside the controller. In our case, as we want to load only the `Util` component, we defined the `$components` array like the following:

```
var $components = array('Util');
```

 Notice, the component name used in the `$components` array is `Util` (without the Component postfix) not `UtilComponent`.

Once loaded, the `UtilComponent` class can be referred and used from the controller. Now instead of using the `strip_and_clean()` method of the `AppController`, we called the `UtilComponent`'s method `strip_and_clean()`.

```
$id = $this->Util->strip_and_clean($id);
```

Everything else in the controller remains unchanged. And it will work, as it was working before. The only difference is, now we have a more reusable code that can be used from any controller or any other application when needed.

Summary

A controller is used to manage the application logic. It controls the application flow and works as a bridge between the model and the view. CakePHP applications use a common format for the URL. From the URL, Cake finds out the appropriate controller action to invoke to handle a particular browser request. Request parameters can be appended to the URL and can be accessed from the actions. Controller can load a model class to interact with the database. By default, CakePHP finds out the related model class from the controller name. We can though override the default and tell the controller to load other model classes using the `$uses` attribute. Every controller action usually renders a view file to send formatted response to the browser. CakePHP has some conventions for saving and naming view files so that they can be loaded and rendered automatically. We can though skip the view rendering by setting controller attribute `$autorender` to `false`. Controller method `set()` is very commonly used to pass data to the relevant view file. Redirection is an established method to forward a user from one action to another and in CakePHP it is done using the method `redirect()`. In Cake, all controllers are subclasses of the `AppController` class. Methods defined inside the `AppController` class that can be called from different controllers. In CakePHP applications, common controller functionalities are written inside components to increase reusability.

Well, that's the end of the controller story. Now, get prepared for the next chapter which is about CakePHP models. We will learn lots of cool stuffs there!

5
Models: Accessing Data

In the previous chapters, we have learned the basics of MVC and have seen CakePHP's MVC implementation in brief. In this chapter, we will focus solely on the M of the MVC—the Model. In short, models are simply the data warehouse of an application. It bridges an application with the database and holds all types of domain/business logics that an application requires.

Most of the today's real life web applications are highly data intensive. Handling data in a smarter way is a crucial need of the time. In usual PHP/MySQL applications, separating domain logics and database operations can be very tricky. But in case of CakePHP, we don't have to think about that at all. Cake provides a simple and smarter solution to this complex problem through its Model.

Theoretically, CakePHP model is a (slightly modified) PHP implementation of the popular design pattern—ActiveRecord. It is much more than a mere database abstraction layer. It helps us to separate domain logics from the application and presentational logics. Moreover, it provides useful functionalities that make it easy to perform database operations without even writing a single line of SQL. In CakePHP, a model is a PHP class that usually represents one single table of the database. All database operations performed on a table are done through its respective model class. Each CakePHP model class, by default, inherits some useful methods for basic database operations. We can, as well, add our own routines to our model classes containing custom application-specific logics.

Models are very important and integral part of the CakePHP framework. And hence, learning how to work with models properly is very essential. In this chapter, we will thoroughly experience some of the model basics. Specifically, we will see:

- How to design a database, according to CakePHP's convention
- How to create a model for our database table
- How to use scaffolding to test out the model
- How some common database tasks like retrieving, saving, and deleting can be effortlessly done using model functions
- How to validate data while saving them into the database

Setting Up Database and Models

As we already know, model classes are generally used to interact with the database. Generally, in CakePHP, a model class represents a certain table in the database. All database operations on the table are done through its corresponding model. A CakePHP model requires no configuration to attach it with a database table. Instead, some simple naming convention is used to name database and models that does the magic. In this section, we will see how to create a model class for a database table. To check out our models and database tables early on, CakePHP offers a tool called 'scaffolding'. We will also see how to use scaffolding for this purpose.

Creating a Model for a Database Table

To see how a model class can be used to interact with a database table, we first need to create a database table. In the following section, we will first create a database table and then see how to create a model class for that table. We will then use scaffolding for a fast test drive through the newly created model class and database table.

Time for Action: Creating a Database Table and Its Model

1. From your MySQL prompt, create a new database named `data-access` by entering the following database command:

    ```
    CREATE DATABASE `data-access`;
    ```

2. Create a `books` table in our database by executing the following SQL commands:

    ```
    USE `data-access`;
    CREATE TABLE `books` (
    `id` int( 11 ) NOT NULL AUTO_INCREMENT PRIMARY KEY ,
    `isbn` varchar( 10 ) NOT NULL ,
    `title` varchar( 127 ) NOT NULL ,
    `description` text NOT NULL ,
    `author_name` varchar( 127 ) NOT NULL
    )
    ```

3. Put a fresh copy of CakePHP inside our web root folder. Rename the Cake folder to `data-access`.

4. Go to the `/app/config` directory inside your Cake installation folder. You will find a file named `database.php.default` there. Rename the file to `database.php`. Open it in any editor. Edit the `$default` array inside the file to configure your database. After editing, it should look like something like the following:

```
var $default = array(
    'driver' => 'mysql',
    'persistent' => false,
    'host' => 'localhost',
    'port' => '',
    'login' => 'username',
    'password' => 'password',
    'database' => 'data-access',
    'schema' => '',
    'prefix' => '',
    'encoding' => ''
);
```

5. Now, enter the following URL from your browser, `http://localhost/data-access/`. It should display a message **Cake is able to connect to the database.** to confirm that our database is configured perfectly. If the configuration is not right, it will show the message: '**Cake is NOT able to connect to the database**'. If so, then probably the database information you provided is incorrect. Please go back to step 4 and fill up the `$default` array with the correct database name, database user name, and password.

6. Create a new PHP file inside `/app/models` folder and name it `book.php`.

7. Write the following code inside the `book.php` file:

```php
<?php
class Book extends AppModel
{
    var $name = 'Book';
}
?>
```

8. Now, create another new PHP file inside `/app/controllers` folder and name it `books_controller.php`.

9. Write down the following code inside the `books_controller.php` file:

```php
<?php
class BooksController extends AppController {
    var $name = 'Books';
    var $scaffold;
}
?>
```

10. Now, go to the following URL and add some test data — `http://localhost/data-access/books/`

What Just Happened?

At first, we created a new database named `data-access`. Then we created a database table named `books` in that database. The `books` table has got the following structure:

books				
id	isbn	title	description	author_name

The database table name and field names we used are not arbitrarily chosen. CakePHP has certain conventions for naming database tables and fields:

- Table names should be lowercased English plural (like `books`, `categories`, `articles` etc.).

- If two or more words are needed to name a table or a field, use underscores to separate the words (like `author_name`, `user_photos` etc.).

- A database table should have a single-field primary key named `id`.

In our case, the table name we used `books` is an English plural. We also have a single-field primary key named `id`. We needed two words to name the 5th field of the table — `author_name`, we connected them using underscore.

 If you have written PHP/MySQL applications before, then you're probably used to naming database tables as you like, and then writing SQL codes to access the database. However, while using CakePHP, you should follow its own naming conventions. It is not that we always have to stick to the convention, but adhering to the convention will save our precious time. It will allow us to avoid tedious configuration and take advantage of CakePHP's automated (euphemistically referred to as "automagic") features for rapid development. Moreover, sticking to a particular convention always increases code quality and maintainability. We will see how conventions of CakePHP help us to do stuff in a much easier and cooler way all through this chapter and in later chapters of this book as well.

Once our database is ready, we have configured our application to connect to the database. In chapter 3, we have already learned how to configure our applications to connect to the database. After configuring our application for the database, we started writing codes for our model.

As we know, in CakePHP, a model class is generally used to access a particular database table. So, to access the `books` table, we need to create its corresponding model class. **CakePHP has a certain convention for naming model classes and model files. By convention:**

- Model filenames are named after the corresponding database table names but in singular form. As an example, if our database table name is `user_photos`, the model filename should be `user_photo.php`.

- Model class names are the CamelCased form of the underscored model filenames. If our model filename is `user_photo.php`, our model class name should be `UserPhoto`.

- Model files are placed under the `/app/models` folder.

 CakePHP automagically understands which model class is tied with which database table through its naming convention. As in our case, the name of our model class `Book` suggests that it is coupled with the database **table** `books`. What a rescue, we don't need to configure it manually!

We then created the model class named `Book`, named the class file `book.php`, and saved it inside the `/app/models` folder. As we have followed the conventions correctly, now CakePHP will automatically detect that our `Book` class is the corresponding model of the database table `books`.

Once we are done with our database tables and models, we can create a simple application with basic database operations (such as add, edit, and delete) out of them very quickly using Cake's scaffolding feature. To scaffold the `Book` model, we have created the related controller class `BooksController` first. And then have added the line `var $scaffold` there. This small piece of code has added scaffolding to our `Book` model for its related database table `books` — yes, it's that simple!

Go to the URL `http://localhost/data-access/books/` and see scaffolding has created a very basic application with create, retrieve, update, and delete functionalities. This is how it looks like after adding some data:

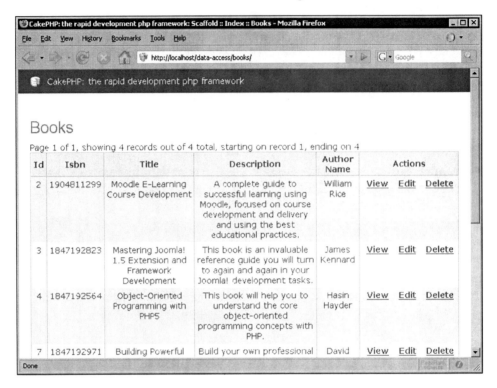

 All that are needed to create a scaffold are a database table, its corresponding model and controller, and some conventions. Once everything is in place, just setting the `$scaffold` attribute in the controller will create a simple working application!

Scaffolding is a quick way to test out the database tables that are often due to change in early parts of the development cycle. But remember, scaffolding is a temporary way to get started. It is not meant to be completely flexible. In professional applications, we will want to customize our logic and user interfaces. To do so, we have to pull the scaffolding down and write some code by ourselves. We will soon see how to write actual codes for these CRUD functionalities.

Retrieving Data

In CakePHP, there are some built-in model methods, which will help the developers to retrieve data from the database tables effortlessly. We will experiment on the Book model that we have already created to see the usage of some of these functions.

Using Model to Retrieve Data

In many cases, we need to search out all the data that matches to some certain conditions. In CakePHP, performing such database queries are done through model methods. CakePHP models have got some built-in methods that make it easy to perform such queries without any real hard effort. In the following section, we will see a step-by-step example of retrieving data from a database table.

Time for Action: Retrieving Data Using Model

1. Take out scaffolding from the BooksController.and add an index() action to it like the following:

```php
<?php
class BooksController extends AppController {
    var $name = 'Books';
function index() {
    $books = $this->Book->find('all',
                array(
                        'fields' => array(
                                        'Book.isbn',
                                        'Book.title',
                                        'Book.author_name'
                                    ),
                        'order' => 'Book.title ASC'
                        )
                        );

    $this->set('books', $books);
                }
}
?>
```

2. Create a view file for the action /books/index (/app/views/books/
index.ctp):

```
<table>
  <thead>
    <th>ISBN</th><th>Title</th><th>Author</th>
  </thead>
  <?php foreach($books as $book): ?>
  <tr>
    <td><?php echo $book['Book']['isbn'] ?></td>
    <td><?php echo $book['Book']['title'] ?></td>
    <td><?php echo $book['Book']['author_name'] ?></td>
  </tr>
  <?php endforeach; ?>
</table>
```

3. Now, point your browser to the following link and see a list of all the books
fetched and shown from the database table

```
http://localhost/data-access/books/
```

What Just Happened?

We first removed scaffolding from the BooksController. And then, we added
a new action named index() there. By calling the BooksController's attribute
$this->Book from the index() action, we can access its respective model Book. In
CakePHP, an instance of the corresponding model class is available in the controller
as a controller attribute. The first line we wrote inside the index() action is
the following:

```
$books = $this->Book->find('all',
          array(
                'fields' => array(
                              'Book.isbn',
                              'Book.title',
                              'Book.author_name'
                            ),
                'order' => 'Book.title ASC'
          )
      );
```

We have called the Book model's built-in method find() with some parameters and
then stored the returned result in a variable named $books. The first parameter all
specifies that we want all the records from the books table.

We can adjust and regulate the returned result of a find() call by
defining some keys like conditions, order, limit in the second
parameter. We will learn more about this nifty method in the next section.

The second parameter contains an associative array with two keys: `fields` and `order`. The `fields` key is an array that is used to specify the fields we want to fetch through the `find()` call. We are interested only in ISBN, title, and author names. And that is why the `fields` key's value is set to an array containing only those field names. The second key `order` is used to specify the sorting order of the query. By setting its value to `Book.title ASC`, we are telling our model to sort the result by book titles.

> All model classes have got some built-in methods that are inherited from their parent classes. These built-in methods make developers life a lot easier, as they don't need to write SQL statements anymore. Methods for all basic CRUD (Create, Read, Update, and Delete) functionalities and many more are already there, we just have to know how to use them. The code looks much cleaner and working with databases no longer remains a boring repetitive job. These neat and smart functions will write SQL queries on behalf of us — the developers.

After setting the `$books` variable with the value returned from the `find()` method, we passed it to the corresponding view file. In our case, the `find()` method returns an array that has got the following structure:

```
Array
(
    [0] => Array
        (
            [Book] => Array
                (
                    [isbn] => 1847192971
                    [title] => Building Powerful and Robust Websites
                                                   with Drupal 6
                    [author_name] => David Mercer
                )
        )
    [1] => Array
        (
            [Book] => Array
                (
                    [isbn] => 1847192823
                    [title] => Mastering Joomla! 1.5 Extension and
                                            Framework Development
                    [author_name] => James Kennard
                )
        )
    . . .
    . . .
)
```

Inside our view file, we just iterated over the $books array and printed out the information we need. Now, visiting the URL http://localhost/data-access/ books/ should show us a page like the following:

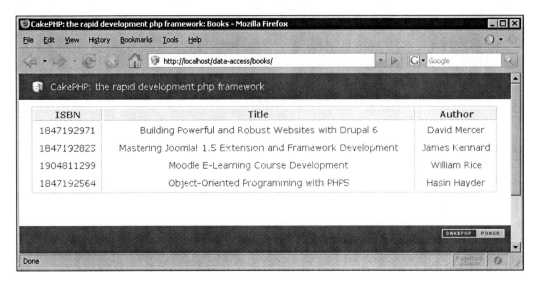

More on Data Retrieval

We have just seen a very basic use of the built-in model method find() for retrieving data from a database table. The find() method is indeed very powerful, and we can accomplish complex queries using it. We will now learn more about the find() method and see how to perform complex queries through it. We will also see how to work with some other data retrieval techniques that CakePHP offers.

More on find()

The find() method is flexible and dynamic enough to achieve the result equivalent to any SQL SELECT query. As an example, to retrieve only the isbn, title and author_name fields of the first two books that have titles starting with the character 'A' and that are sorted by their ISBNs in descending order, we would write the following SQL query:

```
SELECT `Book`.`isbn`, `Book`.`title`, `Book`.`author_name`
FROM `books` AS `Book`
WHERE `Book`.`title` LIKE 'A%'
ORDER BY `Book`.`isbn` DESC
LIMIT 2;
```

In CakePHP, the equivalent query can be performed by calling its `find()` method like the following:

```
find(
    'all',
    array(
        'conditions' => array('Book.title' => 'LIKE A%'),
        'fields' => array(
                        'Book.isbn',
                        'Book.title',
                        'Book.author_name'
                    ),
        'order' => 'Book.isbn DESC',
        'limit'=>2
    )
);
```

> Prefixing conditions with the model's name (like, `Book.title` rather that just `title`) is always a good practice. Particularly, when we were fetching related model data (discussed in Chapter 5) and two or more columns of the result have the same field name. Moreover, it improves clarity of the code.

The `find()` method takes two parameters: `$type` and `$constraints`. The first one `$type` is a string that defines the 'type' of the query. `$type` can be set to one of the following:

- `all`: The method returns all the records that matches the given conditions, sorted by the given order and up to the given limit.

- `first`: The method returns only the first record that matches the given constraints.

- `count`: The method returns the total number of records returned by the query.

As we saw in the last example, we can specify other query constraints in the second parameter `$constraints` as an associative array. The `$constraints` associative array can have the following keys:

- `conditions`: An array of the conditions that will be applied to the WHERE clause of the query. Default is `1=1`, which means no condition is applied.

- `fields`: An array of the fields to be returned by the query. If nothing is specified, it will return all the fields. This parameter is not applicable when the first parameter `$type` of the find function is set to `count`.

- order: A string that defines the ORDER BY clause of the query. If order is not specified, there will be no ORDER BY clause added to the query. This parameter is also not applicable when the type of the function is count.

- limit: An integer that specifies maximum number of records to return. If not specified, the function will return all the records matching given conditions. Only applicable when the type is all.

- offset: An integer that defines the offset of the first record to return. Default is 0. Pertinent only when the type is all.

To understand this concept more clearly, we will now skim through some quick examples showing the usage of the find() method:

1. If we want to know the total number books that have title starting with the character 'A', we would write the following code inside the BooksController:

```
$count = $this->Book->find('count', array('conditions' =>
        array('Book.title' => 'LIKE A%'));
```

It executes the following SQL query:

```
SELECT COUNT(*) AS `count` FROM `books` AS `Book` WHERE
    `Book`.`title` LIKE 'A%';
```

When the $type parameter of the find() method is set to count, the returned result is an integer. In this case, the $count variable may have the value 2.

2. If we want to find the ISBN and title of the book with the biggest id, we would write the following code:

```
$book = $this->Book->find('first',
            array(
                    'fields' => array('isbn', 'title'),
                    'order' => 'Book.id DESC'
            )
                    );
```

It will execute the following SQL statements:

```
SELECT `Book`.`isbn`, `Book`.`title` FROM `books` AS `Book`
WHERE 1 = 1 ORDER BY `Book`.`created` DESC LIMIT 1;
```

The returned result that is stored in the `$book` variable would be something like this:

```
Array
(
    [Book] => Array
        (
            [isbn] => 1847192971
            [title] => Building Powerful and Robust Websites
                        with Drupal 6
        )
)
```

3. If we want to find out all the titles written by an author (say the author's name is 'David Barnes') and sort them by their title, then the following code would work:

```
$books = $this->Book->find('all',
                            array(
                                'fields' => array('title'),
                                'conditions' => array(
                        'Book.author_name' => 'LIKE David Barnes'
                                    ),
                                'order' => 'Book.title ASC'
                                )
                    );
```

The above code will perform the following SQL query:

```
SELECT `Book`.`title` FROM `books` AS `Book` WHERE `Book`.`author_
        name` LIKE 'David Barnes' ORDER BY
`Book`.`title` ASC
```

The output of the above function will be something like the following:

```
Array
(
    [0] => Array
        (
            [Book] => Array
                (
                    [title] => How to write computer books
                )
        )
    [1] => Array
        (
            [Book] => Array
                (
                    [title] => How not to write a technical book!
                )
        )
)
```

Closely look at the difference between the returned arrays when the `$type` parameter of the `find()` method is set to `first` and when it is set to `all`. In case of `first`, the returned array is an associative array containing the book information. Whereas, when the type is set to `all`, the returned array is an array of associative arrays, each containing a single book's information.

In the above examples, we have used pretty simple conditions for the `find()` calls. In real world applications, conditions can be much more complex having many nested conditions with many types of logical and conditional operators. We will now specifically look at the `conditions` key of the `$constraints` parameter and learn how to do more complex things using the `find()`!

Writing Complex Conditions

In its simplest form, the `conditions` key in the `$constraints` parameter has the following structure:

```
'conditions' => array(
                    "ModelName.field_name" =>
                            "comparison_operator value"
            )
```

The good thing about this structure is that it can be expanded to support more than one condition per field with binary operators in between. Let's run through some very quick examples to understand the usage of the 'conditions' key in different situations. We will also discover how to support multiple conditions with different binary operators per field through these examples:

1. If we want to find the book with ISBN '1234567890', we would execute the following SQL command:

    ```
    SELECT * FROM `books` AS `Book` WHERE `Book`.`isbn` = '1234567890';
    ```

    Whereas in CakePHP, we would call the `find()` method from the `BooksController` like the following:

    ```
    $this->Book->find('first', array(
                        'conditions' => array(
                        'Book.isbn' => '= 1234567890'
                                            )
                                )
                );
    ```

    The = (equals) operator used here is needless. As it is used by default if no comparison operator is set.

2. If we want to find all the books that has a title containing the word 'CakePHP', we would execute the following SQL:

```
SELECT * FROM `books` AS `Book` WHERE `Book`.`title` LIKE
'%CakePHP%'
```

In CakePHP, we would use the `find()` method like the following:

```
$this->Book-> find('all', array(
                        'conditions' =>
                array('Book.title' => "LIKE %CakePHP%")
                )
            );
```

3. If we want to find all the books written by the authors – 'Anupom Syam', 'Ahsanul Bari' and 'David Barnes', we would write the following SQL:

```
SELECT * FROM `books` AS `Book` WHERE Book.author_name IN (
'Anupom Syam', 'Ahsanul Bari', 'David Barnes'
)
```

In CakePHP, using the `find()` method, we can do it like the following:

```
$this->Book-> find('all', array(
                        'conditions' => array(
                        'Book.author_name' => array(
                                        'Anupom Syam',
                                        'Ahsanul Bari',
                                        'David Barnes'
                                        )
                                )
                )
            );
```

The identical result of the SQL logical operator `IN()` can be achieved by setting an array of values against a field name.

4. If we want to find all the books written by – 'David Barnes' and has the word 'CakePHP' in title , we would write the following SQL:

```
SELECT * FROM `books` AS `Book` WHERE Book.author_name LIKE 'David
Barnes' AND Book.title LIKE '%CakePHP%'
)
```

In CakePHP, we would write the following,

```
$this->Book-> find('all', array(
                        'conditions' => array(
                'Book.author_name' => 'David Barnes',
                'Book.title' => '%CAKEPHP%'
            )
    )
);
```

To add more than one condition, we just need to have more than one key-value pairs in the conditions array. By default, conditions are joined together using the logical operator AND.

5. If we want to find all the books that are either written by — 'David Barnes' or has the word 'CakePHP' in title , we would write the following SQL:

```
SELECT * FROM `books` AS `Book` WHERE Book.author_name LIKE (
'David Barnes' OR Book.title LIKE '%CakePHP%')
```

In CakePHP, we would write the following:

```
$this->Book-> find('all', array(
                    'conditions' => array(
                        "or" =>
                        array
                        (
                "Book.author_name" => "David Barnes",
                "Book.title" => "%CAKEPHP%"
                    )
                )
            )
        );
```

Cake accepts all valid SQL logical operations. If we want to use something other than the default AND operator, we just have to group together the conditions in an array. And then, we have to set that array to the key named after the logical operation we want to use as value.

6. If we want to find all the 'Drupal' titles written by 'David Mercer' and all the 'Joomla' titles written by 'James Kennard', we would write the following SQL:

```
SELECT * FROM `books` AS `Book` WHERE (
(Book.author_name LIKE 'David Mercer' AND Book.title LIKE
'%Drupal%') OR (Book.author_name LIKE 'James Kennard' AND Book.
title LIKE '%Joomla%')
)
```

In CakePHP, we can perform this query using nested arrays as the value of the conditions key:

```
$this->Book->find('all', array(
                'conditions' => array(
                        'or' => array(
                                        array(
                'Book.author_name'=> 'LIKE David Mercer',
                'Book.title'=> 'LIKE %Drupal%'
                                        ),
                                        array(
                'Book.author_name'=> 'LIKE James Kennard',
                'Book.title'=> 'LIKE %Joomla%'
                                        )
                        )
                )
        );
```

Beside the `find()` method, CakePHP provides some shortcut functions for performing data retrievals. These are collectively known as magic find functions. We will now see how to retrieve data using those magic find functions.

Magic Find Functions

Magic find functions are used as shortcuts to search database tables by a specific field. Take the previous example, where we searched out a book with ISBN 1234567890. We used the `find()` method to perform this search. We can also do the same using the magic functions like the following:

```
$book = $this->Book->findByIsbn('1234567890');
```

It is certainly shorter and it executes exactly the same query as the previous `find()` example.

The `findBy<FieldName>()` function is dynamically created by CakePHP. This magic function can be formed by appending the fieldname (by which we want to search our database tables) just after `findBy` phrase in CamelCased format.

The basic structure of this magic `findBy<FieldName>()` function is like this:

```
findBy<FieldName>(string value, array fields, string order)
```

The first parameter `$value` is the value of the field we are looking for. The second parameter `$fields` is an array containing the fieldnames to be returned by the search. The third one `$order` specifies the order of the result. As like the `find('first')`, the `findBy<FieldName>()` function only returns the first record that matches the supplied criteria.

There's another variant of magic find functions that works like the `find('all')` call — that is it returns all the records that matches the given conditions. These functions have `findAllBy` prefix and the basic prototype looks like the following:

```
findAllBy<FieldName>(string value, array fields, string order, int
$limit)
```

The `findAllBy<FieldName>()` function returns all the records where the field has a value equal to the first parameter `$value`. The second and third parameters are the same as the `findBy<Fieldname>()` function. The fourth parameter `$limit` is used to specify the limit of the query.

Now, let's see a simple example of `findAllBy<FieldName>()` function. Recall the example, where we searched out all the titles written by 'David Barnes' and sorted by their titles. We can also do the same thing using the magic `findAllBy<FieldName>()` function, like the following:

```
$books = $this->Book->findAllByAuthorName('David Barnes', array('Book.
title'),'Book.title ASC'));
```

Outputs of the `findBy<FieldName>()` and `findAllBy<fieldname>()` functions are arrays formatted just like the outputs of `find('first')` and `find ('all')` methods respectively.

Reading a Single Field

In some cases, we may like to read only a single field from a record. It is pretty doable using the `find()` method though. But CakePHP offers a simpler method to accomplish such tasks. As an example, to get the title of the book that has ISBN 1904811299, we can write the following code in our `BooksController`:

```
$this->Book->field('title', array('isbn' => '1904811299'));
```

The prototype of the `field()` method is like the following:

```
field(string $name, string $conditions, string $order)
```

The `field()` method simply returns the value of the single field that is specified as the first parameter `$name` from the first record. The second parameter `$conditions` defines the search criteria and the third one `$order` is used to set the order of the result.

Still now, in this chapter, we have learned how to retrieve data from the database tables using CakePHP's model methods. But there is no point of retrieving if there is no data stored in the database. Saving data into the database is the next thing we are going to learn.

Saving and Updating Data

CakePHP offers some built-in model methods to help us with common database operations—this includes saving and modifying database records. In this section, we will first look at a quick example of saving data and then see another quick one on how to update a database record in CakePHP.

Saving Data

We will continue our experiment on the Book model that we have already created. In the following *Time for action*, we will create a simple application that can take book information from the user and save them into the database.

Time for Action: Saving Data into the Database

1. In the BooksController (app/controllers/books_controller.php), write a new action add():

```php
<?php
class BooksController extends AppController {
    var $name = 'Books';
    var $helpers = array('Form' );
    function index() {
        $books = $this->Book->find('all',
                array(
                        'fields' => array(
                                        'Book.isbn',
                                        'Book.title',
                                        'Book.author_name'
                                    ),
                        'order' => 'Book.title ASC'
                        )
                        );
        $this->set('books', $books);
                        }

    function add() {
        if (!empty($this->data)) {
            $this->Book->create();
            if(!!$this->Book->save($this->data)) {
                $this->Session->setFlash('Book is Saved!', true);
                $this->redirect(array('action'=>'index'));
            }
        }
    }
    }
}
?>
```

2. Now create a view for the action '/books/add' (`app/views/add.ctp`) with the following code:

```
<?php echo $form->create('Book');?>
    <fieldset>
        <legend>Add New Book</legend>
    <?php
        echo $form->input('isbn');
        echo $form->input('title');
        echo $form->input('description');
        echo $form->input('author_name');
    ?>
    </fieldset>
<?php echo $form->end('Submit');?>
```

3. Point your browser to the following URL and add a new book,
   `http://localhost/data-access/books/add`

What Just Happened?

We first added a new action named `add()` inside the `BooksController`. Inside this action, we then checked if there is any form data sent back from the view using the following line of code:

```
if (!empty($this->data)) {
```

When no data is returned from its view, it proceeds with rendering the corresponding view file (`/apps/views/add.ctp`). Inside the view file, we created a form using CakePHP's `FormHelper` for taking book information from the user. The first line of the view file creates a `<form>` start tag:

```
<?php echo $form->create('Book');?>
```

We are binding the form with the `Book` model by providing `Book` as the parameter to the `FormHelper`'s create method. We then added form input fields for taking ISBN, title, description and author's name respectively using `FormHelper`'s `input()` method:

```
<?php
    echo $form->input('isbn');
    echo $form->input('title');
    echo $form->input('description');
    echo $form->input('author_name');
?>
```

We supplied the respective database table fieldnames as parameters to the `input()` calls. It will help CakePHP's `FormHelper` to automatically bind the input fields with their corresponding database table fields. Also, by default, this form's action (where the form is to be submitted) is set to the corresponding controller's `add()` action.

After adding those input fields, we added a submit button and closed the `<form>` tag with the following line of code:

```
<?php echo $form->end('Submit');?>
```

For now, understanding this much about the `FormHelper` will just do. We will discuss much more about this useful helper in Chapter 7.

Now, if we go to the URL `http://localhost/data-access/books/add` it should show us a form like the following:

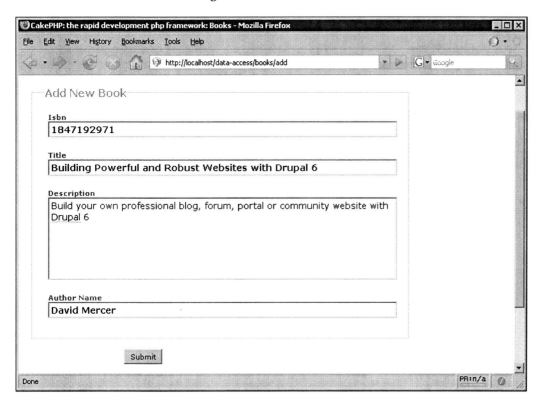

When the form is filled up and submitted, all form data is sent back to the `BooksController`'s `add()` action. Inside the controller action, the submitted form data can be found through the controller attribute `$this->data`. The condition `if (!empty($this->data))` will now return a `true` (as `$this->data` is now filled up with the submitted form data). And code inside the `if{}` block will now get executed. Inside the block, we called the `Book` model's `create()` method first. And right after that we called the model method `save()` with the parameter `$this->data` (that holds the data sent back from the form):

```
$this->Book->create();
$this->Book->save($this->data);
```

 It is important to call the model's `create()` method just ahead of calling the model's `save()` method if the intention is to create a new record.

The `save()` method creates a new record in the database table `books` with data passed into it. When the save operation is done, controller sets a flash message saying **Book is saved!** using the `Session` component's `setFlash()` method. Then, it redirects to the `index()` action of the `BooksController`. The newly added book can now be seen in the list of books. A flash message will appear on top of that list notifying us that the new book is stored successfully in the database table.

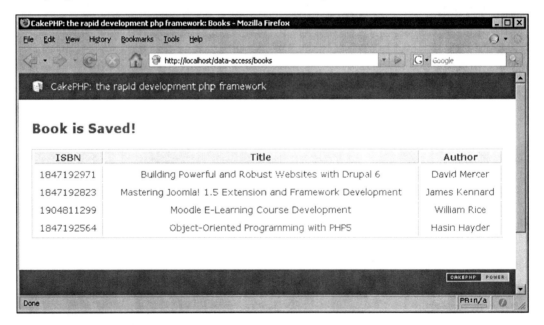

The `save()` method is not used only for creating new record in the database table, it can also be used for updating an existing record. We will now see how the same old `save()` method can be used to modify an already stored record.

Updating a Record

Updating records is one of the four basic database operations that are very commonly used in almost all data intensive web applications. We will now see how to use CakePHP's built-in model method `save()` to update an existing record in the database.

Time for Action: Updating a Database Record

1. Inside the `BooksController` (/app/controllers/books_controller.php), write a new action named `edit()`,

```php
<?php
class BooksController extends AppController {
    var $name = 'Books';
    var $helpers = array('Form' );

    function index() {
        $books = $this->Book->find('all',
                array(
                        'fields' => array(
                                            'Book.id',
                                            'Book.isbn',
                                            'Book.title',
                                            'Book.author_name'
                                        ),
                        'order' => 'Book.title ASC'
                    )
                );
        $this->set('books', $books);
                    }

    function add() {
        if (!empty($this->data)) {
            $this->Book->create();
            if(!!$this->Book->save($this->data)) {
                $this->Session->setFlash('Book is Saved!', true);
                $this->redirect(array('action'=>'index'));
            }
        }
    }
}
```

```
function edit($id=null) {
    if (!$id && empty($this->data)) {
        $this->Session->setFlash('Invalid Book', true);
        $this->redirect(array('action'=>'index'));
    }
    if (empty($this->data)) {
        $this->data = $this->Book->read(null, $id);
    }
    else {
        $this->Book->create();
        if(!!$this->Book->save($this->data)) {
            $this->Session->setFlash('Book is Updated!', true);
            $this->redirect(array('action'=>'index'), null, true);
        }
    }
}
}
?>
```

2. Create a view for the action '/books/edit' (/app/views/edit.ctp).

```
<?php echo $form->create('Book');?>
    <fieldset>
        <legend>Edit Book</legend>
        <?php
            echo $form->input('id');
echo $form->input('isbn');
            echo $form->input('title');
            echo $form->input('description');
            echo $form->input('author_name');
        ?>
    </fieldset>
<?php echo $form->end('Submit');?>
```

3. Inside the view file of the /books/index action (/app/views/books/index. ctp) add an edit link next to the author names:

```
<table>
  <thead>
    <th>ISBN</th><th>Title</th><th>Author</th><th>Actions</th>
  </thead>
  <?php foreach($books as $book): ?>
  <tr>
    <td><?php echo $book['Book']['isbn'] ?></td>
```

```
        <td><?php echo $book['Book']['title'] ?></td>
        <td><?php echo $book['Book']['author_name'] ?></td>
        <td><?php echo $html->link('edit','edit/'.$book['Book']['id'])
           ?></td>
     </tr>
     <?php endforeach; ?>
  </table>
```

4. Point your browser to the following URL and click on an edit button next to a book `http://localhost/data-access/books/`. It should show you a form where we can edit the book information. Modify some information and hit submit to update the database record.

What Just Happened?

In the `BooksController`, we first added a new action named `edit()` that can take a parameter named `$id`.

The first `if{}` block inside the action only gets executed when the `$id` parameter is empty and there is no form data sent back from the view.

```
if (!$id && empty($this->data)) {
        $this->Session->setFlash('Invalid Book', true);
        $this->redirect(array('action'=>'index'));
}
```

In that case, we set a flash message to notify the user that the request is invalid and redirect them to the `/books/index` action. Note the `redirect()` method by default exits just after the redirection. And hence the rest of the part of the code inside that action gets executed only when the `$id` parameter is not empty or some form data is sent back to the action from the view.

```
if (empty($this->data)) {
        $this->data = $this->Book->read(null, $id);
}
else {
    $this->Book->create();
    if(!!$this->Book->save($this->data)) {
        $this->Session->setFlash('Book Updated!', true);
        $this->redirect(array('action'=>'index'), null, true);
    }
}
```

When there is no form data, the `if (empty($this->data))` condition returns a `true` and the following code gets executed:

```
$this->data = $this->Book->read(null, $id);
```

This line actually returns the record with the matching id as an associative array. The returned result is then set to the controller attribute $data.

Just in case you are curious, the returned associative array from the read() method is in the common Cake format. As an example, in our case, it would look something like the following:

```
Array
(
    [Book] => Array
        (
            [id] => 1
            [isbn] => 1904811299
            [title] => Moodle E-Learning Course Development
            [description] => A complete guide...
            [author_name] => William Rice
        )

)
```

 The model method read($fields = null, $id = null) can take two parameters. The firs parameter $fields can be a string or an array specifying a single fieldname or a list of fieldnames that we want to select. When $fields is set to null, all fields are returned. The second parameter specifies the id of the record we want to read. And it returns the record as an associative array having the common Cake format.

After setting up the controller attribute $data with the record returned, the corresponding view file (/app/views/books/edit.ctp) is rendered. The view file has a form that is pretty much similar to the one that we wrote for the /books/add action. The only difference is that it has a new input field for the field id.

```php
<?php echo $form->create('Book');?>
    <fieldset>
        <legend>Edit Book</legend>
        <?php
        echo $form->input('id');
        echo $form->input('isbn');
        echo $form->input('title');
        echo $form->input('description');
        echo $form->input('author_name');
        ?>
    </fieldset>
<?php echo $form->end('Submit');?>
```

It is interesting the way Cake differentiates these two operations—add and edit. When the id field is present in the web form, instead of adding a new record the model performs the update operation on the record with the specified id. Whereas when there is no input field specified in the form for the id field, it just carries out the usual add operation.

We then edited the view file (`/app/views/books/index.ctp`) for the `/books/index` action. We added a new column in the table called `action` and added a new link labeled `edit` next to every author's name there.

```
<table>
  <thead>
    <th>ISBN</th><th>Title</th><th>Author</th><th>Actions</th>
  </thead>
  <?php foreach($books as $book): ?>
  <tr>
    <td><?php echo $book['Book']['isbn'] ?></td>
    <td><?php echo $book['Book']['title'] ?></td>
    <td><?php echo $book['Book']['author_name'] ?></td>
    <td><?php echo $html->link('edit', array('action'=>'edit',
    $book['Book']['id']) ) ?></td>
  </tr>
  <?php endforeach; ?>
</table>
```

The `edit` link is created using the `HtmlHelper`'s link method that was discussed earlier in Chapter 3. These links point to the `edit()` action of the `BooksController` and contains the respective book ids as parameter. So, when someone clicks on the `edit` link of a book, it places a request to the `/books/edit` action and the `id` of the book is passed through the URL. The `edit` action accepts the parameter as `$id`. The code inside the second `if{}` block gets executed. It reads the record with the matching id and sets it to the controller attribute `$data`, and a form shows up in the browser.

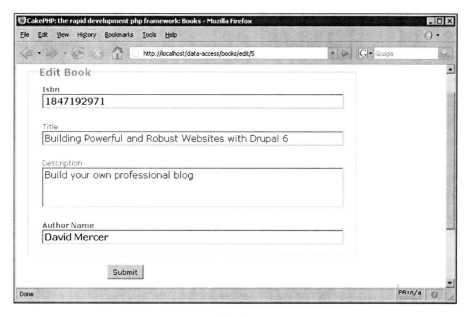

If the controller attribute `$data` is set, `FormHelper` automatically fills up the form inputs with the data set in the `$data` attribute. Also notice that, the HTML input field created for the database table field `id` is a hidden form field. That is quite logical as while editing a record, we obviously must not edit its primary field. The `FormHelper` is pretty intelligent, we must say!

After editing, when the **submit** button is clicked, the form data is sent back to the `edit` action. Now, as the form data is not empty, the following piece of code gets executed:

```
$this->Book->create();
if(!!$this->Book->save($this->data)) {
            $this->Session->setFlash('Book is Updated!', true);
            $this->redirect(array('action'=>'index'), null, true);
}
```

This part of the code is very similar to what we have done for the `/books/add` action. We called the `create()` method of the `Book` model to prepare it for a `save()` operation. And then the `save()` method of the respective model is executed with the submitted form data as the parameter.

 If the `id` field is set in the supplied parameter, instead of inserting a new record, the `save()` method performs a database update operation on the record with matching `id`.

If the update is successful, it takes the user back to the `/books/index` action. A message on top of the table appears to confirm that the edit was successful and a new record shows up in the list of books.

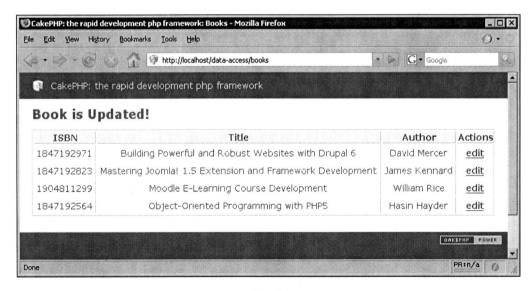

More on the save() Method

We already saw how the handy method `save()` can be used for both storing and updating database records. The `save()` method can take 3 parameters: `$data`, `$validate` and `$fieldList`.

```
save(array $data = null, boolean $validate = true, array $fieldList =
array())
```

The first parameter `$data` is the data to be saved. `$data` is a specially formatted associative array that should have the following structure:

```
Array
(
    [ModelName] => Array
        (
            [fieldname1] => 'value1'
            [fieldname2] => 'value2'
        )
)
```

It is also ok to have the data in a flatter array without the `ModelName` key.

```
Array
(
    [fieldname1] => 'value1'
    [fieldname2] => 'value2'
)
```

In that case, the data will be stored to the corresponding database table of the model that called the `save()` method.

As we already saw, the save method can be used for both save and update operations. The only difference is that in case of update, the 'id' key must be defined in the `$data` array. Whereas for the save operation, it should not contain the 'id'.

Anyway, the good thing is that if we correctly use the `FormHelper` to create our web forms, we don't have to think about the structure. The form data are already formatted and gets saved without putting any extra effort (As we saw in our last two *Time for Actions*). But it is still good to know about the special structure of the `$data` array as in some cases (as an example, where the data to be saved is not sent from a web form etc.), we may need to store them manually.

The second parameter `$validate` can be set to `false` if we want to bypass the CakePHP's validation mechanism (Data validation is discussed later in this chapter) while saving them to the database. By default, `$validate` is set to **true** that imposes the validation on the supplied data.

The third parameter $fieldList is an array containing a list of fieldnames. If the $fieldList parameter is set, the save function will limit the save only to the fields specified in the $fieldList array. That means fields that are not in the $fieldList array will be ignored while saving. It comes especially handy when you want to protect your database from unwanted uses.

The save() method returns false, if for some reason, it fails to save the data or the data do not pass the validation rules. Just when the save operation is finished, the $id attribute of the model is set to the id of the newly created record. So, if the data is stored successfully, we can obtain the id of the last inserted record like the following:

```
$this->Book->save($data);
$last_insert_id = $this->Book->id;
```

Updating a Single Field

Sometimes, we may need to update a single field of a record. CakePHP provides a model function called saveField() to perform that task. Following is a code snippet that shows how to use the saveField() method for updating a field's value:

```
$this->Book->id = 9;
$this->Book->saveField('title','New Title');
```

The above code changes the title to The new title of the record with id = 9. Before we call the saveField() method, we must set the $id attribute of the model to specify which record to update.

The saveField() method can take 3 parameters:

```
saveField(string $fieldName, string $fieldValue, $validate = false)
```

The first parameter $fieldName is the name of the field that is to be modified. The second parameter $fieldValue specifies the new value for that field. The third one $validate is used to turn the validation on and off. By default, validation rules are not applied when the saveField() function is used.

Batch Update

In some cases, we may want to update multiple records at once. CakePHP provides a model method named updateAll() that particularly serves this purpose. Let's assume we have a new field called starred in the books table. Now, to set the starred field to 1 for all the books that are written by 'David Barnes', we can use the updateAll() method like the following:

```
$this->Book->updateAll(
    array('Book.author_name' => "David Barnes"),
    array('Book.starred' => 1)
);
```

The prototype of the method is:

```
updateAll(array $conditions, array $fields)
```

The first parameter $conditions is an array of conditions that identifies all the records to be updated. The format of the $conditions array is the same as of the find() method. The second parameter $fields specifies fields to be updated, along with their new values.

Deleting Data

We have already learned how to perform some basic database operations such as create, read, and update using CakePHP model methods. Now, it's time to look at the last one, that's delete. There are two built-in model functions that CakePHP provides for executing the delete operation. One of them is for deleting a single record and the other is for deleting multiple records. We will first see a step-by-step example of how to delete a single record using the model function del().

Deleting a Single Record

Deleting a record from a database table using CakePHP is pretty easy. CakePHP model by default inherits a method to serve this purpose. We will now see how we can use that model method to delete a record from our books table.

Time for Action: Deleting a Single Record

1. In the BooksController (/app/controllers/books_controller.php) add a new action delete():

```php
<?php
class BooksController extends AppController {
    var $name = 'Books';
    var $helpers = array('Form' );

    function index() {
        $books = $this->Book->find('all',
            array(
                'fields' => array(
                                'Book.id',
                                'Book.isbn',
                                'Book.title',
                                'Book.author_name'
                        ),
                'order' => 'Book.title ASC'
            )
```

```
                );
            $this->set('books', $books);
    }

    function add() {
        if (!empty($this->data)) {
            $this->Book->create();
            if(!!$this->Book->save($this->data)) {
                $this->Session->setFlash('Book is Saved!', true);
                $this->redirect(array('action'=>'index'));
            }
        }
    }
    function edit($id=null) {
        if (!$id && empty($this->data)) {
            $this->Session->setFlash('Invalid Book', true);
            $this->redirect(array('action'=>'index'));
        }
        if (!empty($this->data)) {
            $this->Book->create();
            if(!!$this->Book->save($this->data)) {
                $this->Session->setFlash('Book Updated!', true);
                $this->redirect(array('action'=>'index'), null, true);
            }
        }
        if (empty($this->data)) {
            $this->data = $this->Book->read(null, $id);
        }
    }
    function delete($id = null) {
        if (!$id) {
            $this->Session->setFlash('Invalid Book', true);
        }
        else if($this->Book->del($id)) {
            $this->Session->setFlash('Book is deleted', true);
        }
        else {
            $this->Session->setFlash('Could not delete Book', true);
        }
        $this->redirect(array('action'=>'index'));
    }
}
?>
```

2. Now, in the view file of the /books/index action (/app/views/books/index.ctp) add a delete link next to the edit link,

```
<table>
  <thead>
    <th>ISBN</th><th>Title</th><th>Author</th><th>Actions</th>
  </thead>
  <?php foreach($books as $book): ?>
  <tr>
    <td><?php echo $book['Book']['isbn'] ?></td>
    <td><?php echo $book['Book']['title'] ?></td>
    <td><?php echo $book['Book']['author_name'] ?></td>
    <td>
      <?php echo $html->link('edit', array('action'=>'edit',
                        $book['Book']['id']) ) ?>
      <?php echo $html->link('delete', array('action'=>'delete',
                        $book['Book']['id']) ) ?>
    </td>
  </tr>
  <?php endforeach; ?>
</table>
```

3. Point your browser to the following URL
    http://localhost/data-access/books/
    Now click on a delete link next to a book. It should delete the record and take us back to the index action. A message text should show up on top of the list to notify us that the record has been deleted successfully.

What Just Happened?

First, we wrote and added a new action named delete() inside the BooksController. The delete() action takes a parameter $id. In that method, we first checked if $id is empty. If it is then we set a flash message saying **Invalid book**,

```
if (!$id) {
        $this->Session->setFlash('Invalid Book', true);
}
```

Inside the next if condition, we tried to delete the record by calling the model method del().

$id is passed to the del() method as parameter to specify the record to delete. If the deletion is successful, the if condition returns a true and we set a flash message saying **Book is deleted!**.

```
else if($this->Book->del($id)) {
        $this->Session->setFlash('Book is deleted', true);
}
```

If the deletion fails (it can fail even if the id provided is invalid), the code inside the `else` block gets executed. It sets a flash message saying **Could not delete the book!**.

At the end, we redirect the user back to the `/books/index` action. Notice that the `/books/delete` action does not have any view. In fact, no view is required as for any case, it will redirect the user to the `/books/index` action.

We then added a new link in the view file for the `/books/index` action next to the edit link using the `HtmlHelper`'s link method:

```
<td><?php echo $html->link('delete', array('action'=>'delete',
$book['Book']['id']) ) ?></td>
```

This link is pretty much similar to the `edit` link that we created in the previous *Time for Action*.

Now, if we click on the `delete` link next to any book, it will request the `/books/delete` action to perform the deletion. Then, it will take us back to the `/books/index` action showing a message on top saying **Book is deleted**.

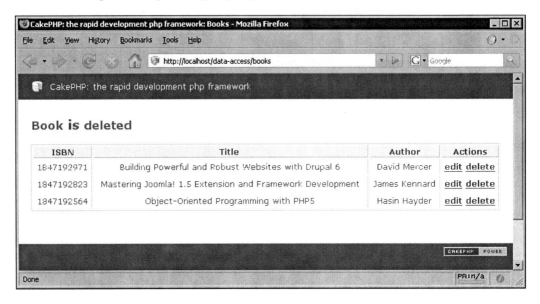

Placing Your Own Logic Inside Model

Any database-related operation is best housed in model classes. Besides, model class often contains domain logics (business rules) that are specific to our applications. For that reason, quite often we need to write our own model methods.

Create and Use Your Own Model Method

We can treat model classes like any other PHP class. The difference is that we should only put business/domain logics inside it. We will now create such a method in a model and use the method from its corresponding controller class.

Time for Action: Create and Use Your Own Model Method

1. Add a new field named `starred` in the `books` table by executing the following SQL command:

```
ALTER TABLE `books` ADD `starred` BINARY NOT NULL DEFAULT '0';
```

2. In the `Book` model (`/app/models/book.php`), create a new method `addStar()`:

```php
<?php
class Book extends AppModel
{
    var $name = 'Book';

    function addStar($id) {
        $this->id = $id;
        $this->saveField('starred', 1);
    }
}
?>
```

3. In the `BooksController` (`/app/controllers/books_controller.php`), write a new action named `star()`,

```php
<?php
class BooksController extends AppController {
    var $name = 'Books';
var $helpers = array('Form' );

    function index() {
        $books = $this->Book->find('all',
            array(
                'fields' => array(
                            'Book.id',
                            'Book.isbn',
                            'Book.title',
                            'Book.author_name'
                        ),
                'order' => 'Book.title ASC'
            )
        );
```

```
        $this->set('books', $books);
    }

    function add() {
        if (!empty($this->data)) {
            $this->Book->create();
            if(!!$this->Book->save($this->data)) {
                $this->Session->setFlash('Book is Saved!', true);
                $this->redirect(array('action'=>'index'));
            }
        }
    }

function edit($id=null) {
    if (!$id && empty($this->data)) {
        $this->Session->setFlash('Invalid Book', true);
        $this->redirect(array('action'=>'index'));
    }
    if (!empty($this->data)) {
        $this->Book->create();
        if(!!$this->Book->save($this->data)) {
            $this->Session->setFlash('Book Updated!', true);
            $this->redirect(array('action'=>'index'), null, true);
        }
    }
    if (empty($this->data)) {
        $this->data = $this->Book->read(null, $id);
    }
}

function delete($id = null) {
    if (!$id) {
        $this->Session->setFlash('Invalid Book', true);
    }
    else if($this->Book->del($id)) {
        $this->Session->setFlash('Book deleted', true);
    }
    else {
        $this->Session->setFlash('Could not delete Book', true);
    }
    $this->redirect(array('action'=>'index'));
}

function star($id = null) {
    if (!$id) {
        $this->Session->setFlash('Invalid Book', true);
    }
```

```
        else {
            $this->Book->addStar($id);
            $this->Session->setFlash('Star is Added', true);
        }
        $this->redirect(array('action'=>'index'));
    }
}
?>
```

4. In the view file of the /books/index action (/app/views/books/index.
    ctp), add the following highlighted codes:

```
<table>
  <thead>
    <th>ISBN</th><th>Title</th><th>Author</th><th>Actions</th>
  </thead>
  <?php foreach($books as $book): ?>
  <tr>
    <td><?php echo $book['Book']['isbn'] ?></td>
    <td>
      <?php echo $book['Book']['title'] ?>
      <?php if($book['Book']['starred']): ?>
          <strong>***</strong>
      <?php endif; ?>
    </td>
    <td><?php echo $book['Book']['author_name'] ?></td>
    <td>
      <?php echo $html->link('edit','edit/'.$book['Book']['id']) ?>
      <?php echo $html->link('delete','delete/
                              '.$book['Book']['id']) ?>
      <?php echo $html->link('add star', array('action'=>'star',
                              $book['Book']['id']) ) ?>
    </td>
  </tr>
  <?php endforeach; ?>
</table>
```

5. Point your browser to the following URL,
    http://localhost/data-access/books/
    Now, click on a add star link next to a book. It should request the /books/
    star action. Then set the starred field of the book to 1 and take us back to
    the index action. A message should appear on top of the list to notify us that
    the record has been starred successfully. Also, now we should find three star
    (*) signs next to that book's title.

What Just Happened?

First, we added a new field called `starred` (of type BINARY) to our database table
`books`. We then wrote a small method named `addStar()` inside our `Book` model.
This method takes a parameter `$id`. This method sets the `starred` field's value to 1
of the record with the matching id in the database table.

```
function addStar($id) {
      $this->id = $id;
      $this->saveField('starred', 1);
}
```

We used model's built-in method `saveField()` for updating the field `starred`
(this method was discussed earlier in this chapter in the section 'Updating a single
record'). It is pretty straightforward.

We then added a new action named `star()` in the `BooksController`.

```
function star($id = null) {
      if (!$id) {
          $this->Session->setFlash('Invalid Book', true);
      }
      else {
          $this->Book->addStar($id);
          $this->Session->setFlash('Star is Added', true);
      }
      $this->redirect(array('action'=>'index'));
}
```

The `star()` method takes a parameter called `$id`. If `$id` is empty, it sets a flash
message saying **Invalid Book**. Otherwise, it calls the `Book` model's `addStar()`
method and passes the `$id` as a parameter to that method.

We then changed the view file of the `/books/index` action. We added an `if`
condition just after the title of the book:

```
<?php if($book['Book']['starred']): ?>
    <strong>***</strong>
<?php endif; ?>
```

If the `starred` field of the book is set to 1, three stars (*) will be printed. We also
added a `add star` link next to the `delete` link in that view file.

Now, if we go to the URL `/books/index` and click on a `add star` link it will
redirect to the `/books/star` action. There the `Book` model's `addStar()` method will
be called. The `addStar()` method will simply change the `starred` field to 1 for

the record with the same id. We will then be redirected to the /books/index page. There, a message will appear on top of the book list saying **Star is Added**. Also, three consecutive star (*) marks will appear next to the starred book names.

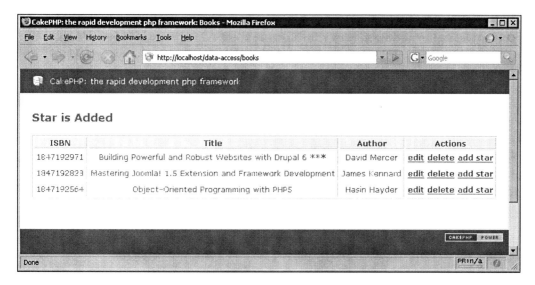

Making Custom SQL Queries

In some cases, we may like to execute custom SQL queries and commands from our custom methods. There are two model methods that allow us to execute SQLs directly.

The first one is the query() method that is used to make custom SQL queries. The following code snippet shows a custom model method that uses the query() method:

```
function getCount()
{
    return $this->query('SELECT count(*) FROM posts');
}
```

The query() method takes an SQL query string as parameter and returns the result of that query as an array. The second one is the execute() method that allows us to execute custom SQL commands. It also takes an SQL string as parameter.

The only difference between these two is that execute() is used to execute SQL commands (INSERT/DELETE/UPDATE), whereas, query() is used for executing SQL queries (SELECT).

Validating Your Data

Data validation is one of the most important aspects of designing secure web applications. It helps to make sure that we are accepting only the correct data while rejecting the bad ones. To check for correctness of data that are input to the application, data validation uses routines, often called validation rules. We are now going to see how we can apply validation rules to ensure the correctness of our input data.

Adding Validation to Our Model

In CakePHP, validation rules are defined in model classes. To let a model class know about the validation rules that we want to apply, we have to define the rules in the $validate attribute of that model. In the following *Time for Action*, we will see how we can add validation rules in our model classes to make sure only the correct input data get saved.

Time for Action: Adding Validation to Our Model

1. In the Book model (/app/models/book.php), create a new attribute $validate like the following:

```php
<?php
class Book extends AppModel
{
    var $name = 'Book';

    var $validate = array(
        'title' => array(
                    'rule' => 'alphaNumeric'
                ),
        'description' => 'alphaNumeric',
        'author_name' => array(
                    'rule' => array('custom', '/[a-z]$/i'),
                    'message' => 'Only letters are allowed!'
                    ),
        'isbn' => array(
            'isbn10' => array(
            'rule' => array('custom', '/^[0-9]{9}[0-9xX]$/'),
            'message' => 'Invalid ISBN!'
        ),
            'unique' => array(
            'rule' => 'isUnique',
```

```
                'on' => 'create',
                'message' => 'The ISBN is already added!'
            )
        )
    );

    function addStar($id) {
        $this->id = $id;
        $this->saveField('starred', 1);
    }
}
?>
```

2. Now, point your browser to the following URL and try adding a book with invalid or no data:
   ```
   http://localhost/data-access/books/add
   ```

What Just Happened?

In CakePHP, data validation is done by the model classes just before saving/updating the data to the database. If the data supplied is not valid, the save/update operation is aborted. To let the model class know about the validation rules to be applied, we have to define the rules in the $validate attribute of the model class.

To add validation to our Book model, we defined the $validate attribute of the model. The $validate attribute contains rules for all the fields that we want to be validated. The first rule we defined is for the title field:

```
'title' => array(
            'rule' => 'alphaNumeric'
        ),
```

As we can see, validation rule for a field is defined as a key-value pair, where the key contains the database field name to be validated and the value contains an array with all the constraints to be applied on those fields. For the title field, the only constraint rule is defined as alphaNumeric—that suggests the data for this field must only contain letters and numbers.

 alphaNumeric is one of the numerous pre-defined validation rules that CakePHP offers. To learn more about the built-in rules, please refer to the official documentation http://book.cakephp.org/

The next validation rule in the $validate array is for the description field:

```
'description' => 'alphaNumeric',
```

If we have only one predefined rule as constraints for a field, we can directly set that as the value instead of using an array. The above line also specifies that the description field should contain only letters and numbers.

The third validation rule we defined is for the author_name field.

```
'author_name' => array(
        'rule' => array('custom', '/[a-z]$/i'),
        'message' => 'Only letters are allowed!'
    )
```

Valid author names should contain only letters. But there is no built-in rule for that. If the pre-defined validation rules cannot meet our requirement, we can anytime create custom rules to fulfill our need. For the author_name field, we created a custom rule using regular expression: array('custom', '/[a-z]$/i'). A custom rule is an array where the first element is the string custom and the second one contains the regular expression against which the data is to be validated. We also added a message key that is set to Only letters are allowed!. This message text will appear next to the respective HTML input field if the validation fails against this specific rule.

> If validation fails for some of the database fields, CakePHP automatically shows some error texts next to their respective HTML form fields (given that FormHelper is used correctly to create the HTML form). We can also override the default error messages by setting the message key in the constraints array.

The last validation rule we defined in the $validate array is for the isbn field:

```
'isbn' => array(
    'isbn10' => array(
        'rule' => array('custom', '/^[0-9]{9}[0-9x]$/'),
        'message' => 'Invalid ISBN!'
    ),
    'unique' => array(
        'rule' => 'isUnique',
        'on' => 'create',
    'message' => 'The ISBN is already added!'
    )
)
```

We defined two validation rules for the isbn field that validates the following specifics:

1. ISBNs must start with 9 digits and end with a digit or the character 'x'.
2. ISBNs must be unique when we are creating a new record.

There is no built-in validation rule provided by CakePHP for validating ISBNs. We used a custom validation for the first rule. The first rule is named isbn10. We used a custom regular expression to define this rule. The second rule is named unique that uses the pre-defined validation rule isUnique. For this rule, we set the on key to create — that specifies Cake should perform this validation only on save operation. We have defined two different messages for these two rules.

Now, we can go to the URL http://localhost/data-access/books/add and try adding some invalid data. Invalid data will not be saved and necessary messages will show up next to the respective form fields.

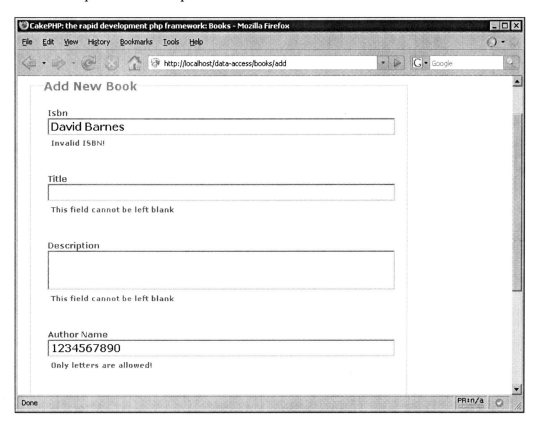

More on Data Validation

As we already saw, we can set the validation in three ways:

1. Simple validation using CakePHP's pre defined rule: The general structure is as follows:

```
var $validate = array(
                'fieldName1' => 'predefinedRuleName',
                . . .
                . . .
            );
```

2. Single rule validation: It has got the following format:

```
var $validate = array(
    'fieldName1' => array(
        'rule' => 'ruleName'/'ruleDefinitionArray',
        . . .
        . . .
    ),
    . . .
    . . .
);
```

3. Multiple rule validation: We can set multiple rules per field by setting the array like the following:

```
var $validate = array(
    'fieldName1' => array(
        'ruleName1' => array(
            'rule' => 'ruleName',
            . . .
            . . .
        ),
        'ruleName2' => array(
            'rule' => 'ruleName2',
            . . .
            . . .
        ),
        . . .
    )
    . . .
    . . .
);
```

In the `$validate` array, we can associate a field with 5 keys for defining
our constraints:

1. `rule`: Defines the validation method and takes either a single string or an
    array as value. It must be present in every validation array, whereas, the
    other keys are optional.

2. `required`: Much like the PHP's `isset()` function—it checks whether the
    field is set in the data to be saved. It can be set to `true` to enable the checking.
    By default, it is set to `false`.

3. `allowEmpty`: It sets whether we should allow empty data to be saved for
    a specific field. By default it is set to `false`, that means `empty` value is
    not allowed. We can set it to `true` to allow empty value to be saved for a
    particular field.

4. `on`: This key specifies on which operation the validation is to be performed.
    We can set it to either `update` or `create`. By default it is set to `null`—that is
    validation is applied for both update and save operations.

5. `message`: It is used to set custom validation message for a rule. The message
    appears next to the respective web form field if the validation fails.

Sometimes, we may find the built-in validation rules and regular expression patterns
are not enough to define our own rule. In those cases, we can create a custom model
method to check the validity of the supplied data. We will now see how we can use
model methods to validate a field.

Custom Validation Methods

For the sake of simplicity, let's assume that the first two digits of ISBN must be a
prime number! Anyway, it's just an example, nothing serious. Now, there is no way
to check this condition using regular expression. To do that we have to use a custom
validation method like this:

```php
<?php
class Book extends AppModel
{
    var $name = 'Book';
    var $validate = array(
        'isbn' => array(
            'rule' => array('isFirstTwoPrime')
        )
    );
    function isFirstTwoPrime($data)
    {
        // take the integer value of the first two digits
        $num = intval( substr($data, 0, 2) );
```

```
                   // if divisible by 2 - not a prime
                   if($num%2==0) return false;
                   //find the square root
                   $limit = sqrt($num);
                   //loop till the limit
                   for($i=3; $i<=$limit; $i++) {
                    //divisible by a number - not a prime
                    if($num%$i==0) return false;
                   }
                   //it's a prime!
                   return true;
             }
       }
       ?>
```

A custom validation method should return only true or false. The data to be validated is passed to the method as a parameter. We can also add extra parameters in the rule array and handle them in our method.

Summary

This chapter was all about models—the data center of a CakePHP application. In CakePHP, a model class usually represents a single database table. All database operations on that database table are done through its corresponding model. Given all necessary conventions are followed correctly, CakePHP automatically ties up a model with its respective database table without any extra configuration.

Every CakePHP model class inherits some useful pre-defined methods that make it easy to perform basic database operations. The built-in method find() is used to retrieve data from the database table. The save() method is used for both storing and updating data into and in a database table. To delete a record from a database table, the pre-defined del() method can be used.

Besides the built-in methods, we can as well write our own methods in a model class. We can add routines containing our application specific business/domain logics there. We can also perform SQL queries directly from models.

In CakePHP, model class also holds the backend validation rules. CakePHP offers a simple validation mechanism that is pretty easy to implement.

Well, it was a pretty extensive chapter covering a lot of ground about CakePHP models. It is pretty important to grasp the essence of the CakePHP's model mechanism before moving to further chapters. Once you find yourself confident about model basics, you are ready to step forward. The next chapter is all about model relationships and associations. Hope you will enjoy that as well!

6
ORM: Modelling the Table Relationship

Database relationship, like every other kind of relationship, is always hard to maintain. It has always been a nightmare for web developers—you know what is meant if you already have developed at least one mid-sized PHP/MySQL application. Particularly, when multiple levels of relationships are involved, it becomes harder to retrieve, store or delete data because complicated SQL queries are needed. To take away this pain from developers, CakePHP offers a simple yet powerful feature called 'object relational mapping' or ORM to handle database relationships with ease. For other types of relationships, you got to find out your own way!

In CakePHP, relations between the database tables are defined through association—a way to represent the database table relationship inside CakePHP. Once the associations are defined in models according to the table relationships, we are ready to use its wonderful functionalities. Using CakePHP's ORM, we can save, retrieve, and delete related data into and from different database tables with simplicity, in a better way—no need to write complex SQL queries with multiple JOINs anymore!

In real life web projects, database table relationship is very commonly used and hence it is important to have a very good understanding of CakePHP's model association. In this chapter, we will have a deep look at various types of associations and their uses. In particular, the purpose of this chapter is to learn:

1. How to figure out association types from database table relations
2. How to define different types of associations in CakePHP models
3. How to utilize the association for fetching related model data
4. How to relate associated data while saving
5. How association helps deleting related and dependent model data
6. How to change associations on the fly when required

Working with Simple Associations

From our previous PHP/MySQL experience, we already know there are basically 3 types of relationship that can take place between database tables:

1. one-to-one
2. one-to-many
3. and many-to-many

The first two of them are simple as they don't require any additional table to relate the tables in relationship. In this section, we will first see how to define associations in models for one-to-one and one-to-many relations. Then we will look at how to retrieve and delete related data from, and save data into, database tables using model associations for these simple associations.

Defining One-To-Many Relationship in Models

To see how to define a one-to-many relationship in models, we will think of a situation where we need to store information about some authors and their books and the relation between authors and books is one-to-many. This means an author can have multiple books but a book belongs to only one author (which is rather absurd, as in real life scenario a book can also have multiple authors). We are now going to define associations in models for this one-to-many relation, so that our models recognize their relations and can deal with them accordingly.

Time for Action: Defining One-To-Many Relation

1. Create a new database and put a fresh copy of CakePHP inside the web root. Name the database whatever you like but rename the cake folder to `relationship`. Configure the database in the new Cake installation.

2. Execute the following SQL statements in the database to create a table named `authors`,

```
CREATE TABLE `authors` (
`id` int( 11 ) NOT NULL AUTO_INCREMENT PRIMARY KEY ,
`name` varchar( 127 ) NOT NULL ,
`email` varchar( 127 ) NOT NULL ,
`website` varchar( 127 ) NOT NULL
);
```

3. Create a `books` table in our database by executing the following SQL commands:

```
CREATE TABLE `books` (
`id` int( 11 ) NOT NULL AUTO_INCREMENT PRIMARY KEY ,
`isbn` varchar( 13 ) NOT NULL ,
```

```
`title` varchar( 64 ) NOT NULL ,
`description` text NOT NULL ,
`author_id` int( 11 ) NOT NULL
)
```

4. Create the `Author` model using the following code (/`app/models/`
   `authors.php`):

```php
<?php
class Author extends AppModel
{
    var $name = 'Author';

    var $hasMany = 'Book';
}
?>
```

5. Use the following code to create the `Book` model (/`app/models/books.php`):

```php
<?php
class Book extends AppModel
{   var $name = 'Book';

    var $belongsTo = 'Author';
}
?>
```

6. Create a controller for the `Author` model with the following code: (/`app/`
   `controllers/authors_controller.php`):

```php
<?php
class AuthorsController extends AppController {
    var $name = 'Authors';
    var $scaffold;
}
?>
```

7. Use the following code to create a controller for the `Book` model (/`app/`
   `controllers/books_controller.php`):

```php
<?php
class BooksController extends AppController {
    var $name = 'Books';
    var $scaffold;
}
?>
```

8. Now, go to the following URLs and add some test data: `http://localhost/`
   `relationship/authors/`

   `http://localhost/relationship/books/`

What Just Happened?

We have created two tables: `authors` and `books` for storing author and book information.

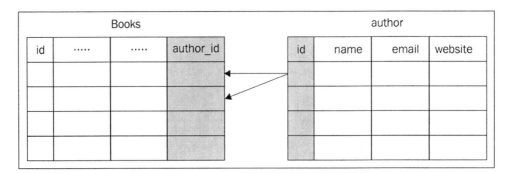

A foreign-key named `author_id` is added to the `books` table to establish the one-to-many relation between `authors` and `books`. Through this foreign-key, an author is related to multiple books, as well as, a book is related to one single author.

 By Cake convention, the name of a foreign-key should be underscored, singular name of target model, suffixed with `_id`.

Once the database tables are created and relations are established between them, we can define associations in models. In both of the model classes, `Author` and `Book`, we defined associations to represent the one-to-many relationship between the corresponding two tables. CakePHP provides two types of association: `hasMany` and `belongsTo` to define one-to-many relations in models.

These associations are very appropriately named:

- As an author 'has many' books, `Author` model should have `hasMany` association to represent its relation with the `Book` model.
- As a book 'belongs to' one author, `Book` model should have `belongsTo` association to denote its relation with the `Author` model.

In the `Author` model, an association attribute `$hasMany` is defined with the value `Book` to inform the model that every author can be related to many books. We also added a `$belongsTo` attribute in the `Book` model and set its value to `Author` to let the `Book` model know that every book is related to only one author.

After defining the associations, two controllers were created for both of these models with scaffolding to see how the associations are working.

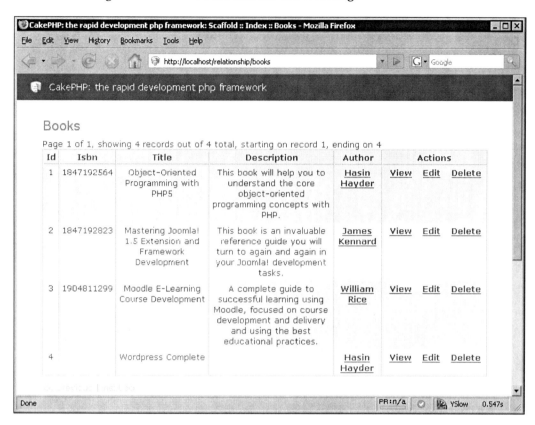

Retrieving Related Model Data in One-To-Many Relation

Once the associations are in place, we can retrieve related data very easily without any trouble. In fact, we don't need to do anything at all—CakePHP's ORM will automatically fetch all the related model data using association. We will work on the previous code-base to see how the related model data can be retrieved.

Time for Action: Retrieving Related Model Data

1. Take out scaffolding from both of the controllers: `AuthorsController` (`/app/controllers/authors_controller.php`) and `BooksController` (`/app/controllers/books_controller.php`).

2. Modify the `AuthorsController` like the following:

```php
<?php
class AuthorsController extends AppController {
    var $name = 'Authors';
    function index() {
        $this->Author->recursive = 1;
        $authors = $this->Author->find('all');
        $this->set('authors', $authors);
    }
}
?>
```

3. Create a view file for the `/authors/index` action (`/app/views/authors/index.ctp`):

```php
<?php foreach($authors as $author): ?>
<h2><?php echo $author['Author']['name'] ?></h2>
<hr />
<h3>Book(s):</h3>
<ul>
<?php foreach($author['Book'] as $book): ?>
<li><?php echo $book['title'] ?></li>
<?php endforeach; ?>
</ul>
<?php endforeach; ?>
```

4. Write down the following code inside the `BooksController`:

```php
<?php
class BooksController extends AppController {
    var $name = 'Books';
    function index() {
        $this->Book->recursive = 1;
        $books = $this->Book->find('all');
        $this->set('books', $books);
    }
}
?>
```

5. Create a view file for the action `/books/index` (`/app/views/books/index.ctp`):

```
<table>
<thead>
```

```
<th>ISBN</th><th>Title</th><th>Author</th>
</thead>
<?php foreach($books as $book): ?>
<tr>
<td><?php echo $book['Book']['isbn'] ?></td>
<td><?php echo $book['Book']['title'] ?></td>
<td><?php echo $book['Author']['name'] ?></td>
</tr>
<?php endforeach; ?>
</table>
```

6. Point your browser to the following links and see how related books and authors show up:
    http://localhost/relationship/authors/
    http://localhost/relationship/books/

What Just Happened?

The first line in the index() action of the AuthorsController sets the model attribute $recursive to 1.

```
$this->Author->recursive = 1;
```

This special attribute is an integer that specifies the number of levels we want our model to fetch associated model data in the next find('all') or find('first') operations. In the AuthorsController, we set it to 1 for the Author model. This means the subsequent Author->find('all') operation will return all associated model data that are related directly to the Author model. The result of the function call Author->findAll() is then stored in a variable $authors. The returned result is an array containing all authors and their book information. This array looks like the following:

```
Array
(
    [0] => Array
        (
            [Author] => Array
                (
                    [id] => 1
                    [name] => Author Name
                    . . .
                )
            [Book] => Array
                (
                    [0] => Array
                        (
                            [id] => 1
```

```
                                        [isbn] => 1847192564
                                        ...
                                        [author_id] => 1
                              )
                      [1] => Array
                          (
                                  [id] => 3
                                  ...
                          )
                  )
          )
  [1] => Array
  ...
  ...
  )
```

Every element of this array contains information about one particular author and his/her related books. Each of these elements has two associated arrays: one is 'an array' containing the author information and the other is 'an array of array' (containing multiple books data as `Author` to `Book` association is `hasMany`) containing information about the books related to that particular author.

We can easily traverse through all the elements of this array and print out all the authors and their related books data. We passed `$authors` to the view file, and in the view file, we used two loops (first loop is to for each author and second loop is for each related book to this particular author) to print out the author and its related book information.

Similarly, in `BooksController`, `Book->recursive` is set to 1 before calling the `Book->find('all')` function.

`Book->find('all')` function also returns a similar array. Every element of this array contains two associated arrays, one contains the book data and the other contains one (not multiple, as `Book` to `Author` association is `belongsTo`) related author data. The returned array looks something like the following:

```
Array
(
    [0] => Array
        (
            [Book] => Array
                (
                    [id] => 1
                    [isbn] => 1847192564
                    . . .
                )
            [Author] => Array
                (
                    [id] => 1
                    [name] => Author Name
                    . . .
                )
        )
    [1] => Array
    . . .
    . . .
)
```

The result of `Book->find('all')` is forwarded to the view. In the view file, we looped through the array and printed out all books' information with their related authors' names.

To have a better understanding of how `$recursive` works, let's assume:

- We have a new model named `Chapter`.
- And `Book` is related to `Chapter` through a `hasMany` association.

We can now set `$recursive` to different values based on the amount of data we want back from a `Author->find('all')` call:

- `$recursive = 0`: Only authors' data is returned.
- `$recursive = 1`: Authors' and their associated books.
- `$recursive = 2`: Author, authors' associated books, and books' related chapters.

In this way, we can fetch out related data of multiple levels by setting the value of $recursive to our desired level.

 Always set $recursive = 0, if you don't need to fetch any associated model data.

By default, $recursive is set to 1. In the last example, it was not required to explicitly set its value to 1.

Saving Related Model Data in One-To-Many Relation

Associations can also make saving related data pretty easy. We will now create a simple program that can save a book and can relate the book with an author at the time of saving. We will add some code to the previous code-base to put in the save functionality.

Time for Action: Saving Related Model Data

1. In the BooksController (/app/controllers/books_controller.php), add the FormHelper and write a new action add(),

```php
<?php
class BooksController extends AppController {
    var $name = 'Books';
    var $helpers = array('Form' );

    function index() {
        $this->Book->recursive = 1;
        $books = $this->Book->find('all',
                array('fields' =>
                    array('Book.isbn','Book.title','Author.name')
                    )
                );
        $this->set('books', $books);
    }

    function add() {
        if (!empty($this->data)) {
            $this->Book->create();
            $this->Book->save($this->data);
            $this->redirect(array('action'=>'index'));
        }
        $authors = $this->Book->Author->generateList();
```

```
                $this->set('authors', $authors);
        }
    }
    ?>
```

2. Create a view for the action '/books/add' (/app/views/add.ctp)

```
<?php echo $form->create('Book');?>
    <fieldset>
        <legend>Add New Book</legend>
    <?php
        echo $form->input('isbn');
        echo $form->input('title');
        echo $form->input('description');
        echo $form->input('author_id');
    ?>
    </fieldset>
<?php echo $form->end('Submit');?>
```

3. Point your browser to the following URL and add a book:
   `http://localhost/relationship/books/add`

What Just Happened?

In the `add()` action of the `BooksController`, we first checked if there is any form data sent back from the view. When no data is returned from its view, a form is displayed to take user input. We have text inputs inside the form to take book information. As well as, we have a select-list to select a related author. This select-list has options for all the authors, from where one single author can be selected. CakePHP model function `generateList()` is used to create this select-list.

`Author->generateList()` returns an array with author's id=>name as key=>value pairs like the following:

```
Array
(
    [1] => Author 1
    [2] => Author 2
    [3] => ...
)
```

 From or through a model class, all model classes related to that model are accessible. Like, `Author` model can be accessed through `Book` model like `Book->Author` and vice-versa.

This function is very handy for creating HTML select tags. We passed the returned result from the function call `Book->Author->generateList()` to the view through `$authors` variable. In the view file FormHelper's `input()` method is used, `$form->input('author_id')` – this `input()` method cleverly creates a select tag with options for every author- where names are used as tag-labels and ids are set as tag-values. The output of `$form->input('author_id')` is something like the following:

```
<select>
<option value="1">Author 1</option>
<option value="2">Author 2</option>
<option value="3">Author 3</option>
...
</select>
```

We will know more about the 'quick and smart' `FormHelper` in Chapter 7.

When the submit button of the form is clicked, all form data is sent back to the `BooksController`'s `add()` action. Then the form data is passed to the `Book->save()` function that stores the book data into the database and automatically relates the newly added book with the selected author (saves the selected author's id in the `author_id` field of `books` table). When the save operation is done, the controller redirects to `index()` action and the newly added book can be seen in the list of books.

The prototype of the `generateList()` function looks like the following:

```
generateList(string $conditions, string $order, int $limit, string
$keyPath, string $valuePath)
```

`$conditions`, `$order`, and `$limit` parameters are just as we would use in the `find()` function. By default, the `generateList()` function takes `id` and `name` fields of the model respectively as keys and values of the returned array. We can change this behavior using `$keyPath` and `$valuePath` parameters.

If we want to get an array of first 10 authors with `id` and `last_name` fields of the `Author` model as key/value pairs and is ordered by the `last_name` field, we could make use of the `$order`, `$limit`, `$keyPath`, and `$valuePath` parameters like the following:

```
$this->Author->generateList(
    null,
    'last_name ASC',
    10,
    '{n}.Author.initial',
    '{n}.Author.last_name'
);
```

Adding More than One Association of the Same Type

In previous examples, the only association that the Author model has is a hasMany association with the Book model. This association was created by the following line of code:

```
var $hasMany = 'Book';
```

Here, a string is used to define the hasMany association. It is also possible to do the same thing using an associative array like the following:

```
var $hasMany = array(
   'Book' => array(
   'className'  => 'Book',
   )
 );
```

Likewise, for the Book model we can do the following:

```
var $belongsTo = array(
    'Author' => array(
    'className'  => 'Author',
    )
  );
```

This alternative method is handy if we want to add more than one association of the same type or we need to customize some of the relationship characteristics.

If we have another model Tutorial and our Author model also has a hasMany association with the Tutorial model, we can use the array approach to define these two associations in the Author model:

```
var $hasMany = array(
   'Book' => array(
   'className'  => 'Book',
   ),
   'Tutorial' => array(
   'className'  => 'Tutorial',
   )
 );
```

One-To-One Relation

Defining associations for one-to-one relation is very much the same as defining association for a one-to-many relation. Let's look at an example to see how a one-to-one relation can be defined in models. Let's assume, we have a `profiles` table and the relation between the `authors` table and the `profiles` table is one-to-one. To establish this relation, we created a `profiles` table with a foreign-key `author_id`.

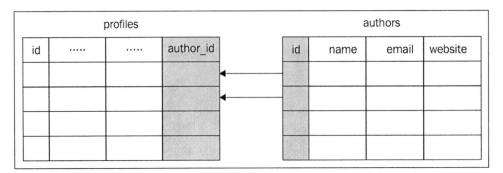

Now, in both of the model classes, `Author` and `Profile`, we have to define associations for this relation. The `belongsTo` association is always defined in the corresponding model of the `table with the foreign-key` and hence in the `Profile` table we have to define a `belongsTo` association. On the other hand, an author can only have one associated profile—to define the relation from `Author` model's perspective, we can use a `hasOne` association.

To resemble this relation, in the `Author` model a `$hasOne` attribute should be defined:

```
var $hasOne = array(
   'Profile' => array(
   'className'  => 'Profile',
    )
  );
```

As well as, a `$belongsTo` attribute should be defined in the `Profile` model:

```
var $belongsTo = array(
   'Profile' => array(
   'className'  => 'Author',
    )
  );
```

In both 'one-to-one' and 'one-to-many' relations, the model that has the foreign-key in its underlying table uses the `belongsTo` association. The only difference between these two relations is: in the other model, the `hasOne` association should be used instead of the `hasMany`.

Customizing Association Characteristics

Defining associations using array has another benefit—we can include some key-value pairs in the associative array to customize the relationship.

A customized `hasMany` association that defines the relation between authors and books may look like the following:

```
var $hasMany = array(
    'Book' => array(
        'className'     => 'Book',
        'foreignKey'    => 'author_id',
        'conditions'    => 'Book.status = 1',
      'fields'          => array('isbn', 'title'),
        'order'             => 'Book.released DESC',
    )
);
```

Let's see how some of these key/value pairs can be used to manipulate a relation:

- `className`: The name of the associated model.
- `foreignKey`: The name of the foreign-key involved in this particular relation. In case of `belongsTo`, it is the name of the foreign-key found in the current model. In case of `hasOne` or `hasMany` associations, it holds the foreign-key name found in the corresponding table of the other model. Default is underscored, singular name of the target model (in case of `belongsTo`, the current model, for `hasOne`/`hasMany`—the other model), suffixed with `_id`.
- `conditions`: A SQL fragment of WHERE clause to filter the related model records. To fetch all the related books that has status = 1, conditions can be set as 'Book.status = 1'.
- `fields`: An array of fields specifies the fields to be retrieved when the associated model data is fetched. If not set, it returns all the fields.
- `order`: A SQL fragment of ORDER BY clause that defines the sorting order for associated records returned. It is not applicable for 'hasOne' and 'belongsTo' associations as there is only one related record.

Working with Complex Associations

A many-to-many relation requires an additional table to relate the two tables in relationship. In this section, we will learn how to define associations in models for many-to-many relations. Then, we will look at how to retrieve, delete, and save related data from and into database tables using model association in this special type of relation.

Defining Many-To-Many Relationship in Models

In the previous examples, we assumed that a book can have only one author. But in real life scenario, a book may also have more than **one** author. In that case, the relation between authors and books is many-to-many. We are now going to see how to define associations for a many-to-many relation. We will modify our existing code-base that we were working on in this chapter to **set** up the associations needed to represent a many-to-many relation.

Time for Action: Defining Many-To-Many Relation

1. Empty the database tables:

   ```
   TRUNCATE TABLE `authors`;
   TRUNCATE TABLE `books`;
   ```

2. Remove the `author_id` field from the `books` table:

   ```
   ALTER TABLE `books` DROP `author_id`
   ```

3. Create a new table, `authors_books`:

   ```
   CREATE TABLE `authors_books` (
   `author_id` INT NOT NULL ,
   `book_id` INT NOT NULL
   ```

4. Modify the `Author` (`/app/models/author.php`) model:

   ```php
   <?php
   class Author extends AppModel
   {
       var $name = 'Author';

       var $hasAndBelongsToMany = 'Book';
   }
   ?>
   ```

5. Modify the `Book` (`/app/models/book.php`) model:

```php
<?php
class Book extends AppModel
{
    var $name = 'Book';
    var $hasAndBelongsToMany = 'Author';
}
?>
```

6. Modify the `AuthorsController` (`/app/controllers/authors_controller.php`):

```php
<?php
class AuthorsController extends AppController {
    var $name = 'Authors';
    var $scaffold;
}
?>
```

7. Modify the `BooksController` (`/app/controllers/books_controller.php`):

```php
<?php
class BooksController extends AppController {
    var $name = 'Books';
    var $scaffold;
}
?>
```

8. Now, visit following URLs and add some test data into the system:

   `http://localhost/relationship/authors/`

   `http://localhost/relationship/books/`

What Just Happened?

We first emptied the database and then dropped the field `author_id` from the books table. Then we added a new join table `authors_books` that will be used to establish a many-to-many relation between authors and books. The following diagram shows how a join table relates two tables in many-to-many relation:

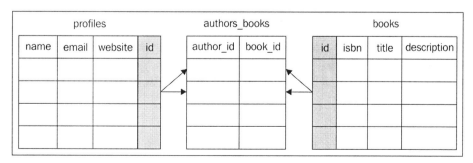

In a many-to-many relation, one record of any of the tables can be related to multiple records of the other table. To establish this link, a join table is used—a join table contains two fields to hold the primary-keys of both of the records in relation.

CakePHP has certain conventions for naming a join table—join tables should be named after the tables in relation, in alphabetical order, with underscores in between. The join table between authors and books tables should be named `authors_books`, not `books_authors`. Also by Cake convention, the default value for the foreign keys used in the join table must be underscored, singular name of the models in relation, suffixed with `_id`.

After creating the join table, we defined associations in the models, so that our models also know about the new relationship that they have. We added `hasAndBelongsToMany` (HABTM) associations in both of the models. HABTM is a special type of association used to define a many-to-many relation in models. Both the models have HABTM associations to define the many-to-many relationship from both ends. After defining the associations in the models, we created two controllers for these two models and put in scaffolding in them to see the association working.

We could also use an array to set up the HABTM association in the models. Following code segment shows how to use an array for setting up an HABTM association between authors and books in the `Author` model:

```
var $hasAndBelongsToMany = array(
    'Book' =>
        array(
            'className'            => 'Book',
            'joinTable'            => 'authors_books',
            'foreignKey'           => 'author_id',
            'associationForeignKey' => 'book_id'
        )
    );
```

Like, simple relationships, we can also override default association characteristics by adding/modifying key/value pairs in the associative array. The `foreignKey` key/value pair holds the name of the foreign-key found in the current model—default is underscored, singular name of the current model suffixed with `_id`. Whereas, `associationForeignKey` key/value pair holds the foreign-key name found in the corresponding table of the other model—default is underscored, singular name of the associated model suffixed with `_id`. We can also have `conditions`, `fields`, and `order` key/value pairs to customize the relationship in more detail.

Retrieving Related Model Data in Many-To-Many Relation

Like one-to-one and one-to-many relations, once the associations are defined, CakePHP will automatically fetch the related data in many-to-many relation.

Time for Action: Retrieving Related Model Data

1. Take out scaffolding from both of the controllers—AuthorsController (/app/controllers/authors_controller.php) and BooksController (/app/controllers/books_controller.php).

2. Add an index() action inside the AuthorsController (/app/controllers/authors_controller.php), like the following:

```php
<?php
class AuthorsController extends AppController {
    var $name = 'Authors';

    function index() {
        $this->Author->recursive = 1;
        $authors = $this->Author->find('all');
        $this->set('authors', $authors);
    }
}
?>
```

Create a view file for the /authors/index action (/app/views/authors/index.ctp):

```php
<?php foreach($authors as $author): ?>
<h2><?php echo $author['Author']['name'] ?></h2>
<hr />
<h3>Book(s):</h3>
<ul>
<?php foreach($author['Book'] as $book): ?>
<li><?php echo $book['title'] ?></li>
<?php endforeach; ?>
</ul>
<?php endforeach; ?>
```

3. Write down the following code inside the BooksController (/app/controllers/books_controller.php):

```php
<?php
class BooksController extends AppController {
    var $name = 'Books';

    function index() {
```

```
      $this->Book->recursive = 1;
      $books = $this->Book->find('all');
      $this->set('books', $books);
   }
}
?>
```

4. Create a view file for the action /books/index (/app/views/books/index.ctp):

```
<?php foreach($books as $book): ?>
<h2><?php echo $book['Book']['title'] ?></h2>
<hr />
<h3>Author(s):</h3>
<ul>
<?php foreach($book['Author'] as $author): ?>
<li><?php echo $author['name'] ?></li>
<?php endforeach; ?>
</ul>
<?php endforeach; ?>
```

5. Now, visit following URLs:

```
http://localhost/relationship/authors/
```

```
http://localhost/relationship/books/
```

What Just Happened?

In both of the models, we first set the value of $recursive attributes to 1 and then we called the respective models find('all') functions. So, these subsequent find('all') operations return all associated model data that are related directly to the respective models. These returned results of the find('all') requests are then passed to the corresponding view files. In the view files, we looped through the returned results and printed out the models and their related data.

In the BooksController, this returned data from find('all') is stored in a variable $books. This find('all') returns an array of books and every element of that array contains information about one book and its related authors.

```
Array
(
      [0] => Array
      (
            [Book] => Array
         (
            [id] => 1
               [title] => Book Title
```

```
            . . .
        )
    [Author] => Array
        (
            [0] => Array
            (
                [id] => 1
            [name] => Author Name
                . . .
        )
            [1] => Array
            (
            [id] => 3
        . . .                    54                    54
    . . .
    . . .
    )
```

Same for the `Author` model, the returned data is an array of authors. Every element of that array contains two arrays: one contains the author information and the other contains an array of books related to this author. These arrays are very much like what we got from a `find('all')` call in case of the `hasMany` association.

Saving Related Model Data in Many-To-Many Relation

Like the simple relations, saving related data in many-to-many relation is also fairly easy. We will now modify our code to add functionality to save a book and relate multiple authors with this book while saving.

Time for Action: Saving Related Model Data

1. Add a controller action `add()` in `BooksController` (`/app/controllers/books_controller.php`),

```php
<?php
class BooksController extends AppController {
    var $name = 'Books';
    var $helpers = array( 'Form' );
    function index() {
        $this->Book->recursive = 1;
        $books = $this->Book->find('all');
        $this->set('books', $books);
    }
    function add() {
        if (!empty($this->data)) {
            $this->Book->create();
            $this->Book->save($this->data);
            $this->redirect(array('action'=>'index'), null, true);
        }
        $authors = $this->Book->Author->generateList();
        $this->set('authors', $authors);
    }
}
?>
```

2. Create a view with a form, for the `/books/add/` action. (`/app/views/books/add.ctp`)

```php
<?php echo $form->create('Book');?>
    <fieldset>
        <legend>Add New Book</legend>
    <?php
        echo $form->input('isbn');
        echo $form->input('title');
        echo $form->input('description');
        echo $form->input('Author');
    ?>
    </fieldset>
```

3. Point your browser to the following URL and add a book:
`http://localhost/relationship/books/add`

What Just Happened?

`Author` model's `generateList()` function is used to get a list of all the authors. This list is passed to the view through `$authors` variable. A form is created in the view with input fields to take book information. In this form, we also created a select list to take all the related authors' names—multiple authors can be selected from this list.

Specifically, the line `$form->input('Author');` creates the select list and automatically. In the input method of the form helper, the related model name: `Author` is supplied as parameter. It tells the method that it has to create a multiple select list from an array `$authors`.

When the form is submitted, the `Book` model's `save()` function automatically gets all the related authors' information along with the book information. The `save()` function first saves the book information and then creates entries in the join table to establish the relations between the book and the selected authors.

Deleting Associated Data

In case of one-to-one and one-to-many relation, to turn on the cascade delete option, we have to set the `dependent` key to `true` in the association definition array of the model. To enable the cascade delete option in `Author` model for its association with the `Book` model, we would add a `dependent` key in the association definition array and set its value to `true` like the following:

```
var $hasMany = array(
      'Book' => array(
          'className'     => 'Book',
          'dependent'=> true
      )
   );
```

When the cascade delete is turned on, if we call the `delete()` method of the `Author` model to delete an author, then all the associated `Book` records related to that particular author are also deleted. To avoid cascade delete even when `dependent` is set to `true`, we can make use of the second parameter `$cascade` of the `delete()` method—which by default has a `true` value. To turn off the cascade delete on the fly, we just have to set this second parameter to `false`.

In case of many-to-many relation, the HABTM association logically does not have any such key/value pair to turn on/off the cascade delete. It is quite rational as in case of HABTM association, we will not like to delete a book if any of its related authors is deleted. Rather, we will want to delete the author and the records in the join table that relates some books with that author. We don't even have to think about that, Cake will automatically delete all such join table entries in `delete()` operations.

Changing Association On The Fly

Let's assume that we have two associations in the `Author` model at the same time:

1. `hasMany` association with `Book` model.

2. `hasOne` association with `Profile` model.

Now, to fetch out all authors and their profile information, we would write the following code:

```
$this->Author->recursive = 1;
$authors = $this->Author->find('all');
```

But this `find('all')` request will also return all associated book information as both `Profile` and `Book` models are on the first level of recursion. We can though ignore all `Book` model data and only use the `User` and `Profile` model data. But it can be costly to performance. We need to somehow destroy the association between the `Author` and `Book` model before the `find('all')` call, so that only the needed data are returned.

The `unbindAll()` method becomes handy in such situations. The following code snippet shows how we can temporarily remove the association between the `Author` and the `Book` model.

```
$this->Author->recursive = 1;
$this->Author->unbindModel(
        array(
                'hasMany' => array(
                        'Book' => array(
                        'className' => 'Book'
                        )
                )
        )
);
$authors = $this->Author->find('all');
```

Sometimes, we may want to temporarily add an association. If we want to temporarily add a `hasMany` association between the `Author` and the `Tutorial` model, we can do it using the model method `bindModel()` like the following:

```
$this->Author->bindModel(
        array(
                'hasMany' => array(
                        'Tutorial' => array(
                        'className' => 'Tutorial'
                        )
                )
        )
);
```

Creating or destroying associations using `bindModel()` and `unbindModel()` only works for the subsequent model operation unless the second parameter of these functions has been set to `true`. If the second parameter has been set to `true`, the bind remains in place for the remainder of the request.

Summary

This chapter was all about model relationships and associations. We learnt how to define different types of associations to epitomize different types of relationships in models. We first learnt basics of simple relationships like one-to-one and one-to-many and then saw how to implicate them in models using `$hasOne`, `$hasmany`, and `$belongsTo` model attributes. Then, we saw how these associations make it easy to retrieve or save related model data. We also learnt how to define model relationship attributes as associated arrays to customize association characteristics and override the defaults.

Then we looked at many-to-many relations — a more complex type of database relation. We learnt that the `$hasAndBelongsToMany` model attribute is defined in both of the models in relation to represent this special type of relationship. Then we saw how Cake makes it easy to handle this complex type of relation and how easy it is to retrieve or store related model data once the associations are defined.

We also learnt that once the associations are in place, deleting related model data takes almost no effort. Cake handles the delete very smartly, for simple relationships you may just need to do some tweaking in the models' association attributes. We also learnt the importance of changing associations on the fly and saw how to do it using `bindModel()` and `unbindModel()` methods.

If you are already done with this chapter, you may be claiming yourself a Cake association expert. Well, honestly you can do it for sure; you have already mastered the Cake association. But don't get too satisfied and please do continue reading the rest of this book. Enough Cake magic left to learn and be proud of knowing. The next thing we are going to learn is Views — files that contain presentational logics.

7
Views: Creating User Interfaces

In CakePHP, everything sent to the web browsers is handled by the views. They are responsible for displaying formatted results of our controller actions to the users. More likely, views contain combinations of (X)HTML and PHP code. As discussed earlier, according to the principle of MVC, views should only contain presentation logics. That means, the code inside views should only perform tasks that relate to generating pages to be displayed in browsers. None of the view code should perform any complicated application logic, nor should it carry out any database operation or domain logic.

We've already seen, how the controller and action decide which view to render back to the user. We've also seen how an action passes data on to the view. We know that view files have a `.ctp` extension and are stored inside the `app/views` folder of our application. In CakePHP, usually every controller action contains a distinct view file that is stored in a folder named after the controller, inside the `/app/views/` directory; and each of the view files is usually named after the action name. As an example, the view file for `BooksController`'s `index()` action should be saved under `app/views/books/` directory and named `index.ctp`.

Beside these actions-specific view files, several other view components are typically involved in an interface creation. They are all parts of the view layer and each of them has different uses. We have 'layouts' that contain common wrapper for different interfaces, 'elements' that contain small reusable view code, and 'helpers'—classes that encapsulates display logics that can be used in different view files in different applications.

In this chapter, we will closely look at those different view components and will learn:

- How to create custom layouts
- How to create and use elements
- How to build our own helper classes
- How to create HTML forms using CakePHP's FormHelper

Working with Layouts

You have certainly noticed that most of the pages of a website share the same top, tails, and maybe sidebars. One of the main philosophies of CakePHP is following the DRY principle that says eliminate the duplication of your work. Cake offers layouts to solve this particular problem. Layouts are site-wide page frames that are used to wrap around all the pages. We can create a layout file containing the common top, tails, and sidebars. And Cake will put all our pages inside that layout while displaying them.

Creating Custom Layouts

All the pages are by default rendered inside the default layout. The default layout should be named `default.ctp` and placed inside `/app/views/layouts/` directory. When the default layout is not provided, CakePHP renders all the pages inside its built-in default layout. We will now see how we can create a new default layout and override the Cake's predefined default one.

Time for Action: Creating a Custom Layout

1. Create a new CakePHP project named `interfaces`.
2. Create a controller class `BooksController` using the following code and save it as `books_controller.php` inside the `/app/controllers/` directory.

```php
<?php
class BooksController extends AppController {
    var $name = 'Books';
    var $uses = array();
    function index() {
        $book    = array (
                'book_title'   => 'Object Oriented Programming
                                              with PHP5',
                'author'       => 'Hasin Hayder',
                'isbn'         => '1847192564',
                'release_date' => 'December 2007'
```

```
                );
        $this->set($book);
        $this->pageTitle = 'Welcome to the Packt Book Store!';
    }
}
?>
```

3. Create a view file named `index.ctp` inside the `/app/views/books/` with the following code:

```
<h2>Book Store</h2>
<dl>
<dt class="header"><?php echo $bookTitle; ?></dt>
<dt>Author:</dt><dd><?php echo $author; ?></dd>
<dt>ISBN:</dt><dd><?php echo $isbn; ?></dd>
<dt>Release Date:</dt><dd><?php echo $releaseDate; ?></dd>
</dl>
```

4. Now, enter the following URL in your browser and see how it looks:
   `http://localhost/interfaces/books/`

5. Save the following code in a file named `default.ctp` under the `/app/views/layouts/` folder to override the Cake's default one.

```
<!DOCTYPE html PUBLIC "-//W3C//DTD XHTML 1.0 Transitional//EN"
        "http://www.w3.org/TR/xhtml1/DTD/xhtml1-transitional.dtd">
<html xmlns="http://www.w3.org/1999/xhtml">
<head>
    <title>
        <?php echo $title_for_layout; ?>
    </title>
    <?php echo $html->css('stylesheet'); ?>
</head>
<body>
    <div id="container">
        <div id="header">
            <h1><a href="http://www.packtpub.com/">PACKT PUBLISHING
                                                </a></h1>
        </div>
        <div id="content">
            <?php echo $content_for_layout; ?>
        </div>
        <div id="footer">
            COPYRIGHT 2008 @ PACKT PUBLISHING
        </div>
    </div>
</body>
</html>
```

6. Create a CSS file named `stylesheet.css` with the following code and save it in the `/app/webroot/css/` folder:

```css
* {
margin:0;
padding:0;
}
body {
    background-color:#333333;
    font-family: Georgia, "Times New Roman", Times, serif;
    font-size:90%;
    margin: 0;
}
h1, h2 {
    background-color: inherit;
    font-weight: normal;
}
h2 {
    color:#000066;
    font-size: 190%;
    margin-top:4px;
}
#header{
    padding: 25px 20px;
}

#header h1 a {
    color: #ffffff;
    text-decoration: none;
}
#header h1 a:hover {
    color: #ff9900;
    text-decoration: none;
}
#content{
    background-color: #fff;
    clear: both;
    color: #666;
    padding: 10px 20px 40px 20px;
    overflow: auto;
}
#footer {
    clear: both;
    padding: 6px 10px;
    text-align: right;
```

```
      color:#CCCCCC;
   }
   dl {
      line-height: 2em;
      margin: 0em 0em;
      width: 60%;
   }
   dt.header {
      color:#333333;
      font-size:124%;
      margin-top: 12px;
   }
   dt {
      font-weight: bold;
      padding-left: 4px;
      vertical-align: top;
   }
   dd {
      margin-left: 10em;
      margin-top: -2em;
      vertical-align: top;
   }
   form {
      clear: both;
      margin: 10px;
   }
   form label {
      width:94px;
      display:block;
      float:left;
   }
   form div.input {
      margin:13px;
   }
   form div.submit {
      margin:20px 0 0 12px;
   }
```

7. Now enter the following URL again in your browser.
   `http://localhost/interfaces/books/`

What Just Happened?

At first, we created a new CakePHP project named `interfaces`. And then, we created a controller class named `BooksController`. Inside the controller, we defined an attribute named `$uses` and assigned it to `null`. This tells the controller that we don't have any associated model for this controller.

We then wrote an action named `index()` inside the `BooksController` and also created the corresponding view file (`/app/books/index.ctp`) for this action. Inside the `index()` action, we defined an associative array `$book` that contains book information and passed that array to its corresponding view file. The view file simply prints out all the book information in a well-formatted manner using (X)HTML.

Now, if we visit the corresponding URL of the `index()` action, it will show us a page, like the following:

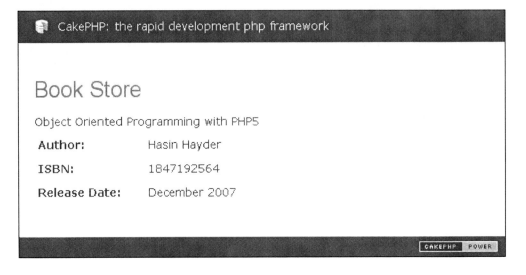

This page displays the book information that we provided from the controller action. Besides, you must have noticed this page has a header and a footer containing CakePHP logo, tagline, and icon.

Now, you must be asking from where are these headers and footers actually coming? We did not add anything like that! This header and footer are in fact coming from the CakePHP's predefined default layout. The default layout is the standard site-wide page frame, inside which, Cake renders all our pages. The pre-defined default layout can be found in a file named `default.ctp` inside the directory `/cake/libs/view/layouts/`. To override this predefined default layout, we don't have to change that core file. We just have to add our own `default.ctp` inside the `/app/views/layouts/` folder.

We then created a customized default layout and put that inside the /app/views/ layouts/ folder. Inside this layout file, we defined our basic (X)HTML page structure. Also, we added some PHP scripts to tell Cake 'where to put what'.

Inside the <title> tag, we added a PHP code snippet:

```
<title>
    <?php echo $title_for_layout; ?>
</title>
```

This PHP script prints out the $title_for_layout variable. The variable $title_for_layout holds the same value as the controller attribute $pageTitle. So, by defining $this->pageTitle in our controllers, we can set the titles of our pages.

We then added a CSS file using the following line:

```
<?php echo $html->css('stylesheet'); ?>
```

Here $html refers to a built-in CakePHP helper class called HtmlHelper. We used HtmlHelper's css() method to link the stylesheet.css file (/app/webroot/css/ stylesheet.css) to the layout.

Helpers are classes that are used to encapsulate presentation logics.

HTMLHelper is one of the built-in helper classes that ships with CakePHP. It helps us to do HTML-related tasks in a faster and easier way. Stay tuned, we will learn more about helpers later in this chapter!

Lastly, somewhere inside the body tag, we added the following line:

```
<?php echo $content_for_layout; ?>
```

This line is mainly responsible for placing controller-rendered view contents inside the layout. We must include this to tell Cake where to place the action-specific controller-rendered views.

As an example, if the index() action of the BooksController is requested, Cake will first render the corresponding view file index.ctp, and then place the rendered output into the $content_for_layout variable of our layout file. So when the content will finally be displayed to the user, the rendered view will be wrapped inside the rendered layout.

Next, we created the stylesheet.css file (that we already have linked in our layout file) with some CSS codes. The directory /app/webroot/css/ is where we put all our CSS files. We placed our stylesheet.css file inside that directory.

Now, if we visit the corresponding URL, we will see a new fresh looking page, like the following:

PACKT PUBLISHING

Book Store

Object Oriented Programming with PHP5

Author: Hasin Hayder

ISBN: 1847192564

Release Date: December 2007

Using Elements

In web applications, we often display the same piece of rendered (X)HTML over and over again in multiple pages. For example, think of a blog site that has two pages. The first page contains the top five posts and the other one contains recent ten posts. In both of these pages, those posts look just same. We can do that by copying the same piece of code and pasting it in all of the pages. But that's not elegant; it's a boring repetitive task! Things get worse when later on, we need to apply some changes on that. Then, we have to apply the same changes in multiple places. CakePHP provides an elegant solution to this problem and it's called elements. Using elements, we can write the code snippet once and use it in any of our pages as many times as we want.

Creating and Using Element

Elements are like functions, written in one place and used in multiple pages, over and over again. Like functions, we can even provide parameters to elements. As an example, for a blog, we can make a 'post element' to display information about a single post. And when we need to display a post from any place, we can call that element and supply the title, body, and the author's name to the element. The 'post element' will display that post information in the format we want.

Now, let's get into some action and see how we can actually create an element and reuse them in different places.

Time for Action: Creating and Using Elements

1. Change the `BooksController`'s code (`/app/controllers/books_controller.php`), like the following:

```php
<?php
class BooksController extends AppController {
    var $name = 'Books';
    var $uses = array();
    var $books     = array (
                    0 => array (
                            'book_title' => 'Object Oriented
                                    Programming with PHP5',
                            'author'    => 'Hasin Hayder',
                            'isbn'          => '1847192564',
                            'release_date' => 'December 2007'
                    ),
                    1 => array (
                            'book_title'  => 'Building Websites
                                    with Joomla! v1.0',
                            'author'      => 'Hagen Graf',
                            'isbn'          => '1904811949',
                            'release_date' => 'March 2006'
                    ),
                    2 => array (
                            'book_title'  => 'Moodle E-Learning
                                    Course Development',
                            'author'     => 'William Rice',
                            'isbn'          => '1904811299',
                            'release_date' => 'October 2006'
                    )
                );
    function index() {
        $this->set('books', $this->books );
        $this->pageTitle = 'Welcome to the Packt Book Store!';
    }
    function view($id = 0) {
        $this->set('book', $this->books[$id] );
        $this->pageTitle = 'Welcome to the Packt Book Store!';
    }
}
?>
```

2. Now, modify the view file `index.ctp` (`/app/views/books/index.ctp`),

```php
<h2>Book Store (All Books)</h2>
<?php
foreach ($books as $book) :
echo $this->element('book_info', array('book' => $book));
endforeach;
?>
```

3. Create a new view file named `view.ctp` under the directory `/app/views/books/` with the following code:

```
<h2>Book Store</h2>
<?php echo $this->element('book_info', array('book' => $book)); ?>
```

4. Create an element named `book_info.ctp` inside the `/app/views/elements/` folder with the following code:

```
<dl>
<dt class="header"><?php echo $book['book_title']; ?></dt>
<dt>Author:</dt><dd><?php echo $book['author']; ?></dd>
<dt>ISBN:</dt><dd><?php echo $book['isbn']; ?></dd>
<dt>Release Date:</dt><dd><?php echo $book['release_date'];
                                                  ?></dd>
</dl>
```

5. Now visit the following links and see what shows up in the browser:

```
http://localhost/interfaces/books/index/
http://localhost/interfaces/books/view/0
http://localhost/interfaces/books/view/1
http://localhost/interfaces/books/view/2
```

What Just Happened?

Inside the `BooksController`, we first created two actions, namely: `index()` and `view()`. Both of these actions used the `$books` array. `$books` is a controller attribute that holds information about some books. The intent of the `index()` is to display information about all the books from `$books`. And the purpose of the `view()` action is to show information about one book from the `$books` array. In both cases, we wanted to show the book information in the same format.

Inside the `index()` action, we passed the whole `$books` array to the view:

```
$this->set('books', $this->books );
```

In the corresponding view of the `index()` action, we looped through the `$books` array:

```
foreach ($books as $book) :
echo $this->element('book_info', array('book' => $book));
endforeach;
```

In each loop, we rendered an element called `book_info` using the view method `element()`. In every iteration, we passed the current `$book` to the element as parameter.

The `element()` method takes two parameters. The first one is the name of the element to render. And the next one is an array of parameters (key=>value pairs) that we want to pass to the element. The parameters passed are available as local variables insides the element as the key-names.

The view file for the `view()` action is much simpler. It has to display only one book information. Inside this view, we asked the `element()` method to render the `book_info` element and passed the `$book` variable to that element as parameter.

When the `element()` method is asked to render an element named `book_info`, it will look for a file called `book_info.ctp` inside the `app/views/elements/` directory. We then created that element file.

 An element file has `.ctp` extension and is placed inside the `app/views/elements/` folder

Every time we rendered the `book_info` element, we passed an array named `$book` that has all information about a book. Inside the element, we printed out the book information inside some (X)HTMLs so that it outputs in a well formatted manner.

Now, if we visit `http://localhost/interfaces/books/index/`, we will see something like the following:

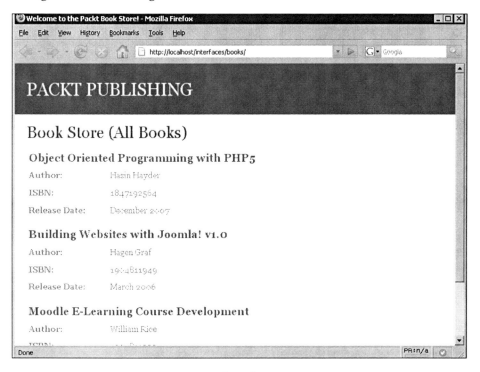

And the URL `http://localhost/interfaces/books/view/1` will display something like this:

In both of these pages, the book information is displayed in the same format. This is the advantage of using elements. We can place the repeating view fragment in a single element file and then render the element where needed. It helps us to reuse a view fragment. Bonus, we will get cleaner and more readable view files. Moreover, if we need to change the way things are displayed, we have to do changes in only one file.

Working with Helpers

Often, we need to include some display logics in our view files. And most of the times, the same logic is repeatedly used in different places. Think about a case where we have some file sizes (in bytes) stored in the database, and we have fetched that information through the model from the controller and supplied them to the view file to display. Now, if we display the file sizes as they are, they will be displayed as simple bytes, which is hard to read. To make it more readable, we have to convert bytes to KB, MB, GB etc, which means we have to apply some computations inside the view. There are two problems with adding our logics directly into the view:

1. It will mess up our view code. We want to have neat views with less PHP codes.

2. If we want to perform the same display logics in different places then we have to write the logic in every place.

Helpers are our friends in such situations. A helper encapsulates presentational logic that can be shared between many views, elements, or layouts. A helper is a normal PHP class that has methods to assist views. It is used to encapsulate 'display logics' that we want to use in different view files (and may be in different applications). It increases scopes of reusability to a great extent. Moreover, it helps us to keep our views neat and clean while performing some logical operations inside.

Creating and Using Your Own Helper

Usually, some similar and related methods containing display logics are grouped together inside a helper. CakePHP ships with some handy helpers like `HtmlHelper`, `FormHelper`, `NumberHelper`, `TextHelper` etc. But still in some cases, we may need to build our own custom helpers. We will now see how to create such a helper to encapsulate some presentation logics and how that helper can be used to assist our views.

Time for Action

1. Create a helper file named `format.php` inside the directory `/app/views/helpers/` using the following code:

```php
<?php
class FormatHelper extends AppHelper {
    function hyphenateISBN( $isbn ) {
        return substr($isbn, 0, 5).'-'.
               substr($isbn, 5, 2).'-'.
               substr($isbn, 7, 2).'-'.
               substr($isbn, 9, 1);
    }
    function shortenDate( $date ) {
        return substr($date, 0, 3).' '.
               substr($date, -4);
    }
}
?>
```

2. Add the following highlighted line to the `BooksController` (`/app/controllers/books_controller.php`):

```php
<?php
class BooksController extends AppController {
    var $name = 'Books';
    var $uses = array();
    var $helpers = array('format');
    ...
    ...
?>
```

3. Change the element `book_info.ctp` (`/app/views/elements/`
   `book_info.ctp`) like the following:

```
<dl>
<dt class="header"><?php echo $book['book_title']; ?></dt>
<dt>Author:</dt><dd><?php echo $book['author']; ?></dd>
<dt>ISBN:</dt>
<dd><?php echo $format->hyphenateISBN($book['isbn']); ?></dd>
<dt>Release Date:</dt>
<dd><?php echo $format->shortenDate($book['release_date']);
                                                      ?></dd>
</dl>
```

4. Now visit the following links and see what shows up in the browser:

   `http://localhost/interfaces/books/index/`

   `http://localhost/interfaces/books/view/0`

   `http://localhost/interfaces/books/view/1`

   `http://localhost/interfaces/books/view/2`

What Just Happened?

We first created a helper class named `FormatHelper`. It has two methods:
`hyphenateISBN()` and `shortenDate()`. Both of them contain some presentation
related logical operations. The first one includes hyphen in a string of ten digits
(ISBN number). As an example, if the number 1847192564 is provided as a
parameter, it would return a formatted ISBN code like 18471-92-56-4. The next
method `shortenDate()` takes a date string like 'December 2007' and returns a
shorter one like 'Dec 2007'.

> A helper should have the word `Helper` appended at the end with the class
> name. Like `TextHelper`, `FormatHelper` etc. The file name of the helper
> should be named after the name of the helper, like—`text.php`, `format.`
> `php` etc. A helper class commonly extends the core class `AppHelper`.
> Helpers are stored inside the directory `app/views/helpers`.

Now, to use this `FormatHelper`, we must first add it to the controller through the
`$helpers` attribute:

```
var $helpers = array('format');
```

When a helper is added to the $helpers array, Cake will automatically create an instance of the helper class and make it available to be used from the view files. The instance name is same as the lowercased helper's name. As our helper's name is Format, we will find its instance as $format.

After adding the helper to the controller, we used it in the element book_info.ctp to format our outputs. Before printing out the ISBN, we hyphenated the number using the FormatHelper's hyphenateISBN() method.

```php
<?php echo $format->hyphenateISBN($book['isbn']); ?>
```

Also, we shortened the release date using the shortenDate() method of the FormatHelper.

```php
<?php echo $format->shortenDate($book['release_date']); ?>
```

Here is how our page looks like after applying the FormatHelper's methods:

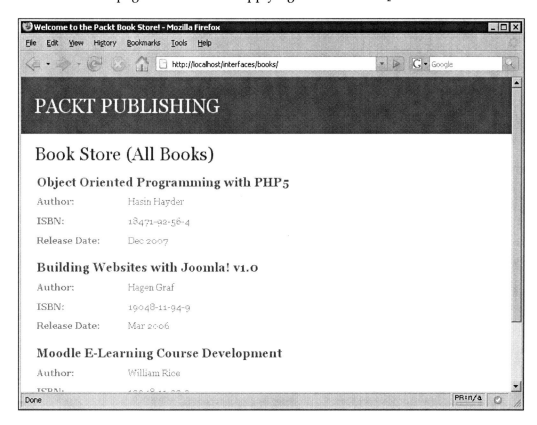

Creating Forms to Take User Input

`FormHelper` is one of the most useful helpers that CakePHP features. Most of the web applications involve forms for taking user inputs. `FormHelper` simplifies the creation of such web forms. There are quite a few reasons of using `FormHelper` instead of writing normal (X)HTML to create web forms:

1. In a Cake standard web form, form inputs are tied with database fields through a standard convention. `FormHelper` makes it easy to create a Cake standard web form.

2. `FormHelper` offers many shortcuts and automagics to create and bind forms with the database.

3. `FormHelper` automatically handles form validation and some security issues.

4. Lastly, we all want to write less and do more!

We will now create a Cake standard web form using the CakePHP's `FormHelper` and check if the above mentioned reasoning is valid.

Time for Action

1. Add an action `add()` at the end of the `BooksController`:

```php
<?php
class BooksController extends AppController {
    var $name = 'Books';
    var $uses = array();
    . . .
    . . .
    . . .
function view($id = 0) {
        $this->set('book', $this->books[$id] );
    $this->pageTitle = 'Welcome to the Packt Book Store!';
}
function add() {
    $this->pageTitle = 'Welcome to the Packt Book Store!';
    }
}
?>
```

2. Create a view file `add.ctp` inside the `/app/views/books/` folder:

```php
<?php
echo $form->create(null, array('url' => '/books/view', 'type' =>
                                                    'post'));
echo $form->input('Book.book_title', array('type'=>'text'));
```

```
echo $form->input('Book.author', array('type'=>'text'));
echo $form->input('Book.isbn', array('type'=>'text'));
echo $form->input('Book.release_date', array('type'=>'date'));
echo $form->end('Submit');
?>
```

3. Change the `BooksController`'s (`/app/controllers/books_controller.php`) `view()` action:

```php
<?php
class BooksController extends AppController {

    var $name = 'Books';
    var $uses = array();
    . . .
    . . .
. . .
    function view() {
      $date_str = $this->data['Book']['release_date']['year'] .'-'.
              $this->data['Book']['release_date']['month'] .'-'.
              $this->data['Book']['release_date']['day'];

      $this->data['Book']['release_date'] = date( 'M Y',
                                      strtotime( $date_str ) );

      $this->set('book', $this->data['Book'] );
      $this->pageTitle = 'Welcome to the Packt Book Store!';
    }
    function add() {
        $this->pageTitle = 'Welcome to the Packt Book Store!';
}
}
?>
```

4. Visit the following link, enter some dummy data, and press submit:

```
http://localhost/interfaces/books/add
```

What Just Happened?

We created a new action `add()` in the `BooksController`. Inside the `add()` action, we just set the title of the page through the `$pageTitle` attribute. In the corresponding view file of the `add()` action, we created a form using the `FormHelper`. The `create()` method of the `FormHelper` creates a formatted opening `<form>` tag:

```
$form->create(null, array('url' => '/books/view', 'type' => 'post'));
```

The above line of code outputs something like the following:

```
<form action="/interfaces/books/view" method="post">
```

The `create()` method of the `FormHelper` takes two parameters: first one `$model` is the default model name for all the fields. The second one `$options` is an associative array that contains number of different `key=>value` pairs to customize the `<form>` tag. In our case, we did not assign any default model name for our form fields. We passed two options through the second parameter. The first one `url` sets the URL where the form is to be submitted. The next one `type` specifies the method of the form submission. The valid values include post, get, file etc.

Then, we added some input fields to the form using the `FormHelper`'s `input()` method. The `input()` method also takes two parameters. The first one `$fieldName` is used to define the field name. And the second one `$options` is an associative array containing different `key=>value` pairs to configure some additional options, like type of the input etc.

We first created a simple text field using the `input()` method to take the title of a book from the user:

```
echo $form->input('Book.book_title', array('type'=>'text'));
```

The first parameter provided to the `input()` method is `Book.book_title`. By setting the fieldname to `Book.book_title`, we actually hooked up this input field to the `Book` model's `book_title` field.

> We could though do it in other ways—by specifying a default model name (in our case, it would be Book) in `$form->create()` method as the first parameter and supplying only the fieldname (that is book_title) in `$form->input()` method.

We also specified the type of the input field to `text` through the second parameter `$options`. Valid `type` values includes: 'text', 'checkbox', 'datetime', 'textarea', 'date', 'time' etc.

This way, we then created two more input fields of type `text` to take author name and the ISBN number of the book:

```
echo $form->input('Book.author', array('type'=>'text'));
echo $form->input('Book.isbn', array('type'=>'text'));
```

And lastly, an input of type `date` to take the release date of the book:

```
echo $form->input('Book.release_date', array('type'=>'date'));
```

The `date` type automatically creates three HTML `<select>` menus to take month, day, and the year.

 To learn more about the `FormHelper` and other helpers that Cake provides, please refer to the CakePHP official manual `http://book.cakephp.org/`

We ended the form using the `$form->end()` method. This method outputs a submit button and a closing HTML form tag `</form>`. This is how the form we created should look like:

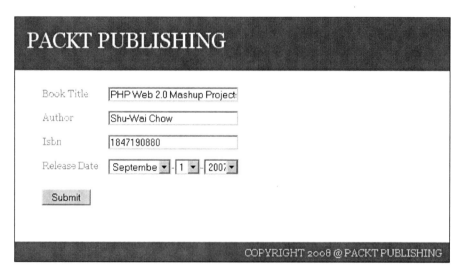

The `view()` action of the `BooksController` is where this form data will be submitted. We will get all the submitted form data in this action through the `$data` attribute.

 If an input field's fieldname is set to `ModelName.fieldname`, it will be available as `$this->data['ModelName']['fieldname']` from the controller action—where the form is submitted.

Like the data entered in the form input with fieldname `Book.book_title` is available as `$this->data['Book']['book_title']` inside the `view()` action of the `BooksController`.

Inside the controller action, we did some manipulation on the submitted form data. Then, we forwarded the submitted book data to its corresponding view to display to the browser.

Now, if we add a book from the URL `http://localhost/interfaces/books/add`, we would see something like the following:

PACKT PUBLISHING

Book Store

PHP Web 2.0 Mashup Projects

Author: Shu-Wai Chow

ISBN: 18471-90-88-0

Release Date: Sep 2007

COPYRIGHT 2008 @ PACKT PUBLISHING

Summary

Views are used to display formatted results of our controller actions. Typically, all outputs are sent to the browser through view files. For every controller action, we have a specific view file.

CakePHP offers some other view aids to make our job simpler. Layout is one of them. We can wrap around all our pages inside a customized (X)HTML page frame by creating our own default layout. We can use elements to reuse view fragments. Elements also help us to make views more readable. We can place the code for a view fragment in an element file and then render that element where needed.

Helper classes are used to encapsulate our display logics and to separate the logics from the view files. Helpers increase reusability to a great extent. CakePHP offers many useful helpers to make developers lives easier. We can, as well, create our own customized helpers to fulfill our particular needs. Amongst the built-in helpers, `FormHelper` is probably the mostly used one. It helps us to create Cake standard web forms easily and offers many shortcuts and automagics to aid quick form creation.

In the next chapter, we will learn how to create a fully functional application without writing a single line of code—using a special Cake tool called 'Bake'. Stay tuned…!

8

Using Shells: Get Further, Faster

Cake gives us the facility to create basic application skeleton/template codes to start working with, without much effort. Rather than having us create all of our application code from scratch, we can use shell commands that will write codes for us! Shells are very powerful tools for automating repetitive tasks. It boosts up the productivity to a great extent, specifically at the starting phase of building an application. It can help us to rapidly generate new models, controllers, and views for our application using commands. Once those building blocks are created, we just have to fill in the application's customized logics in that auto-generated code skeleton.

To execute shells to generate codes in Cake, we use a command called 'cake'. There are a few number of shell scripts come with the cake installation, namely acl, api, bake, console, i18n and schema. Every one of them has different usage. But commonly all of them are used to automate repetitive tasks and speed up our development.

In this chapter, we are specifically interested in one of those shell scripts called `bake`. The `bake` shell script is very cleverly titled — it can write a fully working Cake application with basic CRUD interfaces and functionalities. It is pretty much similar to scaffolding that we learned in chapter 5. The difference is that the bake script actually writes out the codes that can be used to get started with. In this chapter, we will build a simple blog using these tools where a user can post articles and comments.

- How to setup cake shell in Windows and *nix
- How to configure database using shell
- How to use shell to create models
- How to create controllers using `bake`
- How to bake views for our controller actions

Setting Up the Cake Shell

Before we start using the CakePHP shell, we need to set up the Cake shell in our operating system. The process of the setup varies depending on the operating system. But the main idea is to add our /cake/console/ folder to the path variable of the operating system. We will first see how to do that in Windows XP/2000. After that, we will see how we can set it up in Linux.

Setting Up the Cake Shell in Windows

Setting up the Cake shell in Windows is easy. We just have to add our PHP installation path and Cake's console directory's path to the system variable path. We will now see how to do that step by step.

Time for Action: Setting Up the Cake Shell in Windows

1. Create a new Cake project named rapidcake.

2. Go to the **Control Panel** of your operating system. Click on the **System** item. A dialog box will open up. Go to the **Advanced** tab of that window.

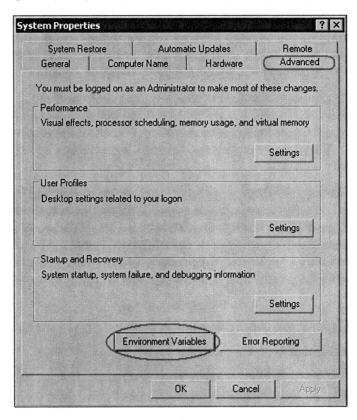

3. At the bottom of this window, find a button named **Environment Variables**. Click on that button, it will pop up another dialog box.

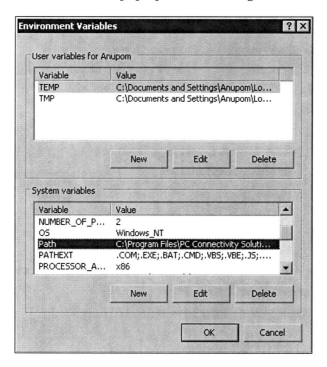

4. Select the **Path** variable under the **System variables** panel. And then click the **Edit** button. It will pop up another dialog box where we can edit the **Path** variables value.

5. Find the **Variable value** text field in this dialog box. At the end of this text field, first add a semicolon (;). Then add your PHP path (that should be something like `C:\wamp\php`) and your Cake console path (something like `C:\wamp\www\rapidcake\cake\console`) separated by semicolons. The whole text that should be appended should look something like this: `;C:\wamp\php;C:\wamp\www\rapidcake\cake\console`
The first semicolon is used to separate our variables from the variables that were there in that text field before.

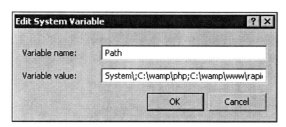

6. Now, open the command prompt and check the installation by entering the **cake** command. If it shows something like the following, then the setup has been successful:

```
C:\Documents and Settings\Anupom>cake

Welcome to CakePHP v1.2.0.7125 RC1 Console

-------------------------------------------------------------

Current Paths:
 -working: C:\Documents and Settings\Anupom
 -root: C:\Documents and Settings
 -app: C:\Documents and Settings\Anupom\
 -core: C:\wamp\www\rapidcake\

...

...
```

Otherwise, if it shows something like the following that means the setup is not working for some reason:

```
'cake' is not recognized as an internal or external command,
operable program or batch file.
```

If so, then please follow the above steps carefully again.

What Just Happened?

As I said before, to use the bake script, we must add the Cake's console directory to our system variable **Path**. In Windows, we can add that from the **Control Panel**. We first opened the **System** window from the **Control Panel** and then opened the **Advanced** tab. We clicked on the **Environment Variables** and then selected **Path** from the list of **System Variables**. We then clicked the **Edit** button that opened up another window. From there, we edited the value of the **Path** variable. We appended a semicolon and the Cake's console directory location at the end of this value. We then opened up the command prompt and entered the command **cake**. It showed us a welcome message and we got confirmed that the Cake console has been installed successfully.

Setting Up the Cake Shell in *nix

Setting up the Cake shell is even easier in Linux. Usually, the **php** command is available via the shell if PHP is correctly installed on a Linux machine. So, we just have to add Cake's console folder to the system path to get the Cake shell up and running. We will now see how to do that in a Linux machine.

Time for Action: Setting Up the Cake Shell in *nix

1. Create a new Cake installation named `rapidcake`.

2. Open up the terminal and enter the following command:

   `anupom@darkhorse:~$ vi .profile`

3. It will open up your `.profile` file. This file may or may not have a line starting with **export PATH=**. If it is already there, then just append a colon (:) and your Cake console directory's path to it.
   Now, this line should look something like the following:

   `export PATH=/opt/local/turbo/bin:/home/netex/bin/:/var/www/rapidcake/cake`

   If there is no line that starts with **export PATH=** then just add a line like the following:

   `export PATH=$PATH:/var/www/rapidcake/cake`

   The part after the colon contains the Cake console path.

   Save the file using *ctrl+o* and exit to the console using *ctrl+x*.

4. Now reload the profile by entering '**. .profile**'

   `anupom@darkhorse:~ $ .  .profile`

5. Now enter the command **cake**. If the setup is successful, then it will show some welcome message:

   `anupom@darkhorse:~$ cake`

   ```
   Hello anupom,

   Welcome to CakePHP v1.2.0.7125 RC1 Console
   ---------------------------------------------------------------
   Current Paths:
    -working: /home/anupom
    -root: /home
    -app: /home/anupom/
    -core: /var/www/rapidcake/

   Changing Paths:
   your working path should be the same as your application path
   to change your path use the '-app' param.
   Example: -app relative/path/to/myapp or -app /absolute/path/to/
   myapp

   Available Shells:

    vendors/shells/:
          - none
   ```

```
cake/console/libs/:
        api
        i18n
        acl
        console
        schema
        bake
```

```
To run a command, type 'cake shell_name [args]'
To get help on a specific command, type 'cake shell_name help'
```

6. If the setup is unsuccessful, then it will show something like the following:

```
bash: cake: command not found
```

If the setup does not work then please carefully follow the steps again.

What Just Happened?

Setting up the Cake shell is much easier in a Linux system. To start using the Cake shell, we first have to add the Cake console directory to the system variable **PATH**. We can set the **PATH** variable in a file named .profile. To do that, we went to the console and opened up the .profile file for editing by entering the command **vi .profile**. We then added our Cake's console directory location to the **PATH** variable. We then saved the file and went back to the shell prompt. From the shell prompt, we reloaded the .profile file by entering the command **. .profile**. We then entered the command **cake** from the shell. It showed us some welcome message to confirm that the installation was successful.

Now that the Cake shell is successfully set up, we can go start baking a simple application with this cool tool!

Baking an Application

In CakePHP, automatic code generation is called Baking. An entire application can be generated with all CRUD operations from a few database tables without writing a single line of code. Baking is a great relief for lazy programmers. Moreover, it can be used to generate a basic skeleton application to get up and running. The bake script can be run from the command line. We will now see how a database can be configured using the 'bake' routine.

Creating and Configuring the Database

The bake script can be used to create the database configuration file. As we already know, a database configuration file is used to associate a database to a Cake application. Let's see how the bake script can help us to create such a database configuration file.

Time for Action: Creating and Configuring the Database

1. Create a database named `rapidcake` with three tables (posts, users, and comments) using the following SQLs:

```
CREATE DATABASE `rapidcake`;
 USE `rapidcake`;
 CREATE TABLE `posts` (
  `id` int(10) NOT NULL auto_increment,
  `title` varchar(256) NOT NULL,
  `body` mediumtext NOT NULL,
  `user_id` int(10) NOT NULL,
  PRIMARY KEY  (`id`),
  KEY `user_id` (`user_id`)
);
 CREATE TABLE `users` (
  `id` int(10) NOT NULL auto_increment,
  `name` varchar(127) NOT NULL,
  PRIMARY KEY  (`id`)
);

 CREATE TABLE `comments` (
  `id` int(10) NOT NULL auto_increment,
  `body` mediumtext NOT NULL,
  `post_id` int(10) NOT NULL,
  `user_id` int(10) NOT NULL,
  PRIMARY KEY  (`id`),
  KEY `post_id` (`post_id`),
  KEY `user_id` (`user_id`)
);
```

2. From the command prompt or terminal, go to `app` directory of the `rapidcake` project:

```
C:\Documents and Settings\Anupom>cd C:\wamp\www\rapidcake\app
```

And then enter the command **cake bake**:

```
C:\wamp\www\rapidcake\app>cake bake
Welcome to CakePHP v1.2.0.7125 RC1 Console
---------------------------------------------------------------
App : app
Path: C:\wamp\www\rapidcake\app
---------------------------------------------------------------
Your database configuration was not found. Take a moment to create
one.
```

3. The script will now ask you to enter some database configuration information. Follow the prompt and enter your database information one by one.

4. It will first ask for the database configuration's name. Enter default.

   ```
   Database Configuration:
   Name:
   [default] > default
   ```

5. Then it will ask for the database driver's name. In our case it is **mysql**.

   ```
   Driver: (db2/firebird/mssql/mysql/mysqli/odbc/oracle/postgres/
   sqlite/sybase)
   [mysql] > mysql
   ```

6. It will then ask if the database connection should be treated as a persistent connection or not. We don't want a persistent connection and so will enter **n**.

   ```
   Persistent Connection? (y/n)
   [n] > n
   ```

7. After that, it's going to ask for the database host name and port number. Enter **localhost** and **n** respectively.

   ```
   Database Host:
   [localhost] > localhost
   Port?
   [n] > n
   ```

8. It will then ask for the database user name and password. Enter your database user name and password correspondingly:

   ```
   User:
   [root] > anupom
   Password:
   >
   ```

9. When the database user name and password is entered, it will ask for the database name. Enter **rapidcake**

   ```
   Database Name:
   [cake] > rapidcake
   ```

10. It will then ask for whether we have any special choice for table prefix, table encoding, and table schema. We don't have any, so for all these enter **n** as answer:

    ```
    Table Prefix?
    [n] > n
    Table encoding?
    [n] > n
    ```

11. At last, the script will show all those information we provided:

```
----------------------------------------------------------------
The following database configuration will be created:
----------------------------------------------------------------

Name:          default
Driver:           mysql
Persistent:    false
Host:              localhost
Port:
User:              root
Pass:
Database:      rapidcake
Table prefix:
Schema:          n
Encoding:
----------------------------------------------------------------
```

And will ask us to reconfirm them. Enter **y** to confirm.

```
Look okay? (y/n)
[y] > y
```

At last, it will ask if we want to add more database configurations. We don't want to, so enter **n**.

```
Do you wish to add another database configuration?
[n] > n
```

It will then create the database configuration file:

```
Creating file C:\wamp\www\rapidcake\app\config\database.php
Wrote C:\wamp\www\rapidcake\app\config\database.php
```

What Just Happened?

If the bake script cannot find the database configuration file database.php inside the /app/config/ folder, it will start baking a new configuration file. Before we bake the database configuration file, we need to create a database. We created a very simple database with three tables named rapidcake. We designed the database according to the Cake convention.

Designing the database according to the Cake convention is pretty much essential for baking. The bake script can intuit the relationship between models from the convention and baking model becomes much easier. We will practically see how this convention helps baking models in the following section.

After creating the database, we entered the command **cake bake** in the command prompt. The bake script then started asking information about the database through the command prompt that is needed to create the configuration file. We just had to enter the answers and at the end, this script generated the configuration file for us.

Now, if we go to the /app/config/ folder, we will see a file named database.php is created with the following code:

```php
<?php
class DATABASE_CONFIG {

    var $default = array(
        'driver' => 'mysql',
        'persistent' => true,
        'host' => 'localhost',
        'port' => '',
        'login' => 'root',
        'password' => '',
        'database' => 'rapidcake',
        'schema' => '',
        'prefix' => '',
        'encoding' => ''
    );

}
?>
```

Now that we have created the database configuration file, we can start baking our models. In the following section, we will see how to generate models from the database tables using the Cake shell script **bake**.

Baking Models

Once the database is configured, the bake script can be used to auto-generate models based on the database. Using bake script, we can generate models, and create associations between models. Moreover, if the database is designed according to Cake convention, the bake script will intuitively suggest the associations between the models. No need to write any code. Even using the bake script, we can add validation rules in models. In the following *Time for Action*, we will see how to create models with their associations using the bake script.

Time for Action: Baking Models

1. From the command prompt or terminal, go to `app` directory of the `rapidcake` project:

   ```
   C:\Documents and Settings\Anupom>cd C:\wamp\www\rapidcake\app
   ```

2. Now, enter the command **cake bake**. It will show some welcome message and your application path. It will also show some options and ask **What would you like to Bake**. Enter **M** to tell the bake script that we want to bake our models:

   ```
   C:\wamp\www\rapidcake\app>cake bake

   Welcome to CakePHP v1.2.0.7125 RC1 Console
   ---------------------------------------------------------------
   App : app
   Path: C:\wamp\www\rapidcake\app
   ---------------------------------------------------------------
   Interactive Bake Shell
   ---------------------------------------------------------------
   [D]atabase Configuration
   [M]odel
   [V]iew
   [C]ontroller
   [P]roject
   [Q]uit
   What would you like to Bake? (D/M/V/C/P/Q)
   > M
   ```

3. It will now intuitively show a list of models based on our database tables and ask to select one to bake. Enter **1** to select the `Comment` model.

   ```
   ---------------------------------------------------------------
   Bake Model
   Path: C:\wamp\www\rapidcake\app\models\
   ---------------------------------------------------------------
   Possible Models based on your current database:
   1. Comment
   2. Post
   3. User
   Enter a number from the list above, or type in the name of another
   model.
   > 1
   ```

4. It will then ask if we want to add validation criteria. For now, we don't want to add any. So, Enter **n**.

```
Would you like to supply validation criteria for the fields in
your model? (y/n)
[y] > n
```

5. Then, it will ask if we want to define any model association. We certainly want. Enter **y**.

```
Would you like to define model associations (hasMany, hasOne,
belongsTo, etc.)?
(y/n)
[y] > y
```

6. The bake script will automatically detect some associations (based on the Cake's database design convention). It will suggest two associations Comment belongsTo Post and Comment belongsTo Author. Confirm them by entering **y**. It will also ask if we want to define some additional associations. Enter **n**.

```
One moment while the associations are detected.
------------------------------------------------------------
Please confirm the following associations:
------------------------------------------------------------
Comment belongsTo Post? (y/n)
[y] > y
Comment belongsTo User? (y/n)
[y] > y
Would you like to define some additional model associations? (y/n)
[n] > n
```

7. The script will then show the information we provided about the Comment model and ask us to reconfirm if everything is alright. If it looks alright, enter **y** to proceed. The bake script will then create the Comment model inside the /app/models/ directory.

```
------------------------------------------------------------
The following Model will be created:
------------------------------------------------------------
Name:        Comment
Associations:
                        Comment belongsTo Post
                        Comment belongsTo User
------------------------------------------------------------
Look okay? (y/n)
[y] > y
Creating file C:\wamp\www\rapidcake\app\models\comment.php
Wrote C:\wamp\www\rapidcake\app\models\comment.php
```

8. After creating the Comment model, it will ask if we want the bake script to write unit test files. Enter **n** as we don't want them now.

```
Cake test suite not installed.  Do you want to bake unit test
files anyway? (y/n
)
[y] > n
```

9. The script will then show the main menu again. Enter **M** again to choose model baking.

```
-----------------------------------------------------------------
Interactive Bake Shell
-----------------------------------------------------------------
[D]atabase Configuration
[M]odel
[V]iew
[C]ontroller
[P]roject
[Q]uit
What would you like to Bake? (D/M/V/C/P/Q)
> M
```

10. This time we will bake out the Post model. It is somewhat similar to what we have done for the Comment model. The only difference is this time we have different associations. Look at the following commands and verbose outputs and do accordingly. It must be trivial by now!

```
-----------------------------------------------------------
Bake Model
Path: C:\wamp\www\rapidcake\app\models\
-----------------------------------------------------------
Possible Models based on your current database:
1. Comment
2. Post
3. User
Enter a number from the list above, or type in the name of another
model.
> 2
Would you like to supply validation criteria for the fields in
your model? (y/n)
[y] > n
Would you like to define model associations (hasMany, hasOne,
belongsTo, etc.)?
(y/n)
[y] > y
```

```
One moment while the associations are detected.
-----------------------------------------------------------------
Please confirm the following associations:
-----------------------------------------------------------------
Post belongsTo User? (y/n)
[y] > y
Post hasOne Comment? (y/n)
[y] > n
Post hasMany Comment? (y/n)
[y] > y
Would you like to define some additional model associations? (y/n)
[n] > n

-----------------------------------------------------------------
The following Model will be created:
-----------------------------------------------------------------
Name:        Post
Associations:
                        Post belongsTo User
                        Post hasMany    Comment
-----------------------------------------------------------------
Look okay? (y/n)
[y] > y

Creating file C:\wamp\www\rapidcake\app\models\post.php
Wrote C:\wamp\www\rapidcake\app\models\post.php
Cake test suite not installed.  Do you want to bake unit test
files anyway? (y/n
)
[y] > n
```

11. When it is done creating the `Post` model, the bake script will show the main bake menu again. Enter 3 to start baking the `User` model. It is also pretty similar to what we have done for the `Comment` model. The only difference is the model association—enter **y** for only the following associations—`User hasMany Comment` and `User hasMany Post`. Following is a sample verbose output:

```
-----------------------------------------------------------------
Interactive Bake Shell
-----------------------------------------------------------------
[D]atabase Configuration
[M]odel
[V]iew
[C]ontroller
```

```
[P]roject
[Q]uit
What would you like to Bake? (D/M/V/C/P/Q)
> M
-----------------------------------------------------------------
Bake Model
Path: C:\wamp\www\rapidcake\app\models\
-----------------------------------------------------------------
Possible Models based on your current database:
1. Comment
2. Post
3. User
Enter a number from the list above, or type in the name of another
model.
> 3
Would you like to supply validation criteria for the fields in
your model? (y/n)


[y] > n
Would you like to define model associations (hasMany, hasOne,
belongsTo, etc.)?
(y/n)
[y] > y
One moment while the associations are detected.
-----------------------------------------------------------------
Please confirm the following associations:
-----------------------------------------------------------------
User hasOne Comment? (y/n)
[y] > n
User hasOne Post? (y/n)
[y] > n
User hasMany Comment? (y/n)
[y] > y
User hasMany Post? (y/n)
[y] > y
Would you like to define some additional model associations? (y/n)
[n] > n

-----------------------------------------------------------------
The following Model will be created:
-----------------------------------------------------------------
Name:      User
```

```
Associations:
User hasMany    Comment
User hasMany    Post
- - - - - - - - - - - - - - - - - - - - - - - - - - - - - - - - - - - - - - - -
Look okay? (y/n)
[y] > y
Creating file C:\wamp\www\rapidcake\app\models\user.php
Wrote C:\wamp\www\rapidcake\app\models\user.php
Cake test suite not installed.  Do you want to bake unit test
files anyway? (y/n

[y] > n
```

12. It will again show the main baking menu. Enter **Q** to quit.

```
- - - - - - - - - - - - - - - - - - - - - - - - - - - - - - - - - - - - - - - -
Interactive Bake Shell
- - - - - - - - - - - - - - - - - - - - - - - - - - - - - - - - - - - - - - - -
[D]atabase Configuration
[M]odel
[V]iew
[C]ontroller
[P]roject
[Q]uit
What would you like to Bake? (D/M/V/C/P/Q)
>Q
```

What Just Happened?

The most crucial and important part of baking is baking models. From the command prompt, we first went to the app directory of the rapidcake project and then entered the command **cake bake**. This time, this script found a database configuration file and showed us a list of things to bake to choose from. We entered **M** to go for model baking. Now, the script will show a list of models that we may like to bake based on the database tables.

We first selected the Comment model by entering **1**. We did not want to add validation rules and so we entered **n** when the script asked if we want to add validations. Then, the script asked if we want to add model associations. We entered **y** to agree. The real benefit of using conventions showed up—Cake suggested some possible associations between the Comment model and other models based on the database convention. As our database followed the Cake convention, most of the time Cake was just accurate. And we just had to enter **y** to confirm the associations. At the end, the bake script showed us the information we provided about the Comment model and asked for reconfirming if everything is alright. We entered **y** to proceed.

Similarly, we baked our `Post` and `User` model by just following up the prompts. Once all the models are baked, we can go and check them out inside the `/app/models/` folder. Now, we will find three new files created inside the `/app/models/` folder namely: `comment.php`, `post.php`, and `user.php`. If you are curious, you can open a file and check out the source code. Our friend 'bake' has compiled them up very nicely!

After creating the models, the next step is to create the corresponding controllers. Baking controllers is much simpler than baking models. In the following section, we will see how we can generate controllers with some basic functionality using the bake script.

Baking Controllers

The next step after creating the models is creating the controllers. For every model, we need a corresponding controller, and the bake script can be used to create controllers for those models. Interestingly, the bake script not only just creates skeleton controller classes but also adds CRUD functionalities to them. Moreover, it almost takes no time to create full fledged controllers with all those cool CRUD operations. Let's see how to auto-generate controllers with the bake script.

Time for Action: Baking Controllers

1. From the command prompt or terminal, go to `app` directory of the `rapidcake` project:

   ```
   C:\Documents and Settings\Anupom>cd C:\wamp\www\rapidcake\app
   ```

2. Enter **cake bake controller** to start baking the controllers.

   ```
   C:\wamp\www\rapidcake\app>cake bake controller


   Welcome to CakePHP v1.2.0.7125 RC1 Console
   ---------------------------------------------------------------
   App : app
   Path: C:\wamp\www\rapidcake\app
   ---------------------------------------------------------------
   ---------------------------------------------------------------
   Bake Controller
   Path: C:\wamp\www\rapidcake\app\controllers\
   ---------------------------------------------------------------
   ```

3. The script will now show a possible list of models we want to build our controllers for and ask you to enter a number from the list. Enter **1** to select `Comments`.

    ```
    Possible Models based on your current database:
    1. Comments
    2. Posts
    3. Users
    Enter a number from the list above, or type in the name of another
    controller.

    > 1
    ```

4. The script will now ask if we want to build our controller interactively. Enter **n** to skip interactive baking.

    ```
    ---------------------------------------------------------------

    Baking CommentsController

    ---------------------------------------------------------------

    Would you like to build your controller interactively? (y/n)

    [y] > n
    ```

5. Then, the bake console will ask if it should include some basic CRUD methods in our controllers. Enter **y** to go for it.

    ```
    Would you like to include some basic class methods (index(),
    add(), view(), edit
    ())? (y/n)
    [y] > y
    ```

6. After that, the script will ask if we want the script to create methods for admin routing. Enter **n** as we don't want it now.

    ```
    Would you like to create the methods for admin routing? (y/n)
    [y] > n
    ```

7. The script will then show the information we provided about the `CommentsController` and ask us to reconfirm if everything is alright. If it look alright, enter **y** to proceed.

    ```
    ---------------------------------------------------------------
    The following controller will be created:
    ---------------------------------------------------------------
    Controller Name:  Comments
    ---------------------------------------------------------------
    Look okay? (y/n)
    [y] > y
    ```

8. The bake console will then create the `CommentsController` based on our provided information and will show a confirmation message.

```
Creating file C:\wamp\www\rapidcake\app\controllers\
                                    comments_controller.php
Wrote C:\wamp\www\rapidcake\app\controllers\
                                    comments_controller.php
```

9. At last, the bake script will ask if it should write down unit test files for this controller. Again we don't need this. Enter **n** to skip.

```
Cake test suite not installed.  Do you want to bake unit test
files anyway? (y/n
)
[y] > n
```

10. Enter the command **cake bake controller** again from the command prompt to start baking the `PostsController`. This time enter **2** to select the `Posts` option.

```
C:\wamp\www\rapidcake\app>cake bake controller

Welcome to CakePHP v1.2.0.7125 RC1 Console
-------------------------------------------------------------
App : app
Path: C:\wamp\www\rapidcake\app
-------------------------------------------------------------
-------------------------------------------------------------
Bake Controller
Path: C:\wamp\www\rapidcake\app\controllers\
-------------------------------------------------------------
Possible Models based on your current database:
1. Comments
2. Posts
3. Users
Enter a number from the list above, or type in the name of another
controller.

> 2
```

11. The bake script will now start baking the `PostsController`. The baking process is similar to what we have done for the `CommentsController`. Follow the command prompt and answer accordingly. The bake script will guide you to the final goal and create the controller file.

```
-------------------------------------------------------------
Baking PostsController
-------------------------------------------------------------
Would you like to build your controller interactively? (y/n)
```

```
[y] > n
Would you like to include some basic class methods (index(),
add(), view(), edit
())? (y/n)
[y] > y
Would you like to create the methods for admin routing? (y/n)
[y] > n

-----------------------------------------------------------------
The following controller will be created:
-----------------------------------------------------------------
Controller Name:  Posts
-----------------------------------------------------------------
Look okay? (y/n)
[y] > y

Creating file C:\wamp\www\rapidcake\app\controllers\posts_
controller.php
Wrote C:\wamp\www\rapidcake\app\controllers\posts_controller.php
Cake test suite not installed.  Do you want to bake unit test
files anyway? (y/n
)
[y] > n
```

12. Similarly, repeat these steps to bake the UsersConroller.

```
C:\wamp\www\rapidcake\app>cake bake controller

Welcome to CakePHP v1.2.0.7125 RC1 Console
-----------------------------------------------------------------
App : app
Path: C:\wamp\www\rapidcake\app
-----------------------------------------------------------------
-----------------------------------------------------------------
Bake Controller
Path: C:\wamp\www\rapidcake\app\controllers\
-----------------------------------------------------------------
Possible Models based on your current database:
1. Comments
2. Posts
3. Users
Enter a number from the list above, or type in the name of another
controller.

> 3
-----------------------------------------------------------------
```

```
Baking UsersController
----------------------------------------------------------------
Would you like to build your controller interactively? (y/n)
[y] > n
Would you like to include some basic class methods (index(),
add(), view(), edit
())? (y/n)
[y] > y
Would you like to create the methods for admin routing? (y/n)
[y] > n

----------------------------------------------------------------
The following controller will be created:
----------------------------------------------------------------
Controller Name:   Users
----------------------------------------------------------------
Look okay? (y/n)
[y] > y

Creating file C:\wamp\www\rapidcake\app\controllers\users_
controller.php
Wrote C:\wamp\www\rapidcake\app\controllers\users_controller.php
Cake test suite not installed.  Do you want to bake unit test
files anyway? (y/n
)
[y] > n
```

What Just Happened?

We started baking our controller by entering the command **cake bake controller**. It is in fact a shortcut to go straight to controller baking, avoiding the main bake menu.

 Similarly, we can enter **cake bake model** to directly go to the model baking skipping the main bake menu.

The bake script then showed a list of possible corresponding models. We first selected the Comments model by entering **1**. The script then started the baking procedure for the CommentsController. It first asked if we want to bake our controllers interactively. We entered **n** to disregard interactive baking. The bake script then asked if it should write down some basic controller methods. We permitted by entering **y**. After that, it asked if it should write controller methods for admin routing. We entered **n** to avoid the admin routing method creation.

We can avoid going through all those prompts by directly entering the command **cake bake controller Comments scaffold**. It will also create the `CommentsController` with basic CRUD methods.

After baking the `CommentsController`, we baked our `PostsControllers` and `UsersController` in the same way.

We can now go to our `/apps/controllers/` folder and check out our just baked controllers there. Try opening a controller file, you will find that the cool bake script has already written some basic methods there.

But without the views, these controllers have no real use. To see our controllers in action, we have to bake our views first. Baking views is the next thing we are going to learn.

Baking Views

Baking views is the simplest amongst all. We already have created models and controllers with all CRUD methods. Now, we just need to create view files for them. We will now see how we can do that rapidly using the bake shell script.

Time for Action: Baking Views

1. From the command prompt or terminal, go to `app` directory of the `rapidcake` project:

    ```
    C:\Documents and Settings\Anupom>cd C:\wamp\www\rapidcake\app
    ```

2. Enter the command **cake bake view** to start baking our views. It will show a list of models to create views for. Enter **1** to select `Comments`.

    ```
    C:\wamp\www\rapidcake\app>cake bake view

    Welcome to CakePHP v1.2.0.7125 RC1 Console
    ---------------------------------------------------------------
    App : app
    Path: C:\wamp\www\rapidcake\app
    ---------------------------------------------------------------
    ---------------------------------------------------------------
    Bake View
    Path: C:\wamp\www\rapidcake\app\views\
    ---------------------------------------------------------------
    ```

```
Possible Models based on your current database:
1. Comments
2. Posts
3. Users
Enter a number from the list above, or type in the name of another
controller.

> 1
```

3. It will then ask if we want to create views for index, add, view, and edit operations. Enter **y** to confirm it.

```
Would you like to create some scaffolded views (index, add, view,
edit) for this controller?
NOTE: Before doing so, you'll need to create your controller and
model classes (including associated models). (y/n)
[n] > y
```

4. After that, it will ask if we want to build views for admin routing. For now, we don't want admin routing stuffs. Enter **n**.

```
Would you like to create the views for admin routing? (y/n)
[y] > n
```

5. The bake script will now start writing view files for CRUD operations on the Comment model. Wait until it shows the message **View Scaffolding Complete**.

```
Creating file C:\wamp\www\rapidcake\app\views\comments\index.ctp
Wrote C:\wamp\www\rapidcake\app\views\comments\index.ctp

Creating file C:\wamp\www\rapidcake\app\views\comments\view.ctp
Wrote C:\wamp\www\rapidcake\app\views\comments\view.ctp

Creating file C:\wamp\www\rapidcake\app\views\comments\add.ctp
Wrote C:\wamp\www\rapidcake\app\views\comments\add.ctp

Creating file C:\wamp\www\rapidcake\app\views\comments\edit.ctp
Wrote C:\wamp\www\rapidcake\app\views\comments\edit.ctp
-----------------------------------------------------------------

View Scaffolding Complete.
```

6. Again, enter the command **cake bake view** and now enter **2** to select Posts. Do the same as we did for baking the views for Comments.

```
C:\wamp\www\rapidcake\app>cake bake view

Welcome to CakePHP v1.2.0.7125 RC1 Console
-----------------------------------------------------------------
App : app
```

```
Path: C:\wamp\www\rapidcake\app
------------------------------------------------------------------
------------------------------------------------------------------
Bake View
Path: C:\wamp\www\rapidcake\app\views\
------------------------------------------------------------------
Possible Models based on your current database:
1. Comments
2. Posts
3. Users
Enter a number from the list above, or type in the name of another
controller.

> 2
Would you like to create some scaffolded views (index, add, view,
edit) for this controller?
NOTE: Before doing so, you'll need to create your controller and
model classes (including associated models). (y/n)
[n] > y
Would you like to create the views for admin routing? (y/n)
[y] > n

Creating file C:\wamp\www\rapidcake\app\views\posts\index.ctp
Wrote C:\wamp\www\rapidcake\app\views\posts\index.ctp

Creating file C:\wamp\www\rapidcake\app\views\posts\view.ctp
Wrote C:\wamp\www\rapidcake\app\views\posts\view.ctp

Creating file C:\wamp\www\rapidcake\app\views\posts\add.ctp
Wrote C:\wamp\www\rapidcake\app\views\posts\add.ctp

Creating file C:\wamp\www\rapidcake\app\views\posts\edit.ctp
Wrote C:\wamp\www\rapidcake\app\views\posts\edit.ctp
------------------------------------------------------------------
View Scaffolding Complete.
```

7. Similarly, repeat these steps for baking the views for Users.

```
C:\wamp\www\rapidcake\app>cake bake view

Welcome to CakePHP v1.2.0.7125 RC1 Console
------------------------------------------------------------------
App : app
Path: C:\wamp\www\rapidcake\app
------------------------------------------------------------------
------------------------------------------------------------------
Bake View
```

```
Path: C:\wamp\www\rapidcake\app\views\
----------------------------------------------------------------
Possible Models based on your current database:
1. Comments
2. Posts
3. Users
Enter a number from the list above, or type in the name of another
controller.

> 3
Would you like to create some scaffolded views (index, add, view,
edit) for this controller?
NOTE: Before doing so, you'll need to create your controller and
model classes (including associated models). (y/n)
[n] > y
Would you like to create the views for admin routing? (y/n)
[y] > n

Creating file C:\wamp\www\rapidcake\app\views\users\index.ctp
Wrote C:\wamp\www\rapidcake\app\views\users\index.ctp

Creating file C:\wamp\www\rapidcake\app\views\users\view.ctp
Wrote C:\wamp\www\rapidcake\app\views\users\view.ctp

Creating file C:\wamp\www\rapidcake\app\views\users\add.ctp
Wrote C:\wamp\www\rapidcake\app\views\users\add.ctp

Creating file C:\wamp\www\rapidcake\app\views\users\edit.ctp
Wrote C:\wamp\www\rapidcake\app\views\users\edit.ctp
----------------------------------------------------------------

View Scaffolding Complete.
```

What Just Happened?

Baking views could not be simpler. We first entered the command **cake bake view**.
A list of models (for which we want to bake views) showed up in the command
prompt. We then selected the Comments model by entering **1**. The baked script then
asked if we want to build our models interactively. We trusted the bake script and
entered **n** to skip the interactive view baking. Then, it asked if we want to create
views for admin routing. We also don't need that and so we again entered **n**. It then
started creating the view files — index.ctp, view.ctp, add.ctp and edit.ctp for
the CommentsController.

Once we are done baking the view files for the CommentsController, we repeated
the same steps for PostsController and UsersController.

Here, every time we selected the model (to bake views for) from the list of models. We could avoid it though by appending the model name at the end of the command like this: **cake bake view Users**. Entering this will start baking the views for the `Users` model.

Baking views is pretty straightforward. We just run the bake script and then followed the prompts. And it generated all those view files for us.

We can now go to the URL—`http://localhost/rapidcake/users/` to check our baked application. First, add a user then add some posts and have fun playing around. Yes, we have created this application without writing a single line of code!

Fascinating, is it not? The following screenshot shows the add post page (`http://localhost/rapidcake/posts/add`) of our application:

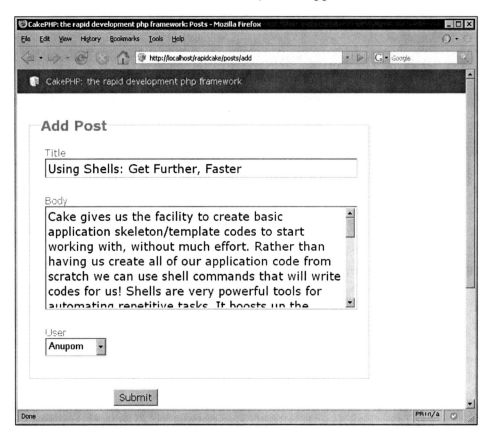

As of now, Cake has created working codes for us, we can work on that to put our customized interfaces and logics in, and make it much like a professional one.

Summary

This chapter was all about baking, the code auto-generation script that comes with CakePHP. One of the prerequisite of a smooth and effortless baking is having a database that follows the Cake convention perfectly. It makes life easier as the bake script becomes more intuitive and can automatically create some basic functionality.

The bake script is a command line tool and is one of the shell scripts that Cake provides. Before we can start using the bake script, we should properly set up the cake shell in our operating system. We just have to add the `/cake/console/` directory to our system variable path and the bake script will be ready to use.

The bake script can be used to create the database configuration file—that is used to associate databases with a Cake application. Once the database configuration file is created, the bake script can be used to generate models. It can, not only create skeleton model classes, but also add associations to them. Based on the database convention, the script can suggest associations among models. We just have to confirm them from the command prompt—bake will write codes for us to create those models and their associations. Similarly, the bake script can be used to create controllers with some basic CRUD methods. We can also auto-generate view files for those controller methods using the bake tool. It is just a matter of some keystrokes and a couple of minutes.

Bake is the best friend of a "lazy type" developer. It helps us to get started quickly. We can have a working application without writing a single line of code. And it almost takes no time and no effort to create a basic application using it.

9
Making Quickwall: The Basics

If we have come this far, we already know a lot about CakePHP. By now, we know what are the goodies in CakePHP that will enable us to develop web applications faster. We know how to install and set up a CakePHP application. We also know about the CakePHP MVC architecture, and how to work with models, controllers, and views.

In this section, we will be utilizing our newfound knowledge to make a web application. We will be calling this application Quickwall. In brief, Quickwall is a simple application that will enable a quick way to ask questions and give answers. Throughout this section, we will be building up this application, adding different features to it, and enhancing it as we go. This chapter is the beginning of it all. In this chapter, we will build the foundations of the application. After going through this chapter, we will:

- Have a quick understanding about Quickwall
- Set up Cake for Quickwall
- Create and configure a database for Quickwall
- Create models and define relationships between them
- Create a controller class and its corresponding views
- Use a custom layout for our application
- Make forms to add new questions and answers

What is This Quickwall All About?

Before we start, let us have a quick idea of what Quickwall is all about. Basically, it will be a simple and easy way to ask questions. Once we post a question, friends, family, or anyone who can help, can answer the question. On the other hand, you will be able to help out friends as well by answering to their questions. Questions can be as simple as:

- What are you having for lunch?
- What should we give David for his birthday?

Or they might be something more important like:

- What features should Quickwall have?
- How do I add custom layouts to CakePHP applications?
- Where can I get some CakePHP developers?

Based on this simple idea, Quickwall will have lots of other functionalities that we will add throughout this section. As we go along, we will also learn how to make a working application with CakePHP.

Setting Up Cake

The first thing that we need to do is set up Cake for a new application. This involves downloading the latest version of Cake, uncompressing it in our web server root, renaming the directory to (you guessed it) Quickwall, and then checking the installation by pointing your browser to the default homepage. Lastly, we will need to change the default security salt. The following *Time for Action* will take us through all these in a step-by-step fashion.

Time for Action: Setting Up Cake

1. Download a fresh copy of Cake and paste the compressed file into the web root. For more details on how to download, please see Chapter 2.

2. Uncompress it into the web root. We will get a directory with a name similar to this: **cake_1.2.0.6311**.

3. Rename the directory to `quickwall`, without the quotations of course.

4. Now open up a browser and go to `http://localhost/quickwall`. If everything is all right, we will get to see the following page:

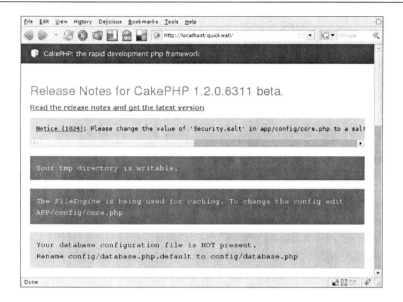

5. Next, we need to change the Security Salt. To do this, open the file /
quickwall/app/config/core.php in a text editor, and find the line
with the following code: Configure::write('Security.salt',
'DyhG93b0qyJfIxfs2guVoUubWwvniR2G0FgaC9mi');. Change the salt string
to something else like: Configure::write('Security.salt', 'DyhG93b
0qyJfIxfs2guVoUubWwvniR2QuickWall');,or anything that you like, and
save the file. Now, refresh the page, and the notice in yellow that the Security
salt will be gone. The following screenshot shows the page after changing the
security salt, and refreshing the page:

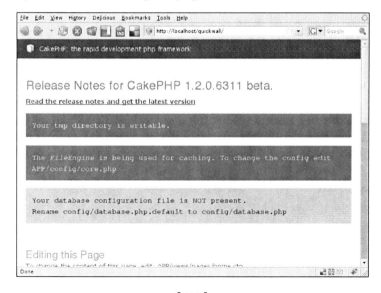

What Just Happened?

In this *Time for Action*, we first downloaded a fresh copy of Cake from the official CakePHP site: `http://cakephp.org`. Of course, if you already have the latest copy, you will be able to use it instead. We then copied the compressed CakePHP file into the web server root. After uncompressing it, we renamed the directory to Quickwall. To check if everything went fine, we then pointed the browser to `http://localhost/quickwall`. We should get a page as shown above.

If, by any chance, you do not end up with the above page, please check back to Chapter 2 for more detailed information for installing cake for a new application.

In this page, you will notice that it has a few text boxes. Some of them are colored yellow and others are green. Green boxes represent issues that have been properly configured. And yellow boxes represent issues that need to be taken care of. For example, the first yellow box asks to change the Security Salt of the application, and that's exactly what we did next.

We then changed the Security Salt for our application. In cryptography, a salt comprises random bits that are used as one of the inputs to a key derivation function. In CakePHP, one of these deviation functions is the hash routine for the Authentication. If no one ever changed their salt value, someone could simply download the CakePHP code, analyze it's working, and use that knowledge to get values for your hashed values. That is why it is a good practice to change the Security Salt just after installing Cake. The Security Salt used is present in the file `/quickwall/app/config/core.php`. This file, as the name suggests, is the main configuration file for CakePHP.

Creating and Connecting the Database

In the default page that we saw in the last section, you will see that there is another yellow box, which says that our database configuration file is not present. CakePHP applications (most web applications these days) commonly use databases. To use a database with our Quickwall application, first we need to create the database. All the tables in the database should follow the conventions that Cake expects. After creating the database, we will need to create a configuration file that will connect the application with the database. The next *Time for Actions* shows this in detail.

Time for Action

1. Create a database named `quickwall` in the local machine's MySQL server. In your favourite MySQL client, execute the following code:

```
CREATE DATABASE quickwall;
```

2. Now create two tables named `questions` and `answers` in our newly created database:

```
CREATE TABLE questions (
    id int(10) unsigned NOT NULL auto_increment,
    question varchar(255) NOT NULL,
    questioner varchar(64) NOT NULL,
    created datetime NOT NULL,
    modified datetime NOT NULL,
    PRIMARY KEY  (id)
);
CREATE TABLE answers (
    id int(10) unsigned NOT NULL auto_increment,
    question_id int(10) unsigned NOT NULL,
    answer varchar(255) NOT NULL,
    answerer varchar(64) NOT NULL,
    created datetime NOT NULL,
    modified datetime NOT NULL,
    PRIMARY KEY  (id)
);
```

3. Move inside the directory `/quickwall/app/config`. In the `config` directory, there will be a file named `database.php.default`. Rename this file to `database.php`.

4. Open the `database.php` file with your favorite editor, and move to line number 73, where we will find an array named `$default`. This array contains database connection options. Assign `login` to the database user you will be using and `password` to the password of that user. Assign `database` to `quickwall`. If we are using the database user `ahsan` with password `sims`, the configuration will look like this:

```
var $default = array(
        'driver' => 'mysql',
        'persistent' => false,
        'host' => 'localhost',
        'port' => '',
        'login' => 'ahsan',
        'password' => 'sims',
        'database' => 'quickwall',
        'schema' => '',
        'prefix' => '',
        'encoding' => ''
    );
```

5. Now, let us check if Cake is being able to connect to the database. Fire up a browser, and point to `http://localhost/quickwall/`. We should get the default Cake page that will have the following two lines: **Your database configuration file is present** and **Cake is able to connect to the database** in green as shown in the following screenshot. If you get the lines, we have successfully configured Cake to use the `quickwall` database:

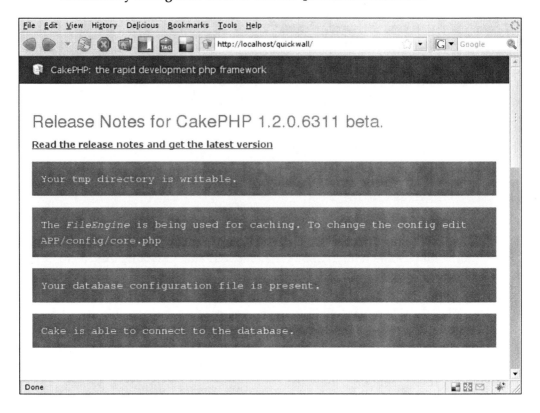

What Just Happened?

In step 1 and 2, we created a database named `quickwall` in our local MySQL server. The database has two tables: `questions` and `answers`. The `questions` table will be used to store all data about questions. To be exact, it will have an auto-generated id for each question, the question itself, the name of the person who asked the question, and the creation and modification time of the question. Similarly, the `answers` table will hold data of all the answers. It will store an auto-generated id for each answer, the id of the question that the answer belongs to, the name of the answerer, and the creation and modification time of the answer.

After the database has been created, we then move to creating the configuration file for connecting the database with our application. For this, we will need to have a configuration file in /quickwall/app/config/ named database.php. This file contains all the necessary information for connecting to the database. We added the database username and password for connecting to the local MySQL server. We also added the name of the database to be used. We then saved the file and checked the default page again. In this page, we made sure that Cake is being able to connect to the database.

Creating and Defining Relationships between Models

In this section, we will create models for our application. By now, we already know that we use models for communicating with database. All our business logic should also be contained inside models. We will be creating two models for our two database tables. After that, we will be defining relationship between these two models. The next *Time for Action* shows us how we are going to do it.

Time for Action

1. Move inside the directory /quickwall/app/models and create two files named question.php and answers.php. This represents the Question and Answer models respectively.

2. In a text editor, open the file question.php and write the following code:

```php
<?php
class Question extends AppModel {
    var $name = 'Question';
}
?>
```

3. Open the file "answer.php" and write the following code:

```php
<?php
class Answer extends AppModel {
    var $name = 'Answer';
}
?>
```

4. Since a question can have many answers, the `Question` model will have a `hasMany` relationship with the `Answer` model. To do this, add a variable named `$hasMany` inside the `Question` class, as shown here:

```php
<?php
class Question extends AppModel {
    var $name = 'Question';
    var $hasMany = array(
        'Answer' => array(
            'className'    => 'Answer'
        )
    );
}
?>
```

5. As all answers belong to a question, the `Answer` model will have a `belongsTo` relationship with the `Question` model. This is achieved by adding a variable named `$belongsTo` in the `Answer` model, as shown here:

```php
<?php
class Answer extends AppModel {
    var $name = 'Answer';
    var $belongsTo = array(
        'Question' => array(
            'className'    => 'Question'
        )
    );
}
?>
```

What just Happened?

We just created two models that we will be needing in our application. In step 1, we created two files with the names, `question.php` and `answer.php`. In step 2 and 3, we declared the the basic classes for these two models.

Next, we define the relationship between the models. We know that a question can have many answers, whereas an answer can only belong to one question only. So, the `Questions` model has a `hasMany` relationship with the `Answer` model. On the other hand, the `Answer` model has a `belongsTo` relationship with the `Question` model. These relationships are defined in step 4 and step 5.

Now, we have two working models with proper relationships defined between them.

Creating the Basic Controller Actions and Their Views

In this chapter, Quickwall will have only two pages: one that will show all the posted questions, along with a form to add a new question, and another that will show a question will all its related answers. The later will also contain a form to add a new answer to the question. For this purpose, we will only be needing one controller with two actions, one for each page. Now we are going to create the `Questions` controller that will have two actions: `home()` and `show()`. We will also be creating the views for these two actions.

Time for Action

1. Inside the directory `/quickwall/app/controllers`, create a file named `questions_controller.php`. This is the `questions` controller.

2. Inside the `questions_controller.php`, write the following code:

```php
<?php
class QuestionsController extends AppController {

    var $name = 'Questions';

}
?>
```

3. Add two actions to the `Questions` controller named `home()` and `show()`:

```php
<?php
class QuestionsController extends AppController {

    var $name = 'Questions';

    function home() {

    }

    function show() {

    }
}
?>
```

4. The `home()` action will show the lists of all the questions. To pass all the questions to the view, write the following code inside the `home()` action:

```php
<?php
class QuestionsController extends AppController {

    var $name = 'Questions';

    function home() {
        $this->Question->recursive = 1;
```

```
        $this->set('questions', $this->Question->find('all'));
    }
    function show() {
    }
}
?>
```

5. The `show()` action will show a particular question and its answers. We need to pass it the id of the question to show. Add the following code inside the `show()` action to pass a question and its answers to the view:

```php
<?php
class QuestionsController extends AppController {
    var $name = 'Questions';
    function home() {
        $this->Question->recursive = 1;
        $this->set('questions', $this->Question->find('all'));
    }
    function show( $id = null) {
        if (!$id) {
            $this->Session->setFlash('Invalid Question.');
            $this->redirect(array('action'=>'home'));
        }
        $this->set('question', $this->Question->read(null, $id));
    }
}
?>
```

6. Now let's add the views for both the actions in the `Questions` controller. Inside the directory `/quickwall/app/views`, create a new directory called `questions`. This will contain the views for all the actions in the `Questions` controller.

7. In the newly created directory `/quickwall/app/views/questions`, create two files with the names: `home.ctp` and `show.ctp`.

8. Inside the file `home.ctp`, which is the view for the `home()` action, add the following code to list all the questions:

```php
<?php if (empty($questions)): ?>
    <p class="no_answer">No Questions yet. Be the first one to
            post a Question!</p>
<?php else: ?>
    <dl>
    <?php foreach ($questions as $question): ?>
        <dt><span><?php e($question['Question']['questioner']);
        ?></span></dt>
```

```
    <dd>
        <?php e($html->link($question['Question']['question']
.'?', array('action' => 'show', $question['Question']['id']))); ?>
        <?php
            $answer_count = count($question['Answer']);
            if(!$answer_count)
                e("(no answers yet)");
            else if($answer_count == 1)
                e("(1 answer)");
            else
                e("(".$answer_count." answers)");
        ?>
    </dd>
    <?php endforeach; ?>
    </dl>
<?php endif; ?>
```

9. The `show.ctp` file is the view for the `show()` action. To display a question and its answers, write the following code in the view:

```
<h2><?php e($question['Question']['question']) ?>?</h2>
<div id="questioner"><div><span><?php e($question['Question']
                            ['questioner']) ?></span></div></div>
<?php if(empty($question['Answer'])): ?>
    <p class="no_answer">No Answers yet. Be the first one to
                                                answer!</p>
<?php else: ?>
    <dl>
    <?php foreach($question['Answer'] as $answer) : ?>
        <dt><span><?php e($answer['answerer']); ?></span></dt>
        <dd><?php e($answer['answer']); ?></dd>
    <?php endforeach; ?>
    </dl>
<?php endif; ?>
```

10. To test the code, let's add some dummy data into the questions and answers table in the `quickwall` database. Using the MySQL client, execute the following queries:

```
USE quickwall;
INSERT INTO questions (id, question, questioner, created,
                                        modified) VALUES
(1, 'Why do you use CakePHP', 'Ahsan', '2008-02-11 22:19:04',
                                '2008-02-11 22:19:04'),
(2, 'Why won''t you use CakePHP', 'Ahsan', '2008-02-11 22:22:06',
                                '2008-02-11 22:22:06');
INSERT INTO answers (id, question_id, answer, answerer, created,
                                        modified) VALUES
```

```
(1, 1, 'Its addictive', 'Anupom', '2008-02-11 22:22:45',
                          '2008-02-11 22:22:45'),
(2, 1, 'I like it.', 'Manzil', '2008-02-11 22:23:06',
                          '2008-02-11 22:23:06'),
(3, 1, 'Coz im lazy and I hate repeating myself', 'AB',
               '2008-02-11 22:23:57', '2008-02-11 22:23:57'),
(4, 2, 'Coz I am stupid', 'Stupid', '2008-02-11 22:24:24',
                          '2008-02-11 22:24:24'),
(5, 2, 'I hate to learn', 'Wanna Be', '2008-02-11 22:25:02',
                          '2008-02-11 22:25:02');
```

11. Open a web browser and go to the following address to check the `home()` action: `http://localhost/quickwall/questions/home`. You should see a page as shown below:

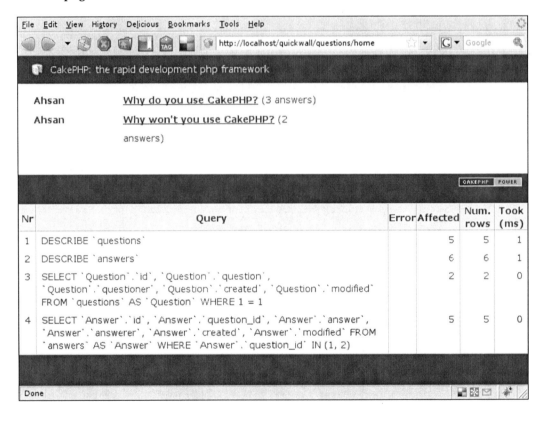

12. To go to the `show()` action, click on any of the questions in the list, you will see a page as shown here:

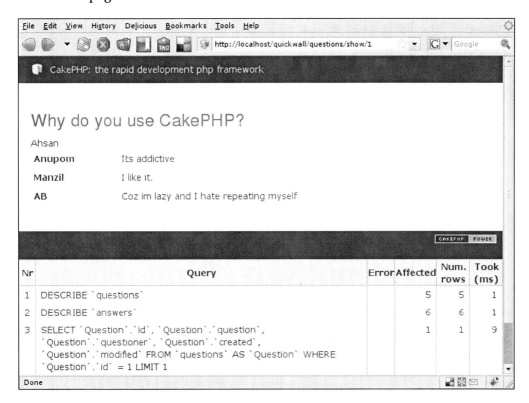

What Just Happened?

We began by creating the `Questions` controller, and adding two actions to it.

The `home()` action will be used to show all the questions. Thus in step 4, we call the `Question` model's `find()` method with the `all` parameter. This will return all the questions stored in the database. We then pass it to the array of questions in the view.

The `show()` action is used to show a question along with all its answers. The id of the question to be shown is passed as a parameter to this action. Without the question id, it is not possible to know which question to display. So we make sure that an id is passed. Or else, if no id is present, an error message is saved in the session, and the page is redirected to the homepage. If an id is passed, the `Question` model's `find()` method is called with the id. This will pass the data of that question in an array. This array is then passed to the view using the `set()` method of the controller.

You will also notice that we do not explicitly pass the associated answers of the question. This is done auto-magically by Cake, as we have already defined the relationship between the `Question` and `Answer` model. So the array structure will also contain the related answers. A sample array that may be passed by this call is shown below:

```
Array
(
    [Question] => Array
        (
            [id] => 1
            [question] => Why do you use CakePHP
            [questioner] => Ahsan
            [created] => 2008-02-11 22:19:04
            [modified] => 2008-02-11 22:19:04
        )

    [Answer] => Array
        (
            [0] => Array
                (
                    [id] => 1
                    [question_id] => 1
                    [answer] => Its addictive
                    [answerer] => Anupom
                    [created] => 2008-02-11 22:22:45
                    [modified] => 2008-02-11 22:22:45
                )

            [1] => Array
                (
                    [id] => 2
                    [question_id] => 1
                    [answer] => I like it.
                    [answerer] => Manzil
                    [created] => 2008-02-11 22:23:06
                    [modified] => 2008-02-11 22:23:06
                )

        )

)
```

This is a very good example of how CakePHP can really make life much easier.

We then move onto making the views for these two actions. As per Cake convention, we create a directory called `questions` in the `views` directory. And create the view files `home.ctp` and `show.ctp` for the two actions.

You will notice the use of a new function `e()`. This is a Cake function that can be used as a shortcut to `echo()`. Basically, it's just a simple wrapper to the echo functions. Given the high usage of `echo()` in applications, this shortcut will save you a lot of keystrokes. Yes, another small reason to use Cake.

Lastly, we enter some dummy data into the database, and check our newly created pages. If everything went all right, you will see the pages as shown. For now, it uses the default Cake layout and styles. But, I am sure, you will not be happy with the way it looks. That is why, in the next section, we will see how to add our own custom layout to Quickwall.

Adding Custom Layout

In this section, we will see how to add our own style and layout to Cake applications. Adding custom layout in Cake is very simple, as you will find out now. We will start with adding our own CSS styles that we would want to use in Quickwall. We will move on to adding a layout file that will be used in all the pages of Quickwall. After we are done doing that, we will see how to set different debug modes in CakePHP. And as a bonus, we will also see how to set a particular page as the default page of the application.

Time for Action

1. First, let us create the CSS file that will style our web application. Go to the directory `/quickwall/app/webroot/css` and create a file named `quickwall.css`. Use the CSS below and save it in `quickwall.css`:

    ```css
    * {
        margin: 0px;
        padding: 0px;
        border: 0px;
    }
    body {
        margin: 0px;
        padding: 0px;
        background-color: #eee;
        font-family: 'Lucida Grande', Helvetica, sans-serif;
    }
    #content {
        width: 570px;
        margin: 0px auto;
        padding: 30px 15px 11px 15px;
        background-color: #fff;
    }
    ```

```
a {
    color: #c00;
}
h1 {
    padding: 0px;
    margin: 0px;
    text-align: center;
    font: Bold 55px 'Arial Black', Tahoma, Helvetica, sans-serif;
    letter-spacing: -2px;
    line-height: 50px;
}
h1 a {
    color:            #444;
    text-decoration:  none;
}
p#strapline {
    font: Bold 28px Helvetica, sans-serif;
    letter-spacing: -1px;
    color: #666;
    text-align: center;
    padding: 0px 0px 30px 0px;
}
p#strapline strong {
    font: Bold 60px Georgia, serif;
    line-height: 8px;
    vertical-align: -20px;
}
form {
    position: relative;
    background-color: #eee;
    border: solid 1px #999;
    padding: 15px;
}
form label {
    position: absolute;
    width: 150px;
    text-align: right;
    left: -166px;
}
form label.questionlabel {
    top: 15px;
}
```

```
form label.questionerlabel {
    top: 50px;
}

form label span {
    background-color: #ccc;
    font: Normal 20px Helvetica, sans-serif;
    letter-spacing: -1px;
    color: #fff;
    padding: 0px 5px 0px 5px;
}

form input.fullwidth {
    width: 500px;
    border: solid 1px #ccc;
    height: 22px;
    margin: 0px 0px 12px 0px;
    font-size: 16px;
}

form span.big {
    font: Bold 60px Georgia, serif;
    position: absolute;
    left: 520px;
    top: -8px;
}

form input.halfwidth {
    width: 200px;
    border: solid 1px #ccc;
    height: 22px;
    font-size: 16px;
}

form input.submitbutton {
    width: 202px;
    height: 24px;
    border: solid 1px #ccc;
    margin: 0px 0px 0px 10px;
    font-size: 16px;
}

dl {
    position: relative;
    padding: 30px 0px;
}

dl dt {
    position: absolute;
```

```
        left: -165px;
        width: 150px;
        text-align: right;
    }
    dl dt span {
        background-color: #ccc;
        font: Normal 20px Helvetica, sans-serif;
        letter-spacing: -1px;
        color: #fff;
        padding: 0px 5px 0px 5px;
    }
    dl dd {
        font-size: 16px;
        color: #444;
        line-height: 20px;
        letter-spacing: -1px;
        padding: 0px 0px 10px 0px;
    }
    dl dd a {
        font-size: 18px;
        font-weight: Bold;
        color: #c00;
         text-decoration:  none;
    }
    div#footer {
        margin:          0px 0px 0px 0px;
        text-align:      right;
        font-size:       12px;
    }

    div#footer a {
        text-decoration:  none;
        color:            #444;
    }

    div#footer a:hover {
        text-decoration:  underline;
    }
    h2 {
        font-size: 20px;
        font-weight: Bold;
        color: #c00;
         text-decoration:  none;
```

```
        line-height: 20px;
        letter-spacing: -1px;
        margin: 0px 0px 30px 0px;
    }
    div#questioner {
        position: relative;
    }
    div#questioner div{
        position: absolute;
        left: -165px;
        top: -53px;
        text-align: right;
        width: 150px;
    }
    div#questioner div span{
        background-color: #ccc;
        font: Normal 20px Helvetica, sans-serif;
        letter-spacing: -1px;
        color: #fff;
        padding: 0px 5px 0px 5px;
    }
    p.no_answer {
        font-size: 16px;
        color: #444;
        line-height: 20px;
        letter-spacing: -1px;
        margin: 30px 0px;
    }
    div.message {
        width: auto;
        height: 24px;
        font-size: 16px;
    }
```

2. Create another CSS file in the same directory named `quickwall_ie6hack.css`. This file will contain the hacks required to render the pages properly in IE6. Copy and save the following code into this file:

```
form label {
    left: -181px;
}
form span.big {
    left: 510px;
```

```
        top: -5px;
    }
    form label.questionlabel {
        top: 17px;
    }
    form label.questionerlabel {
        top: 55px;
    }
```

3. Next, we need to create our layout file. This will be the general page structure that all pages in the application will use. Move to the directory /quickwall/app/views/layout and create a file named default.ctp. Write the following code into the file and save it:

```
<!DOCTYPE html PUBLIC "-//W3C//DTD XHTML 1.0 Strict//EN"
            "http://www.w3.org/TR/xhtml1/DTD/xhtml1-strict.dtd">
<html xmlns="http://www.w3.org/1999/xhtml" xml:lang="en"
                                                lang="en">
<head>
    <meta content="text/html; charset=utf-8" http-equiv=
                                            "Content-Type"/>
    <title>Quick Wall</title>
    <?php e($html->css('quickwall')); ?>
    <!--[if IE 6]>
        <?php e($html->css('quickwall_ie6hack')); ?>
    <![endif]-->
</head>
<body>
    <div id="content">
        <h1><?php e($html->link('Quickwall', '/')); ?></h1>
        <p id="strapline"><strong>"</strong>Quick way to Ask and
                                Answer<strong>"</strong></p>
        <?php
        if ($session->check('Message.flash')):
            $session->flash();
        endif;
        ?>
        <?php e($content_for_layout); ?>
        <div id="footer">
            <a href="http://www.cakephp.org/">
                <?php e($html->image('cake.power.gif')); ?>
            </a>
        </div>
    </div>
</body>
</html>
```

4. To check our new custom layout, open a web browser and point to `http://localhost/quickwall/questions/home`. We should see something like this:

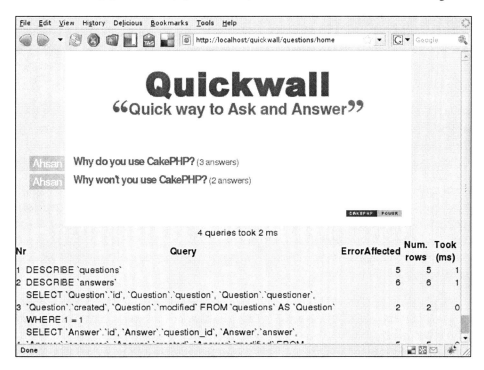

5. You will notice that at the bottom of page, there is information about the queries made to the database. These are useful for debugging purposes. But, for the sake of the beauty of the site, we are going to turn debug off, so that these messages are not shown. To do so, open the file `/quickwall/app/config/core.php` in an editor. You will see the following code at (or near) line 43: `Configure::write('debug', 2);`. Change this to `Configure::write('debug', 0);` and save the file. The debug messages will be turned off.

6. Let's make the `home()` action of the `Questions` Controller the default page of the web application. The default page is shown when no controller and action name are specified in the URL. To make the `home()` action of the `Questions` controller the default action, open the file `quickwall/app/config/routes.php`, and look for the following line: `Router::connect('/', array('controller' => 'pages', 'action' => 'display', 'home'));`. Change this to: `Router::connect('/', array('controller' => 'questions', 'action' => 'home'));`. Now, if we point our web browser to `http://localhost/quickwall/`, we will be taken to the `home()` action of the `Questions` controller.

What Just Happened?

In step 1 and 2, we added two CSS files that we will be using in our layout. All CSS files in CakePHP application reside in the directory /app/webroot/css/. All the CSS files that we want to use should be either located in this directory, or in directories under this one. In step 1, we added the base CSS file for the Quickwall application. Following that, we also added another CSS file that contains hacks to render the page properly in IE6.

Once our CSS files were in place, we moved on to creating the layout. A layout is basically a file that will define the structure of all the pages in the application. Things like the header, footer or menu that are common to all pages are defined in the layout. When no layout is defined, Cake uses its own custom layout and CSS styles.

To define our own layout, we create a file named default.ctp, inside the directory /app/views/layout. This folder contains all the layout files used in the application. An application can use more than one layout file for different views. But, if no layout is explicitly defined in a controller or an action, Cake will use the default.ctp file as the layout. And as already mentioned, if default.ctp is also not present, then Cake will use its own built-in layout.

Now, let's check inside the default.ctp we just created. We will notice that it has the <!doctype> tag, the <head> tag and also the <body> tag. If you remember correctly, we did not include any of these tags in out view files. We will see a line of code like this: <?php e($content_for_layout); ?> in the middle of the layout file. When an action is called, the view is inserted in place of this line and the whole markup of the view, embedded in the layout file, is sent back to the browser. So, if we wanted to use a different layout, we will have to define a layout file, and place the line <?php e($content_for_layout); ?> where we want the content of the view to be placed. It's as simple as that! Thus, using this layout system, we have views that only contain the markup related to that particular action. And all the common markups that will be part of all the pages can reside in the layout. As a result of this layout system, we do not need to include headers and footers to all the pages that we have. Cake will handle that for us, once we have defined the layout file.

Another thing to notice is the way we included the CSS files into the layout. We used the HTML helper of Cake to do it. To include a CSS file, all we need to do is to call css() method of the HTML helper, with the name of the CSS file as its parameter. For example, to include the CSS file quickwall.css, we wrote the following line: <?php e($html->css('quickwall')); ?>. Note that we do not need to include the extension of the file.

Adding Forms to Add New Questions and Answers

With our application, we can view all the questions, we can view all the answers to a question, and we have even added a cool layout for our application. But we still cannot do a very important task. We still cannot add a new question or add a new answer. That is exactly what we are going to do in this section. We are going to add a form to the home() action that will be able to add a new question to Quickwall. And to add a new answer, we will also be adding a new form to the show() action. So, without any delay, let's go and see how to do that.

Time for Action

1. Since we will be using the home() action for both displaying all the questions and also to add a new question, add the following code to the home() action of the Questions controller:

```php
function home() {

    if (!empty($this->data)) {
      $this->Question->create();
      if ($this->Question->save($this->data)) {
       $this->Session->setFlash('Your Question has been added');
          $this->redirect(array('action'=>'home'), null, true);
       } else {
          $this->Session->setFlash('The Question could not be
                                    saved. Please, try again.');
       }
    }

    $this->Question->recursive = 1;
    $this->set('questions', $this->Question->find('all'));
  }
```

2. To display the form that will be used to add a new question, add the following code to the top of the view file of the home() action. As we already know, the view file is /quickwall/app/views/questions/home.ctp.

```php
<?php e($form->create('Question', array('action' => 'home')));?>
    <fieldset>
        <label for="QuestionQuestion" class="questionlabel">
                       <span>Your Question</span></label>
        <?php e($form->text('question', array('class' =>
                   'fullwidth'))); ?><span class="big">?</span>
        <label for="QuestionQuestioner" class="questionerlabel"><spa
```

```
n>Your Name</span></label>
        <?php e($form->text('questioner', array('class' =>
'halfwidth'))); ?>
        <?php e($form->submit('Post Your Question', array('div' =>
false, 'class' => 'submitbutton'))); ?>
    </fieldset>
<?php e($form->end()); ?>

<?php if(empty($questions)): ?>
    <p class="no_answer">No Questions yet. Be the first one
                                to post a Question!</p>
<?php else: ?>
    <dl>
    <?php foreach ($questions as $question): ?>
        <dt><span><?php e($question['Question']['questioner']);
                ?></span></dt>
        <dd>
            <?php e($html->link($question['Question']['question'].
            '?', '/questions/show/'.$question['Question']['id'])); ?>
            <?php
                $answer_count = count($question['Answer']);
                if(!$answer_count)
                    e("(no answers yet)");
                else if($answer_count == 1)
                    e("(1 answer)");
                else
                    e("(".$answer_count." answers)");
            ?>
        </dd>
    <?php endforeach; ?>
    </dl>
<?php endif; ?>
```

3. The show() action is used to display a question and its answers. We will also be using it to add a new answer to question. Add the following code to the show() action of the Questions controller:

```
function show($id = null) {
    if (!$id) {
        $this->Session->setFlash('Invalid Question.');
        $this->redirect(array('action'=>'home'));
    }

    if (!empty($this->data)) {
        $this->Question->Answer->create();
        if ($this->Question->Answer->save($this->data)) {
```

```
        $this->Session->setFlash('The Answer has been saved');
        $this->redirect(array('action' => 'show', $id),
                                            null, true);
    } else {
        $this->Session->setFlash('The Answer could not be
                                saved. Please, try again.');
    }
}

$this->set('question', $this->Question->read(null, $id));
}
```

4. To display the form to add a new answer, add the following code to the view file(/`quickwall/app/views/questions/show.ctp`) of the `show()` action:

```
<h2><?php e($question['Question']['question']) ?>?</h2>
<div id="questioner"><div><span><?php e($question['Question']
                    ['questioner']) ?></span></div></div>

<?php e($form->create('Answer', array('url' => 'show/
                            '.$question['Question']['id'])));?>
    <fieldset>
        <?php e($form->hidden('question_id', array('value' =>
                            $question['Question']['id']))); ?>
        <label for="AnswerAnswer" class="questionlabel"><span>Your
                                    Answer</span></label>
        <?php e($form->text('answer', array('class' =>
                    'fullwidth'))); ?><span class="big">!</span>
        <label for="AnswerAnswerer" class="questionerlabel"><span>
                                    Your Name</span></label>
        <?php e($form->text('answerer', array('class' =>
                                            'halfwidth'))); ?>
        <?php e($form->submit('Post Your Answer', array('div' =>
                        false, 'class' => 'submitbutton'))); ?>
    </fieldset>
<?php e($form->end()); ?>

<?php if(empty($question['Answer'])): ?>
    <p class="no_answer">No Answers yet. Be the first one to
                                            answer!</p>
<?php else: ?>
    <dl>
    <?php foreach($question['Answer'] as $answer) : ?>
        <dt><span><?php e($answer['answerer']); ?></span></dt>
        <dd><?php e($answer['answer']); ?></dd>
    <?php endforeach; ?>
    </dl>
<?php endif; ?>
```

5. Now let's add validation rules so that users cannot enter empty questions and answers. Open the `Question` model in your text editor, and add the following validation rules:

```php
<?php
class Question extends AppModel {
    var $name = 'Question';
    var $hasMany = array(
        'Answer' => array(
            'className'     => 'Answer'
        )
    );
    var $validate = array(
        'question' => array(
            'rule' => array('minLenght', 1),
            'required' => true,
            'allowEmpty' => false,
            'message' => 'Question cannot be empty'
        ),
        'questioner' => array(
            'rule' => array('minLenght', 1),
            'required' => true,
            'allowEmpty' => false,
            'message' => 'Please enter your name'
        )
    );
}
?>
```

6. If there are any validation errors, we should show an error message to the user. To do so, add the following code to /quickwall/app/views/questions/home.ctp:

```php
<?php  e($form->error('Question.question', null, array('class'
                                        => 'message'))); ?>
<?php  e($form->error('Question.questioner', null, array('class'
                                        => 'message'))); ?>

<?php e($form->create('Question', array('action' => 'home')));?>
    <fieldset>
        <label for="QuestionQuestion" class="questionlabel"><span>
                                Your Question</span></label>
```

```php
        <?php e($form->text('question', array('class' =>
                        'fullwidth'))); ?><span class="big">?</span>
        <label for="QuestionQuestioner" class="questionerlabel">
                                <span>Your Name</span></label>
        <?php e($form->text('questioner', array('class'
                                        => 'halfwidth'))); ?>
        <?php e($form->submit('Post Your Question', array('div'
                        => false, 'class' => 'submitbutton'))); ?>
    </fieldset>
<?php e($form->end()); ?>

<?php if(empty($questions)): ?>
    <p class="no_answer">No Questions yet. Be the first one to post
                                        a Question!</p>
<?php else: ?>
    <dl>
    <?php foreach ($questions as $question): ?>
        <dt><span><?php e($question['Question']['questioner']);
                                        ?></span></dt>
        <dd>
            <?php e($html->link($question['Question']['question'].
        '?', '/questions/show/'.$question['Question']['id'])); ?>
            <?php
                $answer_count = count($question['Answer']);
                if(!$answer_count)
                    e("(no answers yet)");
                else if($answer_count == 1)
                    e("(1 answer)");
                else
                    e("(".$answer_count." answers)");
            ?>
        </dd>
    <?php endforeach; ?>
    </dl>
<?php endif; ?>
```

7. Add validation rules to the `Answer` model:

```php
<?php

class Answer extends AppModel {

    var $name = 'Answer';

    var $belongsTo = array(
        'Question' => array(
            'className'     => 'Question'
        )
```

```
        );

    var $validate = array(
        'answer' => array(
            'rule' => array('minLenght', 1),
            'required' => true,
            'allowEmpty' => false,
            'message' => 'Answer cannot be empty'
        ),
        'answerer' => array(
            'rule' => array('minLenght', 1),
            'required' => true,
            'allowEmpty' => false,
            'message' => 'Please enter your name'
        )
    );

    }
    ?>
```

8. Add similar code as step 6 to `/quickwall/app/views/show.ctp`, to show validation errors:

```php
<?php  e($form->error('Answer.answer', null, array('class'
                                        => 'message'))); ?>
<?php  e($form->error('Answer.answerer', null, array('class'
                                        => 'message'))); ?>

<h2><?php e($question['Question']['question']) ?>?</h2>
<div id="questioner"><div><span><?php e($question['Question']
                        ['questioner']) ?></span></div></div>

<?php e($form->create('Answer', array('url' => 'show/
                        '.$question['Question']['id'])));?>
    <fieldset>
        <?php e($form->hidden('question_id', array('value'
                        => $question['Question']['id']))); ?>
        <label for="AnswerAnswer" class="questionlabel"><span>
                                Your Answer</span></label>
        <?php e($form->text('answer', array('class'
                => 'fullwidth'))); ?><span class="big">!</span>
        <label for="AnswerAnswerer" class="questionerlabel"><span>
                                Your Name</span></label>
        <?php e($form->text('answerer', array('class'
                                        => 'halfwidth'))); ?>
        <?php e($form->submit('Post Your Answer', array('div'
                => false, 'class' => 'submitbutton'))); ?>
```

```
        </fieldset>
<?php e($form->end()); ?>

<?php if(empty($question['Answer'])): ?>
    <p class="no_answer">No Answers yet. Be the first one to
                                              answer!</p>
<?php else: ?>
    <dl>
    <?php foreach($question['Answer'] as $answer) : ?>
        <dt><span><?php e($answer['answerer']); ?></span></dt>
        <dd><?php e($answer['answer']); ?></dd>
    <?php endforeach; ?>
    </dl>
<?php endif; ?>
```

9. Point your web browser to `http://localhost/quickwall/` to see the newly created form for adding question. This is how our page should look like:

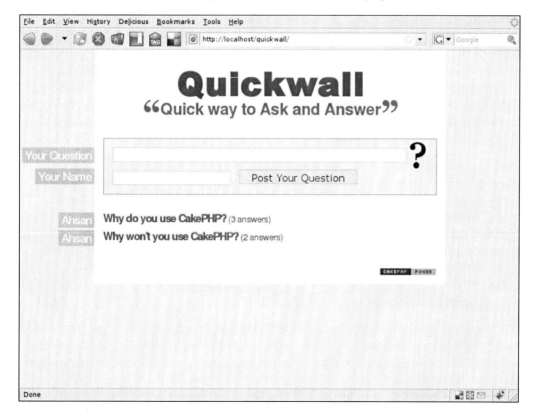

What Just Happened?

In step 1 of this section, we changed the `home()` action of the `Questions` controller, to add the functionality to save a new question if submitted to it. If any data is submitted to the request, Cake will store the POST data into `$this->data`. So, if `$this->data` is not empty, the first thing that is done is to call the `create()` method of the `Question` model. This prepares the model to save new data. Then the `save()` method is called and `$this->data` is passed to it. This saves the data into the database. If the operation is successful, a message is saved into the session, and redirected to the `home()` action. The message is then showed to the user.

Next, in step 2, we change the view of the `home()` action, to add the form. This form will be used to insert new question, so it is related to the `Question` model. To bind the form with the `Question` model, we use the Form helper of CakePHP. A form is created by calling the `create()` function of the Form helper. Two parameters are passed to it: the name of the model to bind, and the name of the action to post the data to. Note that the action name is passed in an array; any other required parameter can be passed through this array. To create a text input that will be used to insert the question, we use the `text()` method of the Form helper. Two parameters are passed to it, the name of the field that will be inserted through it, and an array that contains other options. In this case, we passed the name of the class that this text input should use for styling. Similarly, we use another call, the `text()` function of the Form helper to create the text input to insert the questioner. To create a submit button, we use the `submit()` function of the Form helper. Lastly, we call `$form->end()` to close the form.

Similarly, in step 3 and 4, we create a form in the `show()` action to insert a new answer. To get a more clearer idea of what the Form helper creates, check out the source of the HTML that is generated. An important thing to understand here is how we access the `Answer` model. By default, a controller only loads the model that has the singular name of the controller. So, the `Questions` controller will load the `Question` model by default. But we can also access other models that are related to the loaded model. For example, since the `Question` model is loaded, and it has `hasMany` relationship with the `Answer` model, we can access the `Answer` model by the call `$this->Question->Answer`.

Next in step 5, we add validation rules for the `Question` model. If no validation rules are added, users can submit the form empty, and the empty data will be saved as a new question. This is something that we do not want. To make sure the user cannot enter empty question or name, we add two validation rules to the `Question` model. All validation rules for a model must be added in an array named `$validate`. In the validation array of `Question` model, we add two validation rules, one for each field: question and questioner. Both have similar rules applied. The minimum length of both must be 1, they both are required fields, and none of them can be empty.

The validation rule defined above will not allow to save data that will not pass the validation rule. To show the error messages, in step 6, we added two lines to the view of the action. Again, we use the Form helper to do so. The `error()` function of the Form helper shows the error message of a particular field if there is any. We use this function to show an error message if an error is present.

Similarly in step 7 and 8, we add validation rules for the `Answers` model.

Summary

This was the first chapter of section C, which took us through all the effort that it takes to make a complete CakePHP application. Through out this section we saw how to enhance and build an application that we called Quickwall. We started the chapter by understanding what Quickwall is all about. After quickly setting up Cake for Quickwall, we went through the process of creating and connecting the Quickwall database with the application. We then created two models, and defined relationship between them. After that, we created the controller actions and their corresponding views. Adding custom layout was the natural next step. We saw how we can add our own layout and styles to Cake applications. We discussed the basics of how to add layouts and how views get rendered into them. Also discussed was how we can add CSS files to Cake applications. We ended the chapter, by adding forms to insert new data. The Form helper was used extensively, and we saw how it helped to bind models with forms. Adding validation rules to models were also discussed, along with how to show error messages if there is a validation error.

All in all, this chapter went through the creation of a simple but functional web application. In the following chapters, we will extend this application by adding more useful functionalities to it. And, in the process, we learn how easy and quick it is to make a web application using CakePHP. Read on!

10
Quickwall: User Authentication

In the last chapter, we managed to make a very simple version of Quickwall. Though it was simple, it was a working web application that made it quite usable. More importantly, it will be the base from where we can add more functionalities to it.

In this chapter, we are going to add user authentication to our Quickwall. User authentication is something that is needed in almost all web applications. And whether you like it or not, you have to spend time to make sure the user authentication system is working properly. It is also one of the most important aspect of any web application, because a lot of other functionalities depend on it.

We will see in this chapter, that adding user authentication in CakePHP, like many other stuff, is very easy and quick. So without any delay, let's see the things that we are going to do in this chapter:

- Create the User Model
- Build a simple user sign-up process
- Add email activation to sign up
- Integrate the Authenticating process into the application
- Remembering user with cookie

Creating the User Model and the Users Controller

The first thing that we need to do is create the User model, with its corresponding users table in the database. The users table will store data about each user who will sign up in our web application. The User model is a very important component of the user authentication process. In this section, we are going to create the users table in the database. After that, we are going to create the User model, along with some validation. We are also going to create the skeleton of the Users controller.

Time for Action

1. Create a table in our `quickwall` database with the name `users`. Use the following SQL to do so:

    ```
    CREATE TABLE users (
    id INT( 10 ) UNSIGNED NOT NULL AUTO_INCREMENT PRIMARY KEY ,
    username VARCHAR( 255 ) NOT NULL ,
    password VARCHAR( 40 ) NOT NULL ,
    email VARCHAR( 255 ) NOT NULL ,
    created DATETIME NOT NULL ,
    modified DATETIME NOT NULL
    ) ;
    ```

2. Next, we create a corresponding model for this table. In the `/app/models` directory, we need to create a file named `user.php`, with the following code inside:

    ```php
    <?php

    class User extends AppModel {

        var $name = 'User';

    }

    ?>
    ```

3. We do not want an empty username and password to be saved. Also, we would like to make sure that the email entered is a valid email. For this purpose, we add the following validation code to the `User` model:

    ```php
    <?php

    class User extends AppModel {

        var $name = 'User';

        var $validate = array(
            'username' => array(
                'rule' => array('minLenght', 1),
    ```

```
                'required' => true,
                'allowEmpty' => false,
                'message' => 'Please enter a user name'
            ),
            'password' => array(
                'rule' => array('minLenght', 1),
                'required' => true,
                'allowEmpty' => false,
                'message' => 'Please enter a password'
            ),
            'email' => array(
                'rule' => 'email',
                'required' => true,
                'allowEmpty' => false,
                'message' => 'Please enter a valid email'
            )
        );
    }
?>
```

4. Now, let's create the Users controller. In the /app/controllers directory, create a file with the name users_controller.php, and add the following code to it:

```
<?php
class UsersController extends AppController {
    var $name = 'Users';
}
?>
```

5. To test if our User model and its validation rules are working properly, let's scaffold and check. To do so, add the following line into the Users controller:

```
<?php
class UsersController extends AppController {
    var $name = 'Users';

    var $scaffold;
}
?>
```

6. Make sure we clear the cache. To clear the cache, go to the directory /app/tmp/cache. There are three directories named models, persistent, and views. Delete all the files in these three directories.

7. Now to check the validation rules, point the web browser to
http://localhost/quickwall/users/add. We will see a page as shown
in the following screenshot. Try giving empty user name, password, and
invalid emails, to check.

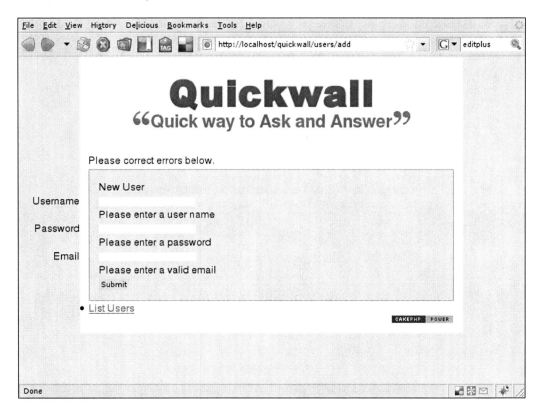

What Just Happened?

In this section, we first added the users table into our quickwall database. The
fields that were included were: id, username, password, email, created, and
modified. Every user who will be added to the application will have a unique id.
The username will be the name that will be used through out the app. to identify the
user. This will also be a unique value. The email field will contain the email address
of the user. We will be using this later to send email notification to the user. And as
usual, the created field will record the time when the user account was created. The
modified field will record the time when the account was last modified.

Next, we added the User model. This model will automatically represent the users
table in the database, as per Cake's convention. We went on adding validation rules
for username, password, and email. For username and password, we do not want
them to be empty. So, we used the built-in validation rule minLenght(), and

sent 1 as its parameter. The `minLenght()` validation rule checks if the data has a the minimum length equal to the parameter passed. Since we sent 1 as the parameter, it has to have a minimum 1 character to pass the validation. For the `email` field, we used the built-in email rule. This checks whether the data is a valid email address. If any of the validation rules are not met, data will not be saved into the database.

The next thing we did was to create the `Users` controller. As per Cake convention, this controller will automatically load the `Users` model. It is a good practice to clear up the cache, after any changes, or sometimes it may result in some unexpected and weird issues. We used the `Users` controller to check whether the model and its validation rules were working fine. For this, we used scaffolding. To make a controller use scaffolding, the only thing that we need to do is to add the line `var $scaffold;` into the controller. Lastly, we tested the model by using scaffolding.

Making the User Sign Up Process

In this section, we are going to create the process by which a user can sign up to Quickwall. We will start by creating an action in the `Users` controller that will handle the sign-up of a new user. We will then move to create its view. The sign-up process will also require the use of special validation rules for situations such as to check if the `username` is unique, and the re-entered password is similar to the first one. This section will also see the use of the `Auth` component. The `Auth` component is a built-in component of CakePHP that makes the process of authenticating very simple and easy. Lastly, we will configure the Cake router to make more meaningful URL for the sign-up process.

Time for Action

1. First, let's remove the scaffolding option that we added at the end of the last section.

2. Next, we will need to add the `Auth` component to the `Users` controller. To do so, add the following line to the `Users` controller:

```php
<?php
class UsersController extends AppController {
    var $name = 'Users';
    var $components = array('Auth');
}
?>
```

3. After adding the `Auth` component, let's add an action named `signup` into the Users controller. Add the following code to the action:

```php
<?php
class UsersController extends AppController {

    var $name = 'Users';
    var $components = array('Auth');

    function signup(){
        if (!empty($this->data)) {
            if(isset($this->data['User']['password2']))
                $this->data['User']['password2hashed'] = $this->
                    Auth->password($this->data['User']['password2']);
            $this->User->create();
            if ($this->User->save($this->data)) {
                $this->Session->setFlash('Congratulations! You have
                                                    signed up!');
                $this->redirect(array('controller' => 'questions',
                                                    'action'=>'home'));
            } else {
                $this->Session->setFlash('There was an error signing
                                            up. Please, try again.');
                $this->data = null;
            }
        }
    }

}
?>
```

4. We will then need to add a function called `beforeFilter()` to the Users controller. Add the following code to this function:

```php
<?php
class UsersController extends AppController {

    var $name = 'Users';
    var $components = array('Auth');

    ...

    function beforeFilter(){
            $this->Auth->allow('signup');
    }

}
?>
```

5. Next, we need to add the view for the sign-up action. Create a directory named `users` inside the `views` directory. Add a file named `signup.ctp` into the `users` directory, and put the following code to it:

```
<h2>Sign Up for Quickwall</h2>
<?php e($form->create('User', array('action' => 'signup')));?>
    <fieldset>
        <label for="UserUsername" class="usernamelabel"><span>
                                        Your Name</span></label>
        <?php e($form->text('username', array('class'
                                        => 'fullwidth'))); ?>
        <label for="UserEmail" class="emaillabel"><span>Your Email
                                        </span></label>
        <?php e($form->text('email', array('class'
                                        => 'fullwidth'))); ?>
        <label for="UserPassword" class="passwordlabel"><span>
                                        Password</span></label>
        <?php e($form->password('password', array('class'
                                        => 'fullwidth'))); ?>
        <label for="UserPasswordRepeat" class="passwordrepeatlabel">
                                <span>Re Password</span></label>
        <?php e($form->password('password2', array('class'
                                        => 'fullwidth'))); ?>
        <?php e($form->submit('Sign Up', array('div' => false,
                                'class' => 'submitbutton'))); ?>
    </fieldset>
<?php e($form->end()); ?>
```

6. We need to make sure that the user name entered by the new user has not been used by some other users. To do so, we first need to add a function to the `User` model. We will name this function `checkUnique()`, as shown here:

```
<?php
class User extends AppModel {
    var $name = 'User';
    var $validate = array(
        ...
    );
    function checkUnique($data, $fieldName) {
        $valid = false;
        if(isset($fieldName) && $this->hasField($fieldName)) {
         $valid = $this->isUnique(array($fieldName => $data));
            }
            return $valid;
    }
}
?>
```

7. We then add another rule for the username field in the validation array, which uses the function defined above, as shown here:

```php
<?php
class User extends AppModel {
    var $name = 'User';
    var $validate = array(
        'username' => array(
            'notempty' => array(
                'rule' => array('minLenght', 1),
                'required' => true,
                'allowEmpty' => false,
                'message' => 'User name cannot be empty'
            ),
            'unique' => array(
                'rule' => array('checkUnique', 'username'),
                'message' => 'User name taken. Use another'
            )
        ),
        'password' => array(
            ...
        ),
        'email' => array(
            ...
        )
    );
    function checkUnique($data, $fieldName) {
        ...
    }
}
?>
```

8. Next, to show the error, if there is any, we add the following line to the view of the `signup` action:

```php
<?php if($form->isFieldError('User.username')) e($form->error
        ('User.username', null, array('class' => 'message'))); ?>

<h2>Sign Up for Quickwall</h2>
<?php e($form->create('User', array('url' => 'signup')));?>
    ...
<?php e($form->end()); ?>
```

9. Next, to check if the two password fields match, we need to add a function in
    the User model to do so. We name this function checkPasswords(). Add the
    following code to it:

```php
<?php
class User extends AppModel {
var $name = 'User';

    var $validate = array(
        ...
    );

    function checkUnique($data, $fieldName) {
            ...
        }

    function checkPasswords($data) {
        if($data['password'] == $this->data['User']
                                        ['password2hashed'])
            return true;
        return false;
    }

}
?>
```

10. Now, let's use the function above in our validation rules to check if both the
    passwords are the same:

```php
<?php
class User extends AppModel {
    var $name = 'User';
    var $validate = array(
        'username' => array(
            ...
        ),
        'password' => array(
            'notempty' => array(
                'rule' => array('minLenght', 1),
                'required' => true,
                'allowEmpty' => false,
                'message' => 'Password cannot be empty.'
            ),
            'passwordSimilar' => array(
                'rule' => 'checkPasswords',
                'message' => 'Different password re entered.'
            )
```

```
            ),
            'email' => array(
                ...
            )
        );
        function checkUnique($data, $fieldName) {
                ...
        }
        function checkPasswords($data) {
            ...
        }
    }
    ?>
```

11. Now, to show the error messages for the password field, add the following line to the view:

```
<?php if($form->isFieldError('User.username')) e($form->error
        ('User.username', null, array('class' => 'message'))); ?>
<?php if($form->isFieldError('User.password')) e($form->error
        ('User.password', null, array('class' => 'message'))); ?>
<h2>Sign Up for Quickwall</h2>
<?php e($form->create('User', array('url' => 'signup')));?>
    ...
<?php e($form->end()); ?>
```

12. To show the error messages, if any error occurs in the email field, add this line to the view:

```
<?php if($form->isFieldError('User.username')) e($form->error
        ('User.username', null, array('class' => 'message'))); ?>
<?php if($form->isFieldError('User.password')) e($form->error
        ('User.password', null, array('class' => 'message'))); ?>
<?php if($form->isFieldError('User.email')) e($form->error
        ('User.email', null, array('class' => 'message'))); ?>
<h2>Sign Up for Quickwall</h2>
<?php e($form->create('User', array('url' => 'signup')));?>
    ...
<?php e($form->end()); ?>
```

13. To access the sign-up process, the URL needed is `http://localhost/quickwall/users/signup`. To make it neat, we will change the URL to `http://localhost/quickwall/signup`. To do so, add the following line in the file `routes.php'` in `/app/config`:

```
/**
 * Here, we are connecting '/' (base path) to controller
                                            called 'Pages',
```

```
 * its action called 'display', and we pass a param to select
                                               the view file
 * to use (in this case, /app/views/pages/home.thtml)...
 */
    Router::connect('/', array('controller' => 'questions',
                                  'action' => 'home'));
    Router::connect('/signup', array('controller' => 'users',
                                       'action' => 'signup'));
/**
 * ...and connect the rest of 'Pages' controller's urls.
 */
    Router::connect('/pages/*', array('controller' => 'pages',
                                       'action' => 'display'));
/**
 * Then we connect url '/test' to our test controller.
                                        This is helpfull in
 * developement.
 */
    Router::connect('/tests', array('controller' => 'tests',
                                      'action' => 'index'));
```

Now point our web browser to `http://localhost/quickwall/signup`. We will see our beautiful sign-up page:

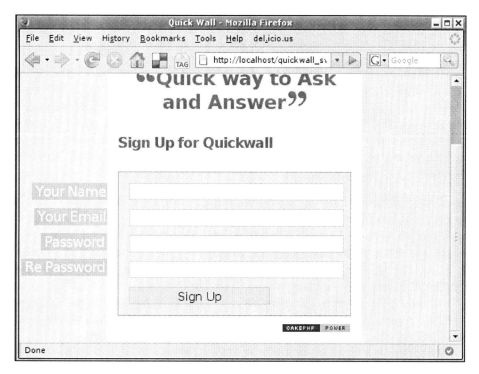

What Just Happened?

This section has gone through the process of adding user sign up to our application. Now, a user can sign up by going to `http://localhost/quickwall/signup`, inputting their user name, email, and password, and get registered to Quickwall. Though, we have not yet added functionality for the user to log in, but that will follow soon. Now, let's have a better understanding of what we have done in this section.

We started by removing the scaffolding option that we added in the last section. Scaffolding can be a very good tool to test our application, but it can never replace hard-coded code. Thus, it was time for it to go.

The next thing that we did was add the `Auth` component to the `Users` controller. As you already know, to add components to a controller, all we need to do is to declare the variable `$components` in our controller, and assign it an array with all the component names. The `Auth` component is the only component that we are using for the `Users` controller, for the time being.

The `Auth` component is a built-in component of CakePHP that makes it very easy to authenticate users in a CakePHP application. As we go along, you will find out just how. Another thing to note is that we added the `Auth` component to the `Users` controller only. But to make the whole application use the `Auth` component, we need to add the `Auth` component to all the controllers in the application. But for the time being, we will keep it to the `Users` controller only. Later, we will add the `Auth` component to all the controllers by adding it to the AppController.

Next, we added an action named `signup()` to the `Users` controller. This action will handle the whole sign-up process. For a user to sign up, they need to call this action. Now, let's understand the code that went into this action. If this action is called without any HTTP POST data, `$this->data` will be empty and nothing is done at all before the view is rendered. Once the user enters the data to sign up and submits the form to this action, the HTTP POST data will be stored in `$this->data`. This time because the `$this->data` is not empty, it will execute the code inside the action.

The first line here checks whether any data named `password2` was passed in. The password2 field contains the re-entered password. If so, then we hash it using the `Auth` component's `password()` function. This function takes in the string to be hashed, and returns the hashed string. The default hashing algorithm used is SHA1. It uses the Security Salt that we defined in `/app/config/core.php` in the last chapter. You may wonder why we are hashing the `password2` field in the first place. And why are we not hashing the `password` field that contains the first entered password? The reason for this is that the Auth component automatically hashes the `password` field. If the `Auth` component is included in a controller and any field named `password` is passed into `$this->data`, it automatically hashes it. But since now we need to compare `password` with `password2` to make sure they are exactly same, we also manually hash the `password2` field. The next few lines of code calls the `User` model and saves the data.

Next up, we add a function called `beforeFilter()` to the `Users` controller. If such a function is defined in a controller, every time any action of the controller is called, the code in `beforeFilter()` is executed before the action code is called. In the `beforeFilter()` function, we call a function of the `Auth` component named `allow()`. The `Auth` Component, by default, does not allow access to any controller action without proper authentication. The only two action names that are an exception is `login` and `logout`. If such actions are defined, they can be assessed without authentication. Other than that, all actions require authentication by default. The `allow()` function of the `Auth` controller can allow other actions that do not need any authentication. For example, in our case, we want the `signup` action to be accessed without authentication. This is exactly what we do here, by calling the `allow()` function of the `Auth` controller.

In the next step, we add the view for our `signup()` action. This has the form that will allow users to enter their preferred user name, email, password, and the re-entered password. As usual, we see the usage of the Form Helper here. Most of the Form Helper functions have been discussed before, so it shouldn't be a problem to understand the code.

Other than the normal validation rules that we added in the last section, the sign-up process requires some other validation rules. We want the user name to be unique for every user. So, we need to check whether the user name entered by the user has not been used before by some other user. Also, we need to check whether the `password` and the `password2` fields are same. We could have also done these checks in our controller action, but doing it in the model makes more sense, as this logic is needed everytime we try to add a new record to the model. Since CakePHP does not have any built-in validation rules to check these two conditions, we need to add our own validation rules. This is what we did in the next few steps.

In step 6, we added a function to the `User` model that we named `checkUnique()`. It takes in two parameters `$data` and `$fieldName`. What this function does is that it checks whether there is a field name with `$fieldname`. If it is present in the table, it checks whether this field has the data passed to `$data`. It uses the model function `isUnique()` to do so.

Next, we add a validation rule to the username field to use the function defined above. Since the username field already had a validation rule from before, we need to define the validation rules for it in multiple format. For each of the rules, we have separate arrays for them. We gave meaningful names to the two rules array, but they could have been anything else too. You will also notice that we did not send the $data parameter to the function. This is because the validation class sends the data to the function automatically as the first parameter. So, if we define our own validation functions, the first parameter should be for the field data. In the next step we add code to the view to show the error message for this validation rule.

Similarly, in the next few steps, we add another validation rule to check whether the passwords are same.

The last thing that we did was to make the URL to access this action more simple. Normally, if we want to access the signup action, the URL needed is http:// localhost/quickwall/users/signup. We made it simpler by adding a routing rule in /app/config/routes.php.

Adding Email Confirmation to Sign Up

In this section, we will enhance the sign-up process by adding email confirmation to it. It is a common practice to make users confirm their sign up by sending them a mail. This makes sure that the email address belongs to the user who is signing in. Normally, just after the user signs up, a mail is sent to his email address. The user account is not activated until the user clicks on a link provided in the mail. Only after the link is visited, the user account is activated. We will accomplish a simplistic implementation of email confirmation is this section.

We will also see the use of the built-in Email component of CakePHP, which simplifies the process of sending a mail.

Time for Action

1. We will begin by adding two more fields to the users database: confirmed and confirm_code:

   ```
   ALTER TABLE users
   ADD confirmed VARCHAR( 1 ) NOT NULL DEFAULT '0',
   ADD confirm_code VARCHAR( 36 ) NOT NULL ;
   ```

2. Next, we need to generate a random string that will be sent in the mail and also be saved in the database. This is done by adding the following line to the Users controller:

   ```
   <?php
   class UsersController extends AppController {
   ```

```php
    var $name = 'Users';
    var $components = array('Auth');
    function signup(){
        if (!empty($this->data)) {
            if(isset($this->data['User']['password2']))
                $this->data['User']['password2hashed'] = $this->
                        Auth->password($this->data['User']['password2']);

            $this->data['User']['confirm_code'] = String::uuid();

            $this->User->create();
            if ($this->User->save($this->data)) {
                ...
            } else {
                ...
            }
            $this->data = null;
        }
    }
    function beforeFilter(){
            ...
    }
    }
    ?>
```

3. Next, we add the Email component to the Users controller:

```php
    <?php
    class UsersController extends AppController {
        var $name = 'Users';
        var $components = array('Auth', 'Email');
        function signup(){
            ...
        }
        function beforeFilter(){
                ...
        }
    }
    ?>
```

4. We will need to add the following code, to compose and send the email to the signing user:

```php
<?php
class UsersController extends AppController {

    var $name = 'Users';
var $components = array('Auth', 'Email');

function signup(){
    if (!empty($this->data)) {

        if(isset($this->data['User']['password2']))
            $this->data['User']['password2hashed'] = $this->
                Auth->password($this->data['User']['password2']);

        $this->data['User']['confirm_code'] = String::uuid();

        $this->User->create();
        if ($this->User->save($this->data)) {
            $this->Email->to = $this->data['User']['email'];
            $this->Email->subject = 'Quickwall Confirmation';
            $this->Email->replyTo = 'noreply@cakequickwall.com';
            $this->Email->from = 'Quickwall
                                        <noreply@cakequickwall.com>';
            $this->Email->sendAs = 'html';
            $this->Email->template = 'confirmation';

            $this->set('name', $this->data['User']['username']);
            $this->set('server_name', $_SERVER['SERVER_NAME']);
            $this->set('id', $this->User->getLastInsertID());
            $this->set('code', $this->data['User']['confirm_code']);

            if ($this->Email->send()) {
                $this->Session->setFlash('Confirmation mail sent.
                                        Please check your inbox');
                $this->redirect(array('controller' => 'questions',
                                        'action'=>'home'));
            } else {
                $this->User->del($this->User->getLastInsertID());
                $this->Session->setFlash('There was a problem sending
                    the confirmation mail. Please try again');
            }

        } else {
            $this->Session->setFlash('There was an error signing up.
                                        Please, try again.');
        }
        $this->data = null;
```

```
            }
        }
        function beforeFilter(){
            ...
        }

    }
    ?>
```

5. Next, we will need to add layout and template file for the email. To add
    the email layout, go into the directory /app/views/layouts and create a
    directory named email. Inside the new directory, create another directory
    named html. Now, inside the html directory, create a new file named
    default.ctp, and copy the following code into it. And save it.

```
<!DOCTYPE HTML PUBLIC "-//W3C//DTD HTML 4.0 Transitional//EN">
<html>
    <body>
        <?php echo $content_for_layout; ?>
    </body>
</html>
```

6. After that, we need to add the template file for the email. Inside the directory
    /app/views/elements, create a new directory named email. Create another
    directory inside the email directory and name it html. Inside the html
    directory, create a new file named confirmation.ctp. Copy and save the
    following code into it:

```
Hi <?php e($name); ?>,<br />
Thank you for signing up in Quickwall. To complete the sign up
                process please click on the link below:<br />
<a href="http://<?php e($server_name) ?><?php e($html->
    url(array('controller' => 'users', 'action' => 'confirm')))
    ?>/<?php e($id) ?>/<?php e($code) ?>">Confirm your account</a>
```

7. Now, we will need to create a new action in the Users controller that will
    accept the link sent via the email. We name it confirm:

```
<?php
class UsersController extends AppController {

var $name = 'Users';
var $components = array('Auth', 'Email');

function signup(){
    ...
}

function confirm($user_id=null, $code=null) {
```

```
        if(empty($user_id) || empty($code)) {
           $this->set('confirmed', 0);
             $this->render();
        }
         $user = $this->User->read(null, $user_id);
        if(empty($user)) {
           $this->set('confirmed', 0);
                $this->render();
         }

        if($user['User']['confirm_code'] == $code){
           $this->User->id = $user_id;
           $this->User->saveField('confirmed', '1');
           $this->set('confirmed', 1);
        } else {
           $this->set('confirmed', 0);
        }
     }
     function beforeFilter(){
           ..
     }
  }
  ?>
```

8. We need to make sure that the confirm action gets by passed by the Auth controller. To do so, add it to the list of allowed actions here:

```
<?php
class UsersController extends AppController {
    var $name = 'Users';
    var $components = array('Auth', 'Email');
    function signup(){
        ...
    }
    function confirm($user_id=null, $code=null) {
    ...
}
    function beforeFilter(){
            $this->Auth->allow('signup', 'confirm');
        }
    }
    ?>
```

9. Lastly, we will need to add the view for the confirm action. Inside the directory /app/views/users, create a file named confirm.ctp. Copy and save the following code into it:

```
<h2>Sign Up Confirmation</h2>
<?php if($confirmed): ?>
    <p>Congratulations! You have successfully confirmed your
                   account. Now you can login.</p>
<?php else: ?>
    <p>Invalid Confirmation. Please sign up.</p>
```

10. Now, try signing up. When a mail has been sent successfully, we will see the following screen:

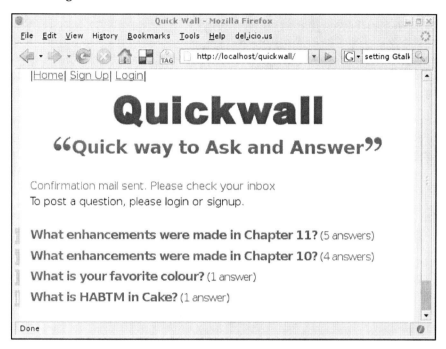

What Just Happened?

We just saw how easy it is to send an email via the Email Component. Now let's get a better understanding of what we actually did.

In step 1, we added two new fields to the users table in the database. These fields are confirmed and confirm_code. The confirmed field will store whether the user account has been confirmed or not. If it's 0 (the default), then the account is yet to be confirmed, and if it's 1, then the account is confirmed and ready to be used. Later, we will be checking this field when a user tries to log in. The confirm_code field will store a randomly generated code. When a user signs up, this random code is generated. It is then saved into the confirm_code field of the account and also is a part of the confirm link sent via the email. Later, when the user clicks on the link from the email, the code in the email is compared to that in the database, to make sure the email address in valid.

In step 2, we added code to generate the random code for the email confirmation. For this, we use the static function `uuid()` of the `String` class. The `String` class has some useful functions that help in string manipulation. It is located in `/cake/libs`. To call any of these functions, just use this format: *String::functionName* e.g. `String::uuid()`. We store the random code into `$this->data['User']['confirm_code']` before `$this->data` is sent to the `User` model for saving the record. This ensures that the code is stored into the `confirm_code` field of the new record.

In step 3, we added the Email Component to the `Users` controller. The Email Component makes it easy to send email from your application. It can send both text or HTML mail. One of the better features of this component is the support for template and layout. We can define templates and all we need to do is to send the data to the template. Another feature that we are not using here is sending attachments. Including an attachment is just a one line code with the Email Component.

In the next step, we used the Email Component to actually send a mail. If the new user record is successfully saved by the `User` model, we define different properties in the Email Component that are necessary for sending the mail. Most of them like `$this->Email->to`, `$this->Email->subject`, `$this->Email->replyTo` and `$this->Email->from` are self explanatory.

`$this->Email->sendAs` defines whether the mail will be sent as HTML or text form. In our case, we are sending it in HTML format.

`$this->Email->template` defines the template that we will be using to send the mail. We are using a template called `confirmation` that we later created in step 6. Next, we used `$this->set()` to send some data to the template. We sent the user name, id, the server name, and the confirm code to the email template. Note, we used `$this->User->getLastInsertID()` to get the id of the last inserted record. We send the email by calling `$this->Email->send()`. This will dispatch an email. Please note, to test the email functionality from your local machine, you will need a working mail server.

In step 5, we added the layout file for email that will be used by the Email Component. This file can be compared to the layout for views. This file does not define the exact content that will go into the email, but just the layout. The content of the email will be placed in place of `<?php echo $content_for_layout; ?>`. In our case, since we are going to send HTML mails, we create a directory named `html` inside `/app/views/layouts/email`. For text layout, we would have created a directory named `text` with the layout file in it. Of course, that file would not have any HTML in it.

After creating the layout file, we created the template file for our email. Remember, we defined in the controller that the template that the Email Component will use for our confirmation mail is called `confirmation`. So, we create a file inside `/app/views/elements/email/html` and we name it `confirmation`. All HTML email templates should be placed here. The data that we sent using `$this->set()` in the controller will be available here. Inside this template file, we compose the structure of the mail we will be sending for confirmation. For text mails, all the templates should be placed in `/app/views/elements/email/text`.

In step 7, we create an action in the `Users` controller that will be called when the user clicks on the link in the confirmation email. The link that we sent in the email had a structure like this: `http://<servername+path>/users/confirm/<user_id>/<confirnation_code>`. When the link is clicked, it will look for an action named `confirm` in the `Users` controller. The user id and the confirmation code will also be sent as parameters. So, the new action that we create is called `confirm` and accepts two arguments: the user id and the confirm code. In the action, we first check where the user id and the confirmation code is present in the URL. We also check whether there is any user with the id sent. If any of the conditions are not true, we send a variable named `confirmed` to the view, with a null value. We force the controller to render the view by calling `$this->render()`. If the request passes the initial checks, the confirmation code sent in the request is checked with that in the database for the user. If it matches, the `confirmed` field in the database is updated to `1`, and `confirmed` is sent to the view with the value of `1`.

Next, we need to make sure that the `confirm()` action can be accessed without any authentication. For this, we have to tell the `Auth` component to allow access to `confirm()` by adding `confirm` to the code in `beforeFilter()`: `$this->Auth->allow('signup', 'confirm')`.

In the last step, we add the view for the `confirm()` action. If `$confirmed` is true here, then it will show a success message or else it will show an invalid confirmation message.

Integrating Authentication: Database and Models

Now, we have a working sign-up process for our application. But we have not yet created a process for logging in, authentication or logging out. To have a good authentication process and to integrate the `User` model with the whole application, we need to make some minor changes into the database, models, controllers, and also the views. This section will show the changes that we will need to make to the database and models.

Time for Action

1. Since we are going to change the database structure, it is a good idea to flush out the old test data that we used so far:

```
TRUNCATE answers ;
TRUNCATE questions ;
TRUNCATE users ;
```

2. In the `questions` table, instead of the questioner's name, we are going to store the id of the user. We will be removing the `questioner` field and instead we are going to have the `user_id` field. Likewise, we are going to remove `answerer` from the `answers` table and add `user_id` to it:

```
ALTER TABLE questions DROP questioner;
ALTER TABLE questions ADD user_id INT( 10 ) UNSIGNED NOT NULL;
ALTER TABLE answers DROP answerer;
ALTER TABLE answers ADD user_id INT( 10 ) UNSIGNED NOT NULL;
```

3. In the `User` model, we are going to add relationships to the `Question` model and the `Answer` model. Since a user can have many questions, and also many answers, the `User` model has a `hasMany` relationship with both the `Question` and `Answer` model. Add the following to the `User` model to do so:

```php
<?php
class User extends AppModel {
    var $name = 'User';
    var $validate = array(
        . . .
    );
    var $hasMany = array(
       'Question' => array(
            'className'     => 'Question'
       ),
       'Answer' => array(
          'className'      => 'Answer'
       )
    );
    function checkUnique($data, $fieldName) {
          . . .
      }
    function checkPasswords($data) {
        . . .
    }
}
?>
```

4. Since a question can have only one questioner, the `Question` model has
    `belongsTo` relationship with the `User` model:

```php
<?php
class Question extends AppModel {
    var $name = 'Question';
    var $hasMany = array(
        'Answer' => array(
            'className'    => 'Answer'
        )
    );
    var $belongsTo = array(
        'User' => array(
            'className'    => 'User'
        )
    );
    var $validate = array(
        ...
    );
}
?>
```

5. Since we do not have any `questioner` field in the `Question` model, let
    us remove the validation rule we added for it. The new validation for the
    `Question` model should look like this:

```php
<?php
class Question extends AppModel {

    ...

    var $validate = array(
        'question' => array(
            'rule' => array('minLenght', 1),
            'required' => true,
            'allowEmpty' => false,
            'message' => 'Question cannot be empty'
        )
    );
}
?>
```

6. Since an answer can have only one answerer, the `Answer` model has `belongsTo` relationship with the `User` model. The `Answer` model already has `belongsTo` relationship defined with the `Question` model. Hence, we modify the `$belongsTo` variable to add the relationship with the `User` model:

```php
<?php

class Answer extends AppModel {

    ...

    var $belongsTo = array(
        'Question' => array(
            'className'    => 'Question'
        ),
        'User' => array(
            'className'    => 'User'
        )
    );

}
?>
```

7. Lastly, since we do not have the `answerer` field in the `Answer` model any more, let's remove the validation rule for it. The new `$validation` array should look like this:

```php
<?php

class Answer extends AppModel {

    ...

    var $validate = array(
        'answer' => array(
            'rule' => array('minLenght', 1),
            'required' => true,
            'allowEmpty' => false,
            'message' => 'Answer cannot be empty'
        )
    );

}
?>
```

What Just Happened?

We started this section by removing any test data that we had in the database. This is because we are going to change the structure of the database and to make sure the old data does not bring any inconsistency. Thanks to God, these are just test data. If this was a working app with real data, this process for porting data from the old structure to the new would have taken a considerable amount of work.

In step 2, we dropped the fields `questioner` and `answerer` from the questions and answers table respectively. Instead, we add a new field to both the tables named `user_id`. Since we have a `users` table that stores user-specific data, it will be redundant to store the name of users in the `questions` and `answers` table. Instead we will use `user_id` as a foreign key to the `users` table.

In the remaining steps, we defined model relationships between the `User` model, `Question` model, and the `Answer` model. Since a user can have many questions and a question can only belong to one user (questioner), the User model has `$hasMany` relation to `Question` model. And the `Question` model has `$belongsTo` relationship with the `User` model. Likewise, since a user can answer many answers, but an answer belongs to one user (answerer) only, the `User` model has a `$hasMany` relationship with the `Answer` model. And the `Answer` model has `$belongsTo` relationship with the `User` model.

We also made sure that we remove the validation rule that we defined for the `questioner` field in `Question` model. We also removed the validation rule for `answerer` in the `Answer` model. No need to validate non-existent fields.

It is not a good idea to run the application now, since we have not yet made changes in the controllers and views. It will surely result in some weird errors. So, be patient and wait till we are done with the next two sections.

Integrating Authentication: Controllers

We continue our effort to integrate the `User` model and the authentication process into our database. This section shows the changes that are required in the controllers:

Time for Action

1. Go into the directory `/app` and create a new file. Name the file `app_controller.php`. Add the following code to it and save:

    ```php
    <?php
    class AppController extends Controller {

    }
    ?>
    ```

2. Now, add the Auth component to the newly created AppController class:

```php
<?php
class AppController extends Controller {

    var $components = array('Auth');

}
?>
```

3. Add the beforeFilter() function to the AppController class, with the following code:

```php
<?php
class AppController extends Controller {

    var $components = array('Auth');

    function beforeFilter(){
        $this->Auth->loginRedirect = array('controller'
                            => 'questions', 'action' => 'home');
            $this->Auth->logoutRedirect  = array('controller'
                            => 'questions', 'action' => 'home');
        $this->Auth->allow('signup', 'confirm', 'home', 'show');
        $this->Auth->authorize = 'controller';
        $this->Auth->userScope = array('User.confirmed' => '1');
        $this->set('loggedIn', $this->Auth->user('id'));
    }

}
?>
```

4. Add a new method to the AppController class named isAuthorized(). Add the following into this method:

```php
<?php
class AppController extends Controller {

    var $components = array('Auth');

    function beforeFilter(){
        ...
    }

    function isAuthorized() {
        return true;
    }

}
?>
```

5. Now, open the `Users` controller file, and remove the `Auth` component and the `beforeFilter()` method from it. It should look as follows:

```php
<?php
class UsersController extends AppController {

    var $name = 'Users';
    var $components = array('Email');

    function signup(){
        ...
    }

    function confirm($user_id=null, $code=null) {
        ...
    }

}
?>
```

6. Add two new actions to the `Users` controller called `login()` and `logout()`. They should have the following code:

```php
<?php
class UsersController extends AppController {

    ...

    function login() {

    }

    function logout() {
        $this->Session->setFlash('Logout');
        $this->redirect($this->Auth->logout());
    }

}
?>
```

7. Now, open the `Questions` controller and modify the `home()` action with the following highlighted code:

```php
<?php
class QuestionsController extends AppController {

    ...

    function home() {
        if (!empty($this->data) && $this->Auth->user('id')) {
            $this->data['Question']['user_id'] = $this->
                                                 Auth->user('id');
            $this->Question->create();
```

```php
        if ($this->Question->save($this->data)) {
            $this->Session->setFlash('Your Question has been added');
        } else {
            $this->Session->setFlash('The Question could not be
                                        saved. Please, try again.');
        }
    }
    $this->data = null;

    $this->Question->recursive = 1;
    $this->set('questions', $this->Question->find('all'));
}
function show( $id = null) {
    ...
    }
}
?>
```

8. Modify the show() action of the Questions controller with the following:

```php
<?php
class QuestionsController extends AppController {

    ...
    function show( $id = null) {
        if (!$id) {
            $this->Session->setFlash('Invalid Question.');
            $this->redirect(array('action'=>'home'));
        }
        if (!empty($this->data) && $this->Auth->user('id')) {
            $this->data['Answer']['user_id'] = $this->
                                                Auth->user('id');
            $this->Answer->create();
            if ($this->Answer->save($this->data)) {
                $this->Session->setFlash('The Answer has been saved');
            } else {
                $this->Session->setFlash('The Answer could not be
                                        saved. Please, try again.');
            }
        }
        $this->data = null;
        $this->Question->recursive = 2;
        $this->set('question', $this->Question->read(null, $id));
    }
}
?>
```

What Just Happened?

We started this section by adding the `AppController`. As you already know, all controllers extend the `AppController`. So if we need to add something that should be defined in all the controllers, it is a very good idea to add it to the `AppController`. We added the file `app_controller.php` in the `/app/` directory. If this file is not present, the default `AppController` is used that can be found in `/cake/libs/controller/app_controller.php`. It is a good idea to add the `AppController` in the `app` directory, instead of changing the cake library file.

In step 2, we added the `Auth` component to the `AppController`. Now, the `Auth` component can be accessed and used in all the controllers that we have on our application.

Next, we added the `beforeFilter()` function to the `AppController`. Now, before executing any controller action code, the code inside the `beforeFilter()` function will be execcuted. In the `beforeFilter()` function, we define a few properties of the `Auth` component.

`$this->Auth->loginRedirect` is used to tell the `Auth` component where to redirect after a successful authentication. Likewise, `$this->Auth->logoutRedirect` tells it where to redirect after a user logs out.

`$this->Auth->allow()` defines which actions do not need any authentication. We included the `home()` and `show()` action of the `Questions` controller, along with the `signup()` and `confirm()` actions of the `Users` controller.

`$this->Auth->authorize` defines the type of authentication that should be done. In our case we use `controller`, which is the simplest form of authentication.

`$this->Auth->userScope` defines any condition that the user needs to fulfil to log in. We set `$this->Auth->userScope` to `array('User.confirmed' => '1')`. For a user to log in, their record should have the confirmed field equal to 1. Any user who has not confirmed cannot log in. Lastly, we send a variable to the view that will contain the id of the currently logged in user. We can get information about the currently logged in user using `$this->Auth->user()`. It will return the value of the field specified in the parameter. If no parameters are passed, it will return all the fields of the record of the currently logged in user. If no user is logged in the current session, it returns null.

Next, we added a new function to the `AppController` named `isAuthorized()`. This is needed for the `Auth` component to work properly. This can be used to run extra logic after a user has successfully authenticated. Since we do not need any such logic, we just include it to return true.

Since we have included the `Auth` component in the `AppController`, we do not need to include it in the `Users` controller. Also, we removed the `beforeFilter()` from the `Users` controller.

In the next step, we add two new actions to the `Users` controller: `login()` and `logout()`. You will notice that the `login()` action is empty. Normally, it contains code that checks the user name and password with the database, and logs in a user. We do not need to include any such code, as this is done automatically by the `Auth` component. In the `logout()` action, we save a logout message to the session, and tell the `Auth` component to logout the currently logged in user. This is done by calling `$this->Auth->logout()`. This function also returns the URL to redirect after logout. So, we just feed it to the `redirect()` function of the controller.

Next, we change the `home()` and `show()` actions of the `Questions` controller. We do not want people to add questions or answers without logging in. So, if a new question or answer is submitted, we check whether the user is logged in using the `$this->Auth->user()` function. To save the id of the questioner, we set `$this->data['User']['user_id']` to the id of the logged in user.

Integrating Authentication: Views

In this section, we make the final set of changes that are required in the view to make the `User` model integrate with the whole app. Also, we will add a user menu from where users can sign up, log in, or log out. Finally, we will have a working authentication system for the application.

Time for Action

1. Let's add a user menu to the application, by adding the following into the layout file at `/app/views/layout/default.ctp`:

```
<!DOCTYPE html PUBLIC "-//W3C//DTD XHTML 1.0 Strict//EN"
            "http://www.w3.org/TR/xhtml1/DTD/xhtml1-strict.dtd">
<html xmlns="http://www.w3.org/1999/xhtml" xml:lang="en"
lang="en">
    <head>

        . . .

    </head>
    <body>
        <div id="content">
        <div id="user_menu">
                |<?php e($html->link('Home', array('controller'
                            => 'questions', 'action' => 'home'))); ?>|
            <?php if($loggedIn): ?>
```

```php
            <?php e($html->link('Logout', array('controller'
                        => 'users', 'action' => 'logout'))); ?>|
        <?php else: ?>
            <?php e($html->link('Sign Up', array('controller'
                    => 'users', 'action' => 'signup'))); ?>|
            <?php e($html->link('Login', array('controller'
                    => 'users', 'action' => 'login'))); ?>|
        <?php endif; ?>
    </div>
    <h1><?php e($html->link('Quickwall', array('controller'
                    => 'questions', 'action' => 'home'))); ?></h1>

        ...

    </div>
</body>
</html>
```

2. Add the view file for the `login()` action of the `Users` controller. Create a file named `login.ctp` in /app/views/users/. Add the following code into it and save:

```php
<h2>Log In To Quickwall</h2>

<?php
    if ($session->check('Message.auth')):
        $session->flash('auth');
    endif;
?>

<?php e($form->create('User', array('action' => 'login')));?>
    <fieldset>
        <label for="UserUsername" class="usernamelabel"><span>
                                        Your Name</span></label>
        <?php e($form->text('username', array('class'
                                    => 'fullwidth'))); ?>
        <label for="UserPassword" class="emaillabel"><span>Password
                                        </span></label>
        <?php e($form->password('password', array('class'
                                    => 'fullwidth'))); ?>
        <?php e($form->submit('Login In', array('div' => false,
                            'class' => 'submitbutton'))); ?>
    </fieldset>
<?php e($form->end()); ?>
```

3. Make the following modifications to the view of the `home()` action of the `Questions` controller:

```php
<?php if($form->isFieldError('Question/question')) e("<div
    class='message'>You haven't entered any question</div>"); ?>
<!-- the validation check for questioner removed -->
<?php if($loggedIn): ?>
    <?php e($form->create('Question', array('action'
                                            => 'home'))); ?>
        <fieldset>
            <label for="QuestionQuestion" class="questionlabel">
                            <span>Your Question</span></label>
            <?php e($form->text('question', array('class' =>
                    'fullwidth'))); ?><span class="big">?</span>
            <!-- Input for Questioner removed -->
            <?php e($form->submit('Post Your Question',
                array('div' => false, 'class' => 'submitbutton'))); ?>
        </fieldset>
    <?php e($form->end()); ?>
<?php else: ?>
    <p>To post a question, please login or signup.</p>
<?php endif; ?>
<?php if(empty($questions)): ?>
    <p class="no_answer">No Questions yet. Be the first one to post
                                a Question!</p>
<?php else: ?>
    <dl>
    <?php foreach ($questions as $question): ?>
        <dt><span><?php e($question['User']['username']);
                                    ?></span></dt>
        <dd>
            <?php e($html->link($question['Question']['question'].
            '?', array('controller' => 'questions', 'action'
            => 'show', $question['Question']['id']))); ?>
            <?php
                $answer_count = count($question['Answer']);
                if(!$answer_count)
                    e("(no answers yet)");
                else if($answer_count == 1)
                    e("(1 answer)");
                else
                    e("(".$answer_count." answers)");
            ?>
        </dd>
    <?php endforeach; ?>
    </dl>
<?php endif; ?>
```

4. In the view file of the `show()` action of the `Questions` controller, make the following modifications:

```php
<?php if($form->isFieldError('Answer/answer')) e("<div
        class='message'>You haven't entered the answer</div>"); ?>
<!-- the validation message check for answerer removed -->

<h2><?php e($question['Question']['question']) ?>?</h2>
<div id="questioner"><div><span><?php e($question['User']
                                    ['username']) ?></span></div></div>

<?php if($loggedIn): ?>
<?php e($form->create('Answer', array('url' => array('controller'
            => 'questions', 'action' => 'show', $question
            ['Question']['id']))));?>
    <fieldset>
        <?php e($form->hidden('question_id', array('value'
                                => $question['Question']['id']))); ?>
        <label for="AnswerAnswer" class="questionlabel"><span>Your
                                            Answer</span></label>
        <?php e($form->text('answer', array('class'
                => 'fullwidth'))); ?><span class="big">!</span>
        <!-- input for the answerer removed -->
        <?php e($form->submit('Post Your Answer', array('div'
                        => false, 'class' => 'submitbutton'))); ?>
    </fieldset>
<?php e($form->end()); ?>
<?php else: ?>
    <p>To post an answer, please login or signup.</p>
<?php endif; ?>

<?php if(empty($question['Answer'])): ?>
    <p class="no_answer">No Answers yet. Be the first one to
                                            answer!</p>
<?php else: ?>
    <dl>
    <?php foreach($question['Answer'] as $answer) : ?>
        <dt><span><?php e($answer['User']['username']); ?>
            </span></dt>
        <dd><?php e($answer['answer']); ?></dd>
    <?php endforeach; ?>
    </dl>
<?php endif; ?>
```

5. Before checking out the new login system, clear the cache. Go to the directory `/app/tmp/cache`. We will find three directories: `models`, `persistent`, and `views`. Delete all the files in these directories.

6. In the user menu, when we click on the login button, we should see a login form as shown:

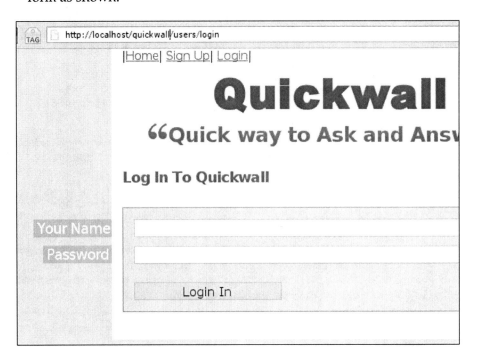

What Just Happened?

We started this section, by adding a user menu. Since we want this menu to be available in all the pages, we added the menu in the layout file in /app/views/layouts/default.ctp.

In step 2, we added the view for the login() action of the Users controller. This is very similar to the signup() action view, but this view only has the user name and password input. Make sure the form in login() view is submitted to the login() action on the Users controller. In the view, we also check if the Auth controller has set any message in the session.

In the next step, we modify the view of the home() action of the Questions controller. If the user is not logged in, we will not show the question submit form. Also, the input for questioner is removed, as we do not need it any more. Also, we change the array from where the user name for questioner will be printed.

Similarly, we make changes to the show() action's view too.

Well, finally we have a working authentication system. It might look like a lot of work, but if see we only added a few lines of code to get a working authentication system. But, we are still not happy with it. As you will see, in the next section, we will add functionality for auto login if the user preferred to remember him.

Remembering User with Cookie

This is a feature that we see commonly in many websites. During log in, if the user prefers to remember his credentials, and next time when the user goes to the site, he is automatically logged in. Of course this is done using cookies.

In this section, we will also introduce the Cookie component. It helps to easily read and write from cookies, but the good work does not end there. The Cookie component automatically encrypts the data in the cookie, adding security to it.

Time for Action

1. Add the following code to the view of the `Users` Controller's `login()` action:

```
<h2>Log In To Quickwall</h2>
<?php
    if ($session->check('Message.auth')):
        $session->flash('auth');
    endif;
?>
<?php e($form->create('User', array('url' => 'login')));?>
    <fieldset>
        <label for="UserUsername" class="usernamelabel"><span>
                                    Your Name</span></label>
        <?php e($form->text('username', array('class'
                                => 'fullwidth'))); ?>
        <label for="UserPassword" class="emaillabel"><span>Password
                                    </span></label>
    <?php e($form->password('password', array('class'
                                => 'fullwidth'))); ?>
        <label for="UserRememberMe" class="passwordlabel"><span>
                                Remember Me</span></label>
        <p><?php e($form->checkbox('remember_me', array('class'
                                => 'bigcheck'))) ?></p>
        <?php e($form->submit('Login In', array('div' => false,
                                'class' => 'loginbutton'))); ?>
    </fieldset>
<?php e($form->end()); ?>
```

2. Add the Cookie Component to the `AppController` class we created in `/app`:

```php
<?php
class AppController extends Controller {

    var $components = array('Auth', 'Cookie');

    function beforeFilter(){
        ...
    }
    ...
}
?>
```

3. Add the following two lines at the end of the `beforeFilter()` method in `AppController`:

```php
<?php
class AppController extends Controller {

    ...

    function beforeFilter(){
        //$this->Auth->loginAction = array('controller'
                             => 'users', 'action' => 'login');
        $this->Auth->loginRedirect = array('controller'
                          => 'questions', 'action' => 'home');
        $this->Auth->logoutRedirect  = array('controller'
                          => 'questions', 'action' => 'home');
        $this->Auth->allow('signup', 'confirm', 'home', 'show');
        $this->Auth->authorize = 'controller';
        $this->Auth->userScope = array('User.confirmed' => '1');
        $this->set('loggedIn', $this->Auth->user('id'));
        $this->Auth->autoRedirect = false;
        $this->Cookie->name = 'QuickWall';
    }
    ...
}
?>
```

4. Open the `Users` controller file, and add the following code into the `login()` action:

```php
<?php
class UsersController extends AppController {

    ...

    function signup(){
        ...
```

```
    }
    function confirm($user_id=null, $code=null) {
        ...
    }
    function login() {
        if ($this->Auth->user()) {
            if (!empty($this->data)) {
                if (empty($this->data['User']['remember_me'])) {
                    $this->Cookie->del('User');
                } else {
                    $cookie = array();
                    $cookie['username'] = $this->data['User']
                                                   ['username'];
                    $cookie['password'] = $this->data['User']
                                                   ['password'];
                    $this->Cookie->write('User', $cookie, true,
                                               '+2 weeks');
                }
                unset($this->data['User']['remember_me']);
            }
            $this->redirect($this->Auth->redirect());
        }
    }

    function logout() {
        ...
    }
}
?>
```

5. Now move back to the AppController, and add the following code to the end of the beforeFilter() method:

```php
<?php
class AppController extends Controller {
    var $components = array('Auth', 'Cookie');
    function beforeFilter(){
        //$this->Auth->loginAction = array('controller'
                                  => 'users', 'action' => 'login');
        $this->Auth->loginRedirect = array('controller'
                                  => 'questions', 'action' => 'home');
        $this->Auth->logoutRedirect  = array('controller'
                                  => 'questions', 'action' => 'home');
```

```
$this->Auth->allow('signup', 'confirm', 'home', 'show');
$this->Auth->authorize = 'controller';
$this->Auth->userScope = array('User.confirmed' => '1');
$this->set('loggedIn', $this->Auth->user('id'));
$this->Auth->autoRedirect = false;

$this->Cookie->name = 'QuickWall';

if(!$this->Auth->user('id')) {
    $cookie = $this->Cookie->read('User');
    if($cookie) {
        $this->Auth->login($cookie);
    }
}
}
}
function isAuthorized() {
    return true;
}
}
?>
```

6. To make sure the cookie is deleted once the user prefers to log out, add the following code to `logout()` action of the `Users` controller:

```
function logout() {
    $cookie = $this->Cookie->read('User');
    if($cookie)
        $this->Cookie->del('User');
    $this->Session->setFlash('Logout');
    $this->redirect($this->Auth->logout());
}
```

7. When we go to the login page now, notice the remember me option:

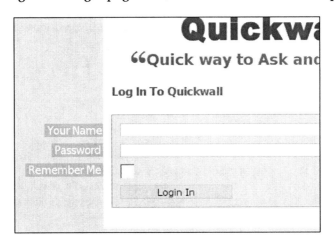

What Just Happened?

The first thing that we did was add a checkbox to the login form. If this checkbox is selected, then it shows that the user is interested to make him remember.

Next, we add the Cookie component to the `AppController`. In that way, all the controllers can now access the Cookie component.

In the next step, we added two lines to the `beforeFilter()` function of the `AppController`. The first one is a property for the `Auth` component: `$this->Auth->autoRedirect`. We set it to false. By default this is set to true. In that case, whenever a user successfully authenticates to the `Auth` component, it redirects to the page specified by `$this->Auth->loginRedirect`. By setting `$this->Auth->autoRedirect` to false, the `Auth` component will return to the `login()` action after successful authentication. The other line that we include sets the name of the cookie to be set.

Next, we add code to the `login()` action. Once a user successfully authenticates, the `login()` action is executed as `$this->Auth->autoRedirect` is set to false. Here, if the user is authenticated and `$this->data` is not empty, it checks for the value of `$this->data['User']['remember_me']`. It is selected, then a cookie is set, that contains the username and password of the user. Normally, it is not a good idea to store passwords in cookies. But, since the Cookie component encrypts the data, it is not a too bad idea. After the cookie is set, the page is redirected to the default redirect page of the `Auth` component.

Finally, we add code in the `beforeFilter()` of the `AppController` that checks the following. First, it checks if the current session has a logged in user. If not, then it checks for the cookie. If it finds a cookie, it sends the cookie data to `$this->Auth->login()` for authentication. If authentication succeeds, then the user is automatically logged in.

Summary

In this chapter, we saw how to create proper user authentication with CakePHP. We started the chapter by adding the User model that is central to the authentication process. We then created a Sign-up process by which users can register to the site. We enhanced the Sign-up process by adding Email confirmation to it. We then moved on to integrate the User model with the other models. We added login and logout processes to the site. At the end of the chapter, we added functionality to remember a user so that he is automatically logged in, if he prefers to.

In more technical terms, this chapter showed us the use of three very important components: Auth, Email, and Cookie component. We saw, how these components can make it so easy to do things that take more time and effort if it was using raw PHP coding.

By the end of this chapter, our Quickwall application has grown into a usable site, where users can not only ask and answer questions, but they things also sign up and log in to it. This was a very important feature to add, as we can make the site more social, based on the authentication process.

11
Quickwall: JavaScript and AJAX

In a time, not so long ago, all a back-end programmer needed to know was how to fetch data from the database, control the logic, and have a good idea about the back-end language used. Fast-forward to present, and all that has changed! A good web programmer needs to be not only good with back-end programming, but also has to have a good idea of front-end technologies like JavaScript.

In this chapter, we are going to see how to use JavaScript and AJAX with CakePHP. We are going to add a bit of interactivity to Quickwall, and you will find out how easy it is (I know it may sound like a cliché, but fortunately it's true) to add AJAX to Cake Applications.

In this chapter, we are going to:

- Add JavaScript validation
- Make AJAX call to update page
- Add AJAX auto-complete to pull data from the database
- Submit a form through an AJAX call
- See how to add in-line editing that changes data with an AJAX call

Adding JavaScript Validation

In this section, we will see how to add JavaScript to a page in CakePHP. To make it easier to manage and work with JavaScript, CakePHP has a built-in helper that is known as the JavaScript helper. We are going to add a simple JavaScript to the main page of Quickwall, so that if users submit a new question that is empty, it instantly shows an error notification. This section will also see the usage of the Prototype JavaScript Framework (http://prototypejs.org/). Some functions of the JavaScript helper, and most of the AJAX helper (we will soon discuss this) uses the Prototype library.

Time for Action

1. In our layout file (`/app/views/layout/default.ctp`), add the following line inside the `<head>` tag:

```
<!DOCTYPE html PUBLIC "-//W3C//DTD XHTML 1.0 Strict//EN"
            "http://www.w3.org/TR/xhtml1/DTD/xhtml1-strict.dtd">
<html xmlns="http://www.w3.org/1999/xhtml" xml:lang="en"
                                                lang="en">
<head>
    <meta content="text/html; charset=utf-8" http-equiv=
                                        "Content-Type"/>
    title>Quick Wall</title>
    <?php e($scripts_for_layout); ?>
    <?php e($html->css('quickwall')); ?>
    <!--[if IE 6]>
        <?php e($html->css('quickwall_ie6hack')); ?>
    <![endif]-->
</head>
<body>
    ...
</body>
</html>
```

2. Next, we will add the JavaScript helper in our `AppController` class (`/app/app_controller.php`). We will also include the HTML and Form helper here:

```
<?php
class AppController extends Controller {

    var $components = array('Auth', 'Cookie');
    var $helpers = array('Html', 'Form', 'Javascript');

    function beforeFilter(){

        ...
    }

    function isAuthorized() {
        return true;
    }
}
?>
```

3. We will be using Prototype, which is a JavaScript library. The version of Prototype that we are using in this book is 1.6.0.2. So next, let us download the library from the Prototype website: `http://prototypejs.org/download`.

4. Put the downloaded file into the following directory: `/app/webroot/js`. The file name of the library should be **prototype-1.6.0.2.js**.

5. Next, let us use the JavaScript helper to include the Prototype library into all the pages. This is done by adding the following line in our layout file:

```
<!DOCTYPE html PUBLIC "-//W3C//DTD XHTML 1.0 Strict//EN"
            "http://www.w3.org/TR/xhtml1/DTD/xhtml1-strict.dtd">
<html xmlns="http://www.w3.org/1999/xhtml" xml:lang="en"
                                            lang="en">
<head>
    <meta content="text/html; charset=utf-8" http-equiv=
                                            "Content-Type"/>
    <title>Quick Wall</title>
    <?php e($javascript->link('prototype-1.6.0.2')); ?>
    <?php e($scripts_for_layout); ?>
    <?php e($html->css('quickwall')); ?>
    <!--[if IE 6]>
        <?php e($html->css('quickwall_ie6hack')); ?>
    <![endif]-->
</head>
<body>
    ...
</body>
</html>
```

6. Also add a <div> into the layout file:

```
<!DOCTYPE html PUBLIC "-//W3C//DTD XHTML 1.0 Strict//EN"
            "http://www.w3.org/TR/xhtml1/DTD/xhtml1-strict.dtd">
<html xmlns="http://www.w3.org/1999/xhtml" xml:lang="en"
                                            lang="en">
...
<body>
    <div id="content">
        <div id="user_menu">
            ...
        </div>
        <h1><?php e($html->link('Quickwall', '/')); ?></h1>
        <p id="strapline"><strong>"</strong>Quick way to Ask and
                                    Answer<strong>"</strong></p>
        <div id='js_errors' class='message' style='display:none'>
                </div>
        <?php
        if ($session->check('Message.flash')):
            $session->flash();
        endif;
        ?>
        <?php e($content_for_layout); ?>
        ...
    </div>
</body>
</html>
```

7. Create a new file in the directory `/app/webroo/js`, and name it `home.js`. Add the following code to the file and save it:

```
Event.observe(window, 'DOMContentLoaded', function() {
    Event.observe('QuestionHomeForm', 'submit',
                                    checkQuestionNotEmpty);
});
function checkQuestionNotEmpty(event) {
    if($F('QuestionQuestion') == '') {
        Event.stop(event);
        $('js_errors').innerHTML = "Cannot Enter Empty Question";
        $('js_errors').show();
        $('QuestionQuestion').focus();
    }
}
```

8. Next, we would like to include the newly created JavaScript file in our homepage. In the file `/app/views/questions/home.ctp`, add the following line:

```
<?php e($javascript->link('home', false)); ?>
```

9. Now, to check if the JavaScript is working, point the web browser to `http://localhost/quickwall/`, log in and try to submit an empty question. We should see an error message as shown:

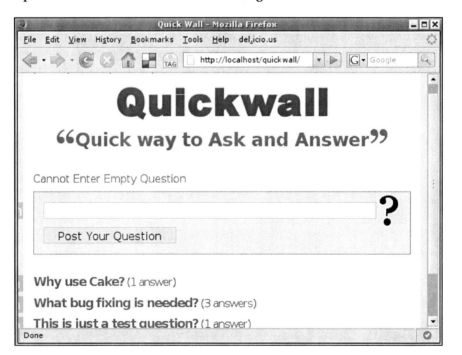

What Just Happened?

In step 1, we added the line `<?php e($scripts_for_layout); ?>` in our layout file. This is similar to `<?php e($content_for_layout); ?>`. But whereas `<?php e($content_for_layout); ?>` is replaced by the view content, `<?php e($scripts_for_layout); ?>` is replaced by any JavaScript link present in the view. Since, we want all the JavaScript link to appear in the `<head>` tag, we insert `<?php e($scripts_for_layout); ?>` inside the `<head>` tag.

In step 2, we added the JavaScript helper in our `AppController`. We are adding it in the `AppController`, so that it is available in all the controllers in our application. Another thing to note here is that we also added the HTML and Form helper to the `AppController`. Normally, the HTML and the Form helper are loaded in the controller by default. But, if any helper is added in the `AppController`, these are overridden. So, it's a good idea to include the HTML and Form helper with any other helper in the `AppController`.

In step 3, we download the Prototype Library. The version that we are using in this book is 1.6.0.2. As you might already know, Prototype is a very popular JavaScript library. It is a rich library with many useful features that help in making AJAX calls, simplify event handling, and traversing DOM elements. Of course, there are many more JavaScript libraries out there. But the reason we are using Prototype here, is because CakePHP's JavaScript helper (part of it, to be exact) and AJAX helper use Prototype.

In step 4, we copied the **prototype-1.6.0.2.js** file in the directory `/app/webroot/js`. This is the directory where all JavaScript files for CakePHP applications are placed. For easy managing, we can place related JavaScript files in directories under this directory.

In step 5, we add the line `<?php e($javascript->link('prototype-1.6.0.2')); ?>` in our layout file. Here, we are using the JavaScript helper to create a link to the Prototype library file. The `link()` function of the JavaScript helper returns a `<script>` tag with links to the specified file. For example, the line above will output the following line:

```
<script type="text/javascript" src="/quickwall_svn/js/prototype-
1.6.0.2.js"></script>
```

Also note that we do not need to include the extension of the JavaScript file.

Next, in step 6, we add a new `<div>` to the layout file. This `<div>`, with `id='js_errors'`, will be used to display the error message. Initially it is kept hidden by using the attribute, `style='display:none'`.

In step 7, we create a new JavaScript file in `/app/webroot/js` that we name `home.js`. Of course, we could have named it anything we wanted. But since we will be linking it to the `home()` action, we name it similarly. Now let's have a look at the code inside `home.js`. The JavaScript code extensively uses the Prototype library. Though explaining the JavaScript code is beyond the scope of this book, here is a general overview of the code. When the DOM has been loaded, it attaches an event to the form with `id = "QuestionHomeForm"`. This is the form present in the homepage, which is used to input a new question. The event attaches the function `checkQuestionNotEmpty()`, so that it is executed whenever the form is submitted. In this function, it is checked whether the question submitted is empty. If so, then it stops the event (submitting of the form), and adds an error message in the `<div>` we added earlier. Lastly, it gets the focus back to the question input text.

Next, in step 8, we added `<?php e($javascript->link('home', false)); ?>` to link the JavaScript file we just created to the view of the `home()` action of the `Questions` controller. We again use the JavaScript helper's `link()` function to create a `<script>` tag. We also added a second parameter `false`. This attaches the JavaScript link to where `<?php e($scripts_for_layout); ?>` is situated. By default, the second parameter is `true`. In that case, the `<script>` tag is included in the view where the call to `$javascript->link()` is made.

AJAX Link to Show Own Questions

Here, we will be using the AJAX helper of CakePHP to make AJAX calls. The AJAX helper uses the Prototype library to produce different JavaScript functionalities. Basically, the AJAX helper is a CakePHP wrapper for Prototype, so that CakePHP developers can easily deploy different JavaScript functionalities without knowing JavaScript at all!

In this section, we will add a new page to the application, the search page. For the time being, this page will only contain a link called **Show My Questions**. When clicked, an AJAX call will be made to the server, and fetch all your questions. The main idea here is to see how to make a successful AJAX call using the AJAX helper.

Time for Action

1. We will start by adding a new action to the `Questions` controller. We name the action `search()`:

```php
<?php
class QuestionsController extends AppController {
    var $name = 'Questions';
    var $uses = array('Question', 'Answer');
function home() {
```

```
      . . .
   }
   function show( $id = null) {
      . . .
   }
   function search() {

   }
}
?>
```

2. Next, we add the view file for this action. Create a new file in `/app/views/questions/` and name it `search.ctp`.

3. We will be using the AJAX helper for this task. So, lets add the helper in our `AppController` (`/app/app_controller.php`):

```php
<?php
class AppController extends Controller {
   var $components = array('Auth', 'Cookie');
   var $helpers = array('Html', 'Form', 'Javascript', 'AJAX');

   . . .

}
?>
```

4. In the view of the `search()` action, add the following lines:

```php
|<?php e($ajax->link(
   'Show Your Questions',
   array('controller' => 'questions', 'action' =>
                               'user_questions', $loggedIn),
   array('update' => 'questionList', 'loading' => "$('loader').
                        show()", 'loaded' => "$('loader').hide()")
)); ?>|
<div id="questionList"></div>
```

5. The above will create a link that will make an AJAX call to `Questions` controller's `user_questions` action. Let us create the `user_questions`, and add the following code to it:

```php
<?php
class QuestionsController extends AppController {
   var $name = 'Questions';
   var $uses = array('Question', 'Answer');
   function home() {
      . . .
```

```
    }
    function show( $id = null) {
        ...
    }
    function search() {

    }
    function user_questions($user_id = null) {
        $this->layout = 'ajax';
        Configure::write('debug', '0');

        $this->set('questions', $this->Question->find('all',
            array('conditions' => array('user_id' => $user_id))));
    }
}
?>
```

6. To reuse code, we will now create an element. Inside the directory /app/
   views/elements, create a new file named question_list.ctp. Add the
   following code to the file and save it:

```
<dl>
<?php foreach ($questions as $question): ?>
    <dt><span><?php e($question['User']['username']); ?>
                                                </span></dt>
    <dd>
        <?php e($html->link($question['Question']['question'].'?',
            array('controller' => 'questions', 'action'
                => 'show', $question['Question']['id']))); ?>
        <?php
        $answer_count = count($question['Answer']);
        if(!$answer_count)
            e("(no answers yet)");
        else if($answer_count == 1)
            e("(1 answer)");
        else
            e("(".$answer_count." answers)");
        ?>
    </dd>
<?php endforeach; ?>
</dl>
```

7. To make use of the element we just created, refactor the code in the view of the `home` action of the `Questions` controller:

```php
<?php e($javascript->link('home', false)); ?>

...

<?php if($loggedIn): ?>
    ...
<?php endif; ?>
<?php if(empty($questions)): ?>
    <p class="no_answer">No Questions yet. Be the first one to post
                                            a Question!</p>
<?php else: ?>
    <?php e($this->renderElement('question_list')); ?>
<?php endif; ?>
```

8. Let's use the same element in the view of the `user_questions` action we created in step 5. Create a file named `user_questions.ctp` in `/app/views/questions`, and add the following code:

```php
<?php if(empty($questions)): ?>
    <p class="no_answer">No question asked by this user.</p>
<?php else: ?>
    <?php e($this->renderElement('question_list')); ?>
<?php endif; ?>
```

9. Now, let's add a link to the new search page we created. Also, we will add a loading image to show when the AJAX call is made. In the layout file, add the following lines:

```php
<!DOCTYPE html PUBLIC "-//W3C//DTD XHTML 1.0 Strict//EN"
            "http://www.w3.org/TR/xhtml1/DTD/xhtml1-strict.dtd">
<html xmlns="http://www.w3.org/1999/xhtml" xml:lang="en"
                                                        lang="en">
<head>
    ...
</head>
<body>
    <div id="content">
        <div id="user_menu">
            |<?php e($html->link('Home', '/')); ?>|
            <?php if($loggedIn): ?>
                <?php e($html->link('Search', array('controller' =>
                        'questions', 'action' => 'search'))); ?>|
                <?php e($html->link('Logout', array('controller' =>
                        'users', 'action' => 'logout'))); ?>|
            <?php else: ?>
```

```
                <?php e($html->link('Sign Up', array('controller' =>
                                            'signup'))); ?>|
                <?php e($html->link('Login', array('controller' =>
                            'users', 'action' => 'login'))); ?>|
            <?php endif; ?>
          </div>
          <?php e($html->image('loading.gif', array('id' => 'loader',
                                'style' => 'display:none'))); ?>
          <h1><?php e($html->link('Quickwall', '/')); ?></h1>
          ...
        </div>
      </body>
    </html>
```

10. Lastly, add the loading image file to /app/webroot/img/ directory with the
    name loading.gif.

What Just Happened?

We started this section by adding a new action to the Questions controller that we
call search. We also added a view file for this action.

To use the AJAX helper, we will need to load it into our controller. Since, we want to
use it in all the controllers, we add the AJAX helper in the AppController.

Step 4 is where the main action of this section happens. We call the AJAX helper with
the following code:

```
<?php e($ajax->link(
   'Show Your Questions',
   array('controller' => 'questions', 'action' => 'user_questions',
$loggedIn),
   array('update' => 'questionList', 'loading' => "$('loader').
show()", 'loaded' => "$('loader').hide()")
)); ?>
```

We call the link() function of the AJAX helper. This function takes three
parameters. The first one is the label of the link. In this case, our label is Show Your
Question. The second one should be an array that specifies the controller action to
which the AJAX request will be made.

We specified to call the user_questions action of the Questions controller by
passing this array: array('controller' => 'questions', 'action' => 'user_
questions', $loggedIn). We also send the logged in user's id as a parameter to the
action. The third and the last parameter takes an array with different options that we
can specify for the AJAX call. In this case, we sent three options: update, loading,
and loaded. The update option specifies a HTML tag in the page. The result sent
back from the AJAX response will be put inside this HTML tag. Here, we specified
questionList, the <div> that is added below the code that calls the AJAX helper.

BORDERS.

BORDERS BOOKS MUSIC A
2 Penn Plaza
Manhattan (Penn Plaza), NY 10121

212.244.1814

STORE: 0582   REG: 09/88   TRAN#: 0758
SALE   06/22/2009   EMP: 00669

CAKEPHP APPLICATION DEVELOPMEN
    9648688   SP T   39.99

              Subtotal   39.99
BR: 8421566640   S

          Subtotal   39.99
          NY 8.375%   3.35
1 Item   Total   43.34
          MASTERCARD   43.34
ACCT # /S XXXXXXXXXXXXX0983
              AUTH: 022372
NAME: SETTRO/MONJAY

        CUSTOMER COPY

    06/22/2009 02:07PM
TRANS BARCODE: 0582090758006906229

      Shop online
      24 hours a day
      at Borders.com

aScript code that we want to execute
AJAX response. Here, we specified
ᵣ". This is an image to show the user
ᵢe last option we used was loaded.
ᵢe that we want to run after the AJAX
hide the loader image again.

er to make an AJAX call to the
on. In step 5, we add this action to the

eter, the $user_id. Remember, in the
l in user. In the first line of this action,
this is an AJAX call, we do not want
se. Instead, we only what the content of
yout to be ajax, only the content of the
.gure::write('debug', '0'). This
As we know, database query information
We do not want any debug information
e change the Debug to 0. Next, we send
id sent, and pass them to the view.

ns action returns has exactly the same
ᵢe home action. So, we will want to use the
. To reuse and separate view segments,
nts that can be called from many views
ᵗt repeated everywhere. Instead the
ᵣm different places where it is needed. All
nts. We created an element that we name
t from both the views of user_questions
m a view using the renderElement()
nd 8, we call the question_list element
ᵢestion_list')); ?>.

in the layout. We also add an image link
image is kept hidden. Lastly, we add the
/img. This is where all the image files in a

AJAX AutoComplete to Search Users

Our search page looks pretty empty with one link only. In this section, we are going to add more functionalities to it. We will start by adding another link with the label Show Questions of Others. When clicked, this will show an input text to enter user name. This is where we will use AJAX AutoComplete. What AJAX AutoComplete will do is that it will fetch all the user names matching the text we enter, and show them below the text field. We can choose any one of the names. Once chosen, it will show all the questions asked by that user.

We will be creating the AJAX AutoComplete by using the AJAX helper. But, for it to work, we will need to have another JavaScript library based on Prototype: Scriptaculous (http://script.aculo.us/). It is a JavaScript library that uses Prototype to add different effects in the front-end.

Time for Action

1. We will start by adding a link and a form to the view of the search page (/app/views/questions/search.ctp):

```
|<?php e($ajax->link(
   'Show Your Questions',
   array('controller' => 'questions', 'action' =>
                                'user_questions', $loggedIn),
   array('update' => 'questionList', 'loading' => "$('loader').
                       show()", 'loaded' => "$('loader').hide()")
)); ?>|
<a href='javascript:;' id='showOthersQuestion'>Show Questions of
                                               Others</a>|

<form id='user_search_form'  style="display:none">
  <fieldset>

  </fieldset>
</form>
<div id="questionList"></div>
```

2. Create a JavaScript file named search.js in the directory /app/webroot/js. Add the following code to the file, and save:

```
Event.observe(window, 'DOMContentLoaded', function() {
    Event.observe('showOthersQuestion', 'click',
                                        showUserSearchForm);
});

function showUserSearchForm(event) {
    $('user_search_form').show();
}
```

3. Add a link to the JavaScript file we just created to the view of the search page
   (`/app/views/questions/search.ctp`):

```
<?php e($javascript->link('search', false)); ?>
|<?php e($ajax->link(
        'Show Your Questions',
        array('controller' => 'questions', 'action' =>
                             'user_questions', $loggedIn),
        array('update' => 'questionList', 'loading' =>
            "$('loader').show()", 'loaded' => "$('loader').hide()")
)); ?>|
<a href='javascript:;' id='showOthersQuestion'>Show Questions of
                                                Others</a>|
<form id='user_search_form'  style="display:none">
   ...
</form>
<div id="questionList"></div>
```

4. We will be using Scriptaculous, which is a JavaScript library based on
   Prototype. It is used to add different front-end effects and functionality.
   In this case, we will be using its AutoComplete feature. The version of
   Scriptaculous we are using is 1.8.1. Download it from `http://script.`
   `aculo.us/downloads`.

5. Uncompress the ZIP file downloaded, and we will find a directory named
   `src` inside the root directory. Copy all the JavaScript files from the `src`
   directory to `/app/webroot/js` of our application.

6. Link the main Scriptaculous file to the layout file, by adding the following:

```
<!DOCTYPE html PUBLIC "-//W3C//DTD XHTML 1.0 Strict//EN"
            "http://www.w3.org/TR/xhtml1/DTD/xhtml1-strict.dtd">
<html xmlns="http://www.w3.org/1999/xhtml" xml:lang="en"
                                            lang="en">
<head>
    ...
    <title>Quick Wall</title>
    <?php e($javascript->link('prototype-1.6.0.2')); ?>
    <?php e($javascript->link('scriptaculous')); ?>
    <?php e($scripts_for_layout); ?>
    <?php e($html->css('quickwall')); ?>
    <!--[if IE 6]>
       <?php e($html->css('quickwall_ie6hack')); ?>
    <![endif]-->
</head>
<body>
    ...
</body>
</html>
```

7. In the view of the search page, add the following code to make an AJAX call that will retrieve all the matching user names:

```php
<?php e($javascript->link('search', false)); ?>

|<?php e($ajax->link(
    'Show Your Questions',
    array('controller' => 'questions', 'action' =>
                                'user_questions', $loggedIn),
    array('update' => 'questionList', 'loading' => "$('loader').
                            show()", 'loaded' => "$('loader').hide()")
)); ?>|
<a href='javascript:;' id='showOthersQuestion'>Show Questions of
                                                        Others</a>|
<form id='user_search_form'  style="display:none">
    <fieldset>
        <label for="UserUsername" class="questionlabel"><span>
                                    Username</span></label>
        <?php echo $ajax->autoComplete('User.username',
            array('controller' => 'users', 'action' =>
            'show_usernames'), array('class' => 'fullwidth'))?>
    </fieldset>
</form>
<div id="questionList"></div>
```

8. The above code makes an AJAX call to /questions/show_usernames. Add the action named show_usernames to the Users controller, with the following code:

```php
<?php
class UsersController extends AppController {

    ...

    function logout() {
        ...
    }

    function show_usernames() {
        $this->layout = "ajax";
        Configure::write('debug', '0');

        $this->set(
            'usernames',
            $this->User->find('all', array(
                'conditions' => array(
                    'username LIKE' => $this->data['User']
                                                ['username'].'%',
                    'confirmed' => '1'
```

```
            )
        ))
    );}
}
?>
```

9. We will now add the view for the action we just created. Create a new file named `show_usernames.ctp` in the directory `/app/views/users`. Then, add the following code to it:

```
<ul>
<?php foreach($usernames as $username): ?>
    <li><?php e($username['User']['username']); ?></li>
<?php endforeach; ?>
</ul>
```

10. To apply proper styling to our autocomplete list, add the following to the end of our main css file `quickwall.css` in `/app/webroot/css`:

```css
div#UserUsername_autoComplete {
    position         :absolute;
    width            :250px;
    background-color :white;
    border           :1px solid #888;
    margin           :0px;
    padding          :0px;
}

div#UserUsername_autoComplete ul{
    list-style-type: none;
}

div#UserUsername_autoComplete ul li.selected {
    background-color: #ffb;
}
```

11. To test the autocomplete functionality we just added, point your browser to `http://localhost/quickwall/questions/search`, log in, click on the **Show Questions of Others**, and start typing in the username input. We will see an autocomplete list with matching user names:

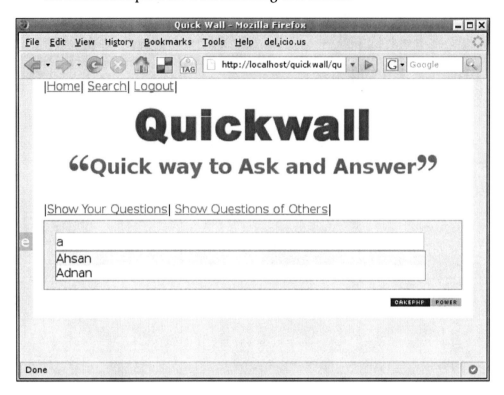

What Just Happened?

In step 1 of this section, we add a normal HTML link and a form with `id="user_search_form"`. This is kept hidden initially.

Next, we add another JavaScript file in `/app/webroot/js` and named it `search.js`. Later, we will be linking it with the view of the `search` action. In this JavaScript file, we add events, so that when a user clicks on the **Show Questions of Others**, the form below is displayed.

As promised, in step 3, we create a JavaScript link in the view of the `search` action, using the JavaScript Helper.

In step 5, 6, and 7, we download the Scriptaculous library and put it into our `/app/webroot/js` directory. We also add a link in our layout file to the main Scriptaculous file.

In step 7, we call the `autoComplete()` function of the AJAX helper in the view of the search page by adding the following code to it:

```php
<?php echo $ajax->autoComplete('User.username',
array('controller' => 'users', 'action' => 'show_usernames'),
array('class' => 'fullwidth'))?>
```

Just like the `link()` function of the AJAX helper, the `autoComplete()` function also takes three parameters. The first is the name of the field that we are interested to AutoComplete. This should have a format like this: Modelname.fieldname. In the above code we used `User.username` as we want it to AutoComplete the user name. The next parameter is used to point the controller function to which the AJAX request will be sent to. Above, we specified: `array('controller' => 'users', 'action' => 'show_usernames')`. We will be creating this action in the next step. The third parameter is used to send extra options to the function. For example, here we specified that the class of the input text created should have a `class = "fullwidth"`.

In step 8, we added the action `show_usernames` to the `Users` controller. In the action, we first defined the layout to be `ajax`, so that only the content of the view is returned. We changed the Debug level to 0, so that no debug messages are returned. The AutoComplete code in the previous step also sends the user name (or the partial user name) entered by the user. This can be accessed in `$this->data['User']['username']`. Lastly, we send any user name that is "like" the entered text, and who has confirmed their email address to the view of the action.

In step 9, we create the view of the action. We put the matching user names into an unordered list and send it back to the browser.

Lastly, we add styles for the unordered list that will appear below the user name input.

AJAX Form Submit to View Questions of a User

In the previous section, we used AJAX AutoComplete to pull all the matching usernames from the database and show them in a list. When the user selects one of the names, it is put into the input text box. In this section, we will carry on from there. We will be adding a submit button to the form that will submit the form through an AJAX call. The AJAX call will return all the questions asked by the user.

Time for Action

1. Add the following code to `search.ctp` in /app/views/questions/ to
    submit the name of the user select, and show the questions of that user:

```php
<?php e($javascript->link('search', false)); ?>
|<?php e($ajax->link(
    'Show Your Questions',
    array('controller' => 'questions', 'action' =>
                                'user_questions', $loggedIn),
    array('update' => 'questionList', 'loading' => "$('loader').
                        show()", 'loaded' => "$('loader').hide()")
)); ?>|
<a href='javascript:;' id='showOthersQuestion'>Show Questions of
                                                    Others</a>|
<form id='user_search_form'  style="display:none">
    <fieldset>
        <label for="UserUsername" class="questionlabel"><span>
                                Username</span></label>
        <?php echo $ajax->autoComplete('User.username',
            array('controller' => 'users', 'action' =>
            'show_usernames'), array('class' => 'fullwidth'))?>
        <?php echo $ajax->submit('Search', array('div' => false,
        'class' => 'submitbutton', 'url' => array('controller'
        => 'questions', 'action' => 'user_questions'), 'update'
        => 'questionList', 'loading' => "$('loader').show()",
            'loaded' => "$('loader').hide()")) ?>
    </fieldset>
</form>
<div id="questionList"></div>
```

2. The code added above will make an AJAX call to /questions/user_
    questions. The AJAX call will also submit the name of the user selected.
    To process the user name sent, and return that user's questions, add the
    following code to Questions controller's user_questions action:

```php
<?php
class QuestionsController extends AppController {
    ...
    function user_questions($user_id = null) {
        $this->layout = 'ajax';
        Configure::write('debug', '0');
        if(empty($user_id)) {
            if($this->data['User']['username']) {
                $user = $this->Question->User->findByUsername
                            ($this->data['User']['username']);
                if(isset($user['User']['id'])){
                    $user_id = $user['User']['id'];
                } else {
                    $this->set('nouser', true);
```

```
            }
        } else {
            $user_id = $this->Auth->user('id');
        }
    }
    ;
    $this->set('questions', $this->Question->find('all', array
            ('conditions' => array('user_id' => $user_id))));
    }
}
?>
```

3. Next, we will need to modify the view of this action. Add the following code to the file `user_questions.ctp` in the directory `/app/views/questions/`:

```
<?php if(isset($nouser)) : ?>
    <p class="no_answer">No such user found</p>
<?php else: ?>
    <?php if(empty($questions)): ?>
        <p class="no_answer">No question asked by this user.</p>
    <?php else: ?>
        <?php e($this->renderElement('question_list')); ?>
    <?php endif; ?>
<?php endif; ?>
```

4. To try it out, point the browser to `http://localhost/quickwall/` `questions/search`, log in, click on **Show Questions of Others**, start typing in a name, select a user name for the autocomplete list, and click on **Search**. You should be presented with the questions of that user:

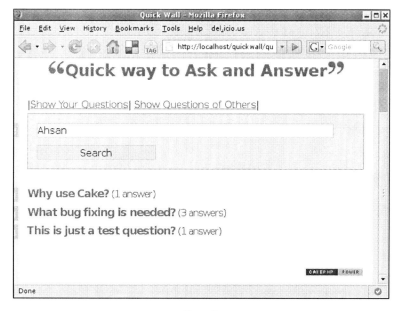

What Just Happened?

Here we added a submit button to the hidden form in the view of the search page. This was done by adding the following code:

```
<?php echo $ajax->submit('Search', array('div' => false,
'class' => 'submitbutton', 'url' => array('controller' =>
'questions', 'action' => 'user_questions'), 'update' =>
'questionList', 'loading' => "$('loader').show()", 'loaded' =>
"$('loader').hide()")) ?>
```

The `submit()` function of the AJAX helper submits the form using an AJAX call to the controller action specified. It takes two parameters here. The first is the label of the submit button created. The second parameter is an array that can take many different options. We pass the following options into the array: `div`, `class`, `url`, `update`, `loading`, and "`loaded`". By specifying `div` to false, it does not create a wrapping `<div>` element for the submit button.

`class` specifies the class name for the submit button.

`url` is used to point to the controller action to which the AJAX call should be made. The `update` option is used to specify the DOM element that will be filled with the returned text.

`loading` and `loaded` has the same functions as discussed previously.

In the next step, we modify the `users_question` action in the `Questions` controller. This is the same action that returns the questions of the logged in user. Previously, the id of the logged in user was sent, so it was easy to find all the questions with that `user_id`. But this time, we are supplied with the user name. So, we need to use the user name to get the id of that user. To do so, we need to access the `User` model. Since the `User` model is related to the `Question` model, we can access the User mode through the `Question` model. As a result, we do not have to explicitly load `User` model. We use this to find the id of the user name, and then send the questions with that particular `user_id`.

Lastly, we modify the view of this action to accommodate the changes.

In-Line Editing to Edit Own Answers

This is the last section of the chapter. We will end this chapter by showing another eye catching functionality. We would like our users of Quickwall to edit the answers that they have given. But to do so, we would like to do so in the same position where the answer in shown. When a user will click on the answer, it will be replaced by input field, where our beloved user can edit it. This is called in-line editing. Thanks to the CakePHP AJAX helper and Scriptaculous, doing this will be very easy.

Time for Action

1. Modify the file `/app/views/questions/show.ctp`, as shown below:

```
. . .
<h2><?php e($question['Question']['question']) ?>?</h2>
<div id="questioner"><div><span><?php e($question['User']
                          ['username']) ?></span></div></div>
<?php if($loggedIn): ?>
  . . .
<?php else: ?>
  <p>To post an answer, please login or signup.</p>
<?php endif; ?>
<?php if(empty($question['Answer'])): ?>
    . . .
<?php else: ?>
  <dl>
  <?php foreach($question['Answer'] as $answer) : ?>
    <dt><span><?php e($answer['User']['username']);
                              ?></span></dt>
    <dd ><span id='answer_<?php e($answer['id'])
              ?>'><?php e($answer['answer']); ?></span></dd>
    <?php if(!empty($loggedIn) && $answer['user_id']
                              == $loggedIn): ?>
      <?php e($ajax->editor('answer_'.$answer['id'],
        array('controller' => 'questions', 'action' =>
        'edit_answer', $answer['id']), array('callback' =>
        "return 'data[Answer][answer]=' + escape(value)"))); ?>
    <?php endif; ?>
  <?php endforeach; ?>
  </dl>
<?php endif; ?>
```

2. The code added in the first step will make an AJAX call to `/questions/edit_answer`. Add this new action to the `Questions` controller, with the code below:

```php
<?php
class QuestionsController extends AppController {
  var $name = 'Questions';
  var $uses = array('Question', 'Answer');
  function home() {
    . . .
  }
  function show( $id = null) {
    . . .
  }
  function search() {
  }
```

```php
function user_questions($user_id = null) {
    ...
}
function edit_answer($answer_id = null) {
    $this->layout = 'ajax';
    Configure::write('debug', '0');

    $answer = $this->Question->Answer->findById($answer_id);
    if(!empty($this->data['Answer']['answer']) &&
        $answer['Answer']['user_id'] == $this->Auth->user('id')) {
        $this->Question->Answer->id = $answer_id;
        $this->Question->Answer->saveField('answer',
        $this->data['Answer']['answer']);
        $this->set('answer', $this->data['Answer']['answer']);
    } else {
        $this->set('answer', $answer['Answer']['answer']);
    }
}
}
?>
```

3. Lastly, add the view file for the `edit_answer` action. In `/app/views/questions`, add a new file named `edit_answer.ctp`. Just add this single line to it, and save:

```php
<?php e($answer) ?>
```

4. Now from the browser, log into Quickwall, and go to the page of a question that has your answers. Hover the mouse over any one of your answer and click. You will be presented with a input to edit the answer:

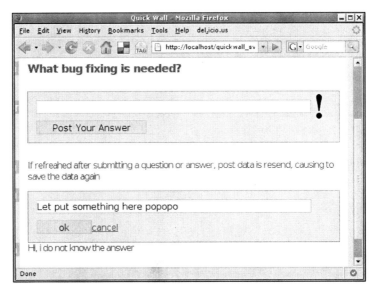

What Just Happened?

Inline editor is created by adding the following code to the view of the `show` action:

```
<?php e($ajax->editor('answer_'.$answer['id'],
array('controller' => 'questions', 'action' => 'edit_answer',
$answer['id']), array('callback' => "return 'data[Answer]
[answer]=' + escape(value)"))); ?>
```

This code will only work if the answer belongs to the currently logged in user. The `editor()` function of the AJAX helper is passed two parameters. The first is the id of the DOM element that will be replaced by the inline editor. You will notice we added a unique id attribute to each `<dd>` tag that holds an answer. This id is passed as the first parameter. The second parameter is an array that contains the controller action that will save the edited data. The third parameter is used to pass extra options. We pass only one option named `callback`. This points to JavaScript code that will be executed before data is sent via the AJAX call. Normally, the `editor()` function sends the edited data in a variable named `value`. But this is not included in `$this->data` variable once in the server side. POST data is only included in `$this->data` if the name of the variable passed is in this format: `data[ModeName][fieldname]`. We use the `callback` option to change the name of the variable passed to `data[Answer][answer]`, so that it is included in `$this->data`.

Next, we create the `edit_answer` action in the `Questions` controller. It accepts the AJAX request made by the AJAX helper function in the previous step. What this does is that it saves the edited data into the database, and sends it back to browser.

Summary

In this chapter, we saw the usage of the JavaScript and the AJAX helpers. We started this chapter by showing how to add JavaScript to Cake views and layouts. We saw the use of `<?php e($scripts_for_layout); ?>` to add JavaScript links to the layout. We also saw the use `$javascript->link())` to link JavaScript files in the views.

We then moved into the usage of the AJAX helper. We found out that the AJAX helper in CakePHP depends on the Prototype and Scriptaculous Javascript Libraries. We first created an AJAX link, using `$ajax->link()`, that retrieved data from the server and populated a DOM element. We saw how easy it is to add AJAX AutoComplete(`$ajax->autocomplete()`) that retrieved matching data from the database. Next, we saw how to submit a form through an AJAX call (`$ajax->submit()`). We ended the chapter by creating an AJAX Inline Editor using `$ajax->editor()`.

12

Quickwall: Making It Better

During the last three chapters, we have slowly developed Quickwall into a small but working web application. In chapter 9, we built the basics of the application. In chapter 10, we saw how to integrate authentication to it. And in chapter 11, we saw the use of the AJAX helper to make our application more interactive.

In this last chapter, we will continue the evolution of Quickwall, and yet again add more features to it. And in the process, we will see many more features of CakePHP that can make the life of web developers much easier.

In this chapter, we will see how to do the following stuff with CakePHP:

- Making dates more human readable
- Make a user page in Quickwall
- Integrating the user page with the search page
- Adding pagination using CakePHP
- Adding RSS Feeds to our application.

Making Dates More Readable

If you remember, we have fields in our database tables called `created` and `modified`. CakePHP automatically saves the time when a row has been inserted to `created`. Similarly, it saves the time when a row has been changed in the `modified` field. But, we have not really used these two fields. In this section, we will use the `created` field to show the time, so that the users know when a question or answer has been posted. We will also show the use of the Time Helper that is a default helper present in CakePHP. The Time Helper has many different functions that help to show the time in a nicely presented format.

Time for Action

1. Add the Time helper to the App controller:

```php
<?php
class AppController extends Controller {

    . . .
    var $helpers = array('Html', 'Form', 'Javascript',
                                        'Ajax', 'Time');

    function beforeFilter(){

        . . .
    }

    function isAuthorized() {
      return true;
      }
}
?>
```

2. In the element `question_list.ctp`, add the following lines to show a well formatted date:

```php
<dl>
<?php foreach ($questions as $question): ?>
    <dt>
       <span><?php e($question['User']['username']); ?></span>
    </dt>
    <dd>
       <?php e($html->link($question['Question']['question'].'?',
           array('controller' => 'questions', 'action' => 'show',
                              $question['Question']['id']))); ?>
       <?php e($time->niceShort($question['Question']
                                        ['created'])) ?>
       <?php
          if(!$question['Question']['answer_count'])
              . . .
       ?>
    </dd>
<?php endforeach; ?>
</dl>
```

3. To add the time when an answer was given, add the following line to view of the `show()` action:

```php
<?php  e($form->error('Answer.answer', null, array('class'
                                        => 'message'))); ?>

<h2><?php e($question['Question']['question']) ?>?</h2>
```

```
<div id="questioner"><div><span><?php e($question['User']
                                ['username']) ?></span></div></div>
<?php if($loggedIn): ?>
   ...
<?php endif; ?>
<?php if(empty($question['Answer'])): ?>
   ...
<?php else: ?>
   <dl>
   <?php foreach($question['Answer'] as $answer) : ?>
      <dt><span><?php e($answer['User']['username']); ?>
                                </span></dt>
      <dd>
         <span id='answer_<?php e($answer['id']) ?>'>
                        <?php e($answer['answer']); ?></span>
         <?php e($time->niceShort($answer['modified'])) ?>
      </dd>
      <?php if(!empty($loggedIn) && $answer['user_id']
                                      == $loggedIn): ?>
         ...
      <?php endif; ?>
   <?php endforeach; ?>
   </dl>
<?php endif; ?>
```

4. To make sure that the questions are shown in order, add the following lines in the home() action of the questions controller:

```
<?php
class QuestionsController extends AppController {

   ...

   function home() {

      ...

      this->Question->unbindModel(
         array('hasMany' => array('Answer'))
      );
      $this->set('questions', $this->Question->find('all',
               array('order' => 'Question.created DESC')));
}

   ...

}
?>
```

5. Do the same for the user questions, add the following code to the user_questions() action of the Question controller:

```php
<?php
class QuestionsController extends AppController {

    ...
    function user_questions($user_id = null) {
        $this->layout = 'ajax';
        Configure::write('debug', '0');

        ...
        $this->Question->unbindModel(
            array('hasMany' => array('Answer'))
        );
        $this->set('questions', $this->Question->find('all',
            array('conditions' => array('Question.user_id'
            => $user_id), 'order' => 'Question.created DESC')));
    }
    ...
}
?>
```

6. Now, if you point your browser to the homepage (http://localhost/ quickwall/), we should be able to see the data and time when the questions were asked, in a nice format:

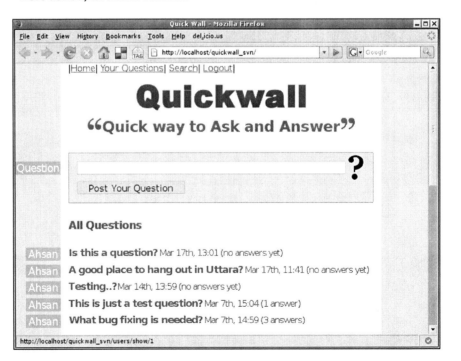

What Just Happened?

We just saw a simple usage of the Time Helper. Like most things in CakePHP, formatting time in a human readable format is not really very hard to do. Now, let us understand in more details what have we accomplished in the above *Time for Action*.

We started by adding the Time Helper to our App controller. Adding the Time Helper here has the advantage that we can use it in all the views of our application. Though we will not be using it in all the views, adding it in the App Controller is a good idea, since the Time Helper is used very frequently.

In the next step, we changed the element `question_list.ctp`. This element is used to show the lists of questions. To show the time when a question has been posted, we use the function `$time->niceShort()` of the Time Helper. This function takes the raw time as a parameter and formats the time in a human readable format. There are some more functions in the Time Helper that can be used to format time in different formats. To check out the other functions in the Time Helper, we can check the source of the helper which can be found in `/cake/libs/view/helpers/time.php`.

Next, we do the same thing for the answers of the questions. In the view file of the `show()` action of the `Questions` controller, we again use the `$time->niceShort()` function of the Time Helper, to format the time when an answer has been last modified.

In Step 4 and 5, we made sure that the questions are shown in a descending order depending on the time they have been posted. We achieved this by mentioning the order in the `find()` method of the `Question` model, which is used to get the questions from the database. The code `$this->Question->find('all', array('order' => 'Question.created DESC'))` tells the `find()` method to return an array of questions that are ordered in descending order in respect to the created field.

Creating a User Page

In this section, we will create a user page that will be showing the questions posted by a particular user. In addition to that, the page will also contain information about the user such as the number of questions posted by the user, the number of answers given, and the user's joining date. Lastly, we will be adding a link so that the user can easily check their own page.

Time for Action

1. First, lets add an action to the `Users` controller, named `show()`, for the user page. Add the following code to it:

```php
<?php
class UsersController extends AppController {
    var $name = 'Users';
    var $components = array('Email');
    function signup(){
        ...
    }

    ...

    function show($id = null) {
        if (!$id) {
            $this->Session->setFlash('Invalid User.');
            $this->redirect(array('controller' => 'questions',
                                    'action'=>'home'));
        }
        $this->User->recursive = 2;
        $this->set('user', $this->User->find(array('User.id'
                => $id), array('id', 'username', 'created')));

        $this->User->Answer->recursive = -1;
        $this->set('answer_count', $this->User->
            Answer->find('count', array('conditions'
            => array('Answer.user_id' => $id))));
    }
}
?>
```

2. Next, let's add the view file for the new action. In the directory `/views/users`, create a new file named `show.ctp`. Add the following code to it:

```php
<h2><?php e($user['User']['username']) ?></h2>
<div id="questioner"><div><span>Name</span></div></div>
<dl>
    <dt><span>Joined On</span></dt>
    <dd><?php e($time->niceShort($user['User']['created'])) ?></dd>
    <dt><span>Asked</span></dt>
    <dd><?php e(count($user['Question'])) ?> questions</dd>
    <dt><span>Answered</span></dt>
    <dd><?php e($answer_count) ?> answers</dd>
</dl>
<h2><?php e($user['User']['username']) ?>'s Questions</h2>
<?php if(empty($user['Question'])): ?>
    <p class="no_answer">No Questions yet asked by this user</p>
<?php else: ?>
    <dl>
```

```php
<?php foreach ($user['Question'] as $question): ?>
  <dt>
    <span><?php e($user['User']['username']); ?></span>
  </dt>
  <dd>
    <?php e($html->link($question['question'].'?',
          array('controller' => 'questions', 'action'
          => 'show', $question['id']))); ?>
    <?php e($time->niceShort($question['created'])) ?>
    <?php
      $answer_count = count($question['Answer']);
      if(!$answer_count)
        e("(no answers yet)");
      else if($answer_count == 1)
        e("(1 answer)");
      else
        e("(".$answer_count." answers)");
    ?>
  </dd>
<?php endforeach; ?>
</dl>
<?php endif; ?>
```

3. Next, let's add a link to this page, so that a logged in user can see their own page:

```php
<!DOCTYPE html PUBLIC "-//W3C//DTD XHTML 1.0 Strict//EN"
          "http://www.w3.org/TR/xhtml1/DTD/xhtml1-strict.dtd">
<html xmlns="http://www.w3.org/1999/xhtml" xml:lang="en"
                                           lang="en">
<head>
  ...
</head>
<body>
  <div id="content">
    <div id="user_menu">
      |<?php e($html->link('Home', '/')); ?>|
      <?php if($loggedIn): ?>
        <?php e($html->link('Your Questions',
          array('controller' => 'users', 'action' => 'show',
          $loggedIn))); ?>|
        <?php e($html->link('Search', array('controller' =>
          'questions', 'action' => 'search'))); ?>|
        <?php e($html->link('Logout', array('controller' =>
          'users', 'action' => 'logout'))); ?>|
      <?php else: ?>
        <?php e($html->link('Sign Up', array('controller' =>
          'users', 'action' => 'signup'))); ?>|
        <?php e($html->link('Login', array('controller' =>
          'users', 'action' => 'login'))); ?>|
```

```
            <?php endif; ?>
        </div>

        ...
    </div>
</body>
</html>
```

4. To make sure no one can view these pages without logging in, we add the following code to `App` controller:

```php
<?php
class AppController extends Controller {

    ...

    function beforeFilter(){

        ...
        $this->Auth->allow('signup', 'confirm', 'home', 'show');
        if($this->name == 'Users') $this->Auth->deny('show');
        ...
    }

    ...

}
?>
```

5. Now, if we log in and go to the homepage, and click on the link **Your Questions**, we will get to see the user page:

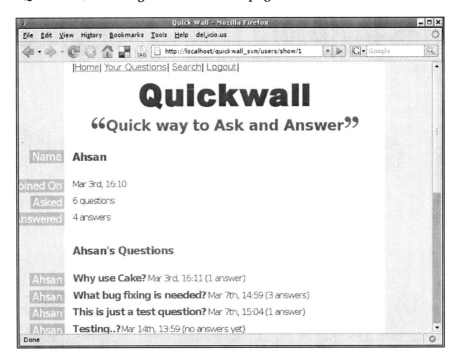

What Just Happened?

In step 1, we added an action to the Users Controller named show(). This is the action of the user page that we created. The action accepts a parameter named $id.

$id should be a valid user id. If the $id parameter is not present, it will not be possible to tell which user page needs to be shown, and this it will be redirected to the homepage. In the next line, we use the find() method of the User model to fetch the user info, and send it to the view using in the set() method of the Users controller. Also note, that in the find() method, the second argument we passed is an array that indicates the fields the query should return. We are also interested to know the number of answers the user has given. For that, we will need to use the Answers model. Since the Users model is the only model that is accessible in the Users controller by default, we will need to instantiate the Answer model, and call its find() method to get the number of answers given by the user. This value is passed to the view in the variable $answer_count.

In step 2, we create the view for the user page. In the view, we print the name of the user, his joining date, the number of questions he posted, the number of answers he gave, and a list of all the questions posted by the user. Also, note the use of the Time Helper for showing dates.

Next, we add a link to the menu in the layout, so that the user can easily access his page. This link will only be visible if the user is logged in.

In the next step, we made sure that the user page cannot be accessed without proper authentication. This means that only users who are logged in, can access the page. By, default, all actions are not accessible in the Authentication component. By calling the Auth Component's allow() function, we can allow actions to be accessed without authentication. The problem here is that both the Questions controller and the Users Controller have actions named show(). The show() action of the Questions controller is allowed to be accessed without authentication. Since the allow() function of the Auth component takes action names only, the show() actions of both the controllers are accessible without authentication. To make sure that the show() action of the Users controller is not accessible without authentication, we first check whether the current controller is the Users controller. This is done by checking the property $name of the controller. The $name property stores the name of the controller. If the controller name is Users, we call the deny() function of the Auth component to deny access to the action if the user is not authenticated.

Linking the Search Page to the User Page

In this section, we will link the user page that we just created, to the search page. When a user name is selected in the search page, we will redirect the page to the page of that user. To do this, we will need to undo some of the stuff that we did in the last chapter.

Time for Action

1. To link the user page to the search page, let us first remove the two links we created in the search page. To do so, go to the view (/views/questions/search.ctp), and remove the two links we created there.

2. Next, remove the link to the JavaScript file search.js that we had in this view. We will not be needing it anymore.

3. We had the form in this view hidden by default. We do not want to hide it anymore. So remove the attribute for hiding the form.

4. Now replace the AJAX submit we had in this view, with a normal submit button.

5. Redefine form action and method for the form. Our search.ctp should look like this now:

```
<form id="user_search_form" method="POST" action="
        <?php e($html->url(array('controller' => 'questions',
        'action' => 'search'))) ?>">
    <fieldset>
        <label for="UserUsername" class="questionlabel"><span>
                Username</span></label>
        <?php echo $ajax->autoComplete('User.username',
                array('controller' => 'users', 'action' =>
                'show_usernames'), array('class' => 'fullwidth'))?>
        <?php e($form->submit('Search', array('div' => false,
                                'class' => 'submitbutton'))); ?>
    </fieldset>
</form>
<div id="questionList"></div>
```

6. Next, add the following code to the search action of the Questions controller:

```
<?php
class QuestionsController extends AppController {

    ...

    function search() {
        if($this->data) {
            if($this->data['User']['username']) {
                $user = $this->Question->User->findByUsername
                                ($this->data['User']['username']);
```

```
            if(isset($user['User']['id'])){
                $user_id = $user['User']['id'];
            } else {
                $user_id = null;
            }
        } else {
            $user_id = $this->Auth->user('id');
        }
        $this->redirect(array('controller' => 'users', 'action'
                                        => 'show', $user_id));
        }
    }
    ...
}
?>
```

What Just Happened?

In this section, we linked the search page to the user page. After removing some of the stuff that we added in the last chapter, we populated the `search()` action of the `Questions` controller with code that will do this for us. If no data has been submitted to the `search()` action, it will just render the view and show the search page. When a user selects a user name from the search result, and submits the page, the POST data is submitted back to the `search()` action. It instantiates the User mode, and checks whether such a user exists. If so, the id of this user is collected through the `User` model and the page is redirected to the user page of that user.

Adding Pagination

As we already know, the homepage of Quickwall shows all the questions that have been posted. This is a good thing, but what will happen when there will be many more questions? All the questions will be shown in the page, and as a result the page might be a big one! Also, it is not a good idea in terms of performance. One solution may be user paginations—so that all the questions are not shown together in a page, but divided into many pages.

Implementing pagination using CakePHP can be ridiculously easy. It is a default functionality in version 1.2.

Time for Action

1. In the `Questions` controller, add the following variable:

```php
<?php
class QuestionsController extends AppController {

    var $name = 'Questions';
    var $paginate = array('limit' => 5, 'page' => 1, 'order' =>
                            array('Question.created'=>'desc'));

    ...

}
?>
```

2. In the home action of the `Questions` controller, change the following line:

```php
<?php
class QuestionsController extends AppController {

    ...

    function home() {
        if (!empty($this->data) && $this->Auth->user('id')) {
            $this->data['Question']['user_id'] =
                                        $this->Auth->user('id');
            $this->Question->create();
            if ($this->Question->save($this->data)) {
                $this->Session->setFlash('Your Question has
                                            been added');
                $this->redirect(array('action'=>'home'), null, true);
            } else {
                $this->Session->setFlash('The Question could not be
                                            saved. Please, try again.');
            }
        }

        $this->Question->recursive = 1;$this->set('questions',
                                $this->paginate('Question'));
    }

    ...

}
?>
```

3. Add the following lines to the view of the `home()` action:

```php
<?php e($javascript->link('home', false)); ?>

...

<h2>All Questions</h2>
```

```
<?php if(empty($questions)): ?>
    ...
<?php else: ?>
    <?php e($this->renderElement('question_list')); ?>
    <?php e($paginator->prev()); ?>
    <?php e($paginator->numbers()); ?>
    <?php e($paginator->next()); ?>
<?php endif; ?>
```

4. If we check the homepage now, and we have more than five questions, we
   will see the cool pagination links:

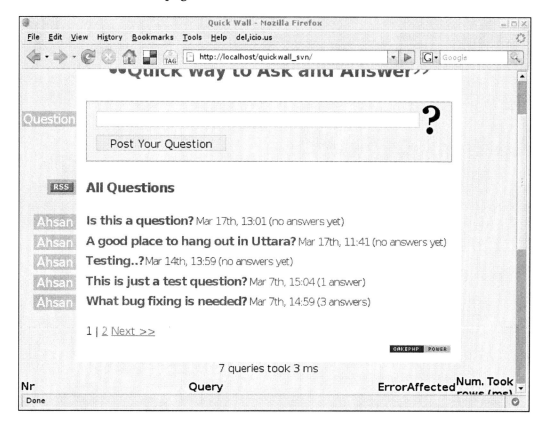

What Just Happened?

To use pagination, the first thing that we need to do is to add the variable $paginate
in the controller. This variable is assigned an array that contains arguments that
are needed to be passed to the Pagination component. In this case, we passed the
arguments limit, page, and order. The limit argument is used to indicate the
number of rows that will be shown in a page. The page argument indicates the page
number that should be the default page. And order indicates the ordering of the rows.

In the next step, we change the line that sends the questions to the views, using the `set()` method. Instead of using the model's `find()` method, we used `$this->paginate('Question')`. The pagination component sends the appropriate rows to the views, depending on the page viewed.

Pagination in CakePHP consists of a component and a helper. As you have noticed, we do not need to manually include them as it is included by default.

In the next step, we change the view of the `home()` action, to include the pagination links. Pagination in CakePHP provides different functions to include pagination links like the next button, previous button, current page etc. The `$paginator->prev()` function creates a link that will take the user to the previous page. Similarly, the `$paginator->next()` function creates a link to the next page. The `$paginator->numbers()` function creates a list of page numbers that also act as links.

As we say, using pagination in CakePHP is very simple indeed. Just think how much effort it would take if we wanted to create the same functionality using raw PHP!

Adding RSS Feeds

In this section, we will be adding a feature that will enable Quickwall users to subscribe to RSS Feeds. We will be creating a RSS link so that users can subscribe to Quickwall. Whenever a new question has been posted, users can see that using their RSS readers. And, yes, you guessed it right, implementing RSS feeds using CakePHP is very easy indeed.

Time for Action

1. In the file `routes.php` found in `/app/config`, add the following line at the end of the file:

    ```php
    <?php

        . . .

        Router::parseExtensions();

    ?>
    ```

2. Next, add the Request Handler component in the `App` controller:

    ```php
    <?php
    class AppController extends Controller {

        var $components = array('Auth', 'Cookie', 'RequestHandler');

    }
    ?>
    ```

3. In the directory `/app/views/questions`, add a new directory called `rss`.

4. In the newly created folder, add a new file named `home.ctp`. Add the following code to it:

```php
<?php
echo $rss->items($questions, 'transformRSS');
function transformRSS($question) {
                return array(
                        'title' => $question['Question']
                                                ['question']."?",
                        'link' => array('action' => 'show',
                                $question['Question']['id']),
                        'guid' => array('action' => 'show',
                                $question['Question']['id']),
                        'description' => $question['User']
                         ['username'].' asked a new question at
                         Quickwall: '.$question['Question']
                         ['question'].'?',
                        'author' => $question['User']
                                                ['username'],
                        'pubDate' => $question['Question']
                                                ['created']
                );
}
?>
```

5. Next, in the home action of the `Questions` controller, add the following line:

```php
<?php
class QuestionsController extends AppController {

    ...

    function home() {

        ...

        $this->set('questions', $this->paginate('Question'));

        $this->set('channel', array('title' => 'Quickwall'));
    }

    ...

}
?>
```

6. Add the image file for RSS, the `img` directory in `/app/webroot/img`. Name the image file `rss.gif`.

7. Lastly, in the view of the `home()` action, add a link for the RSS, as shown below:

```php
<?php e($javascript->link('home', false)); ?>

<?php e($javascript->link('home', false)); ?>

<?php  e($form->error('Question.question', null, array('class'
                                            => 'message'))); ?>

<?php if($loggedIn): ?>
    <?php e($form->create('Question', array('action'
                                        => 'home'))); ?>
        <fieldset>
            <label for="QuestionQuestion" class="questionlabel">
                            <span>Your Question</span></label>
            <?php e($form->text('question', array('class'
                    => 'fullwidth'))); ?><span class="big">?</span>
            <!-- Input for Questioner removed -->
            <?php e($form->submit('Post Your Question', array('div'
                    => false, 'class' => 'submitbutton'))); ?>
        </fieldset>
    <?php e($form->end()); ?>
<?php else: ?>
    <p>To post a question, please login or signup.</p>
<?php endif; ?>
<h2>All Questions</h2>
<div id="questioner">
    <div>
        <span>
            <?php e($html->link($html->image('rss.gif', array('alt'
                    => 'RSS')), array('action' => 'home.rss'), null,
                    false, false)); ?>
        </span>
    </div>
</div>
<?php if(empty($questions)): ?>
    ...
<?php endif; ?>
```

We will see the new RSS link in the homepage:

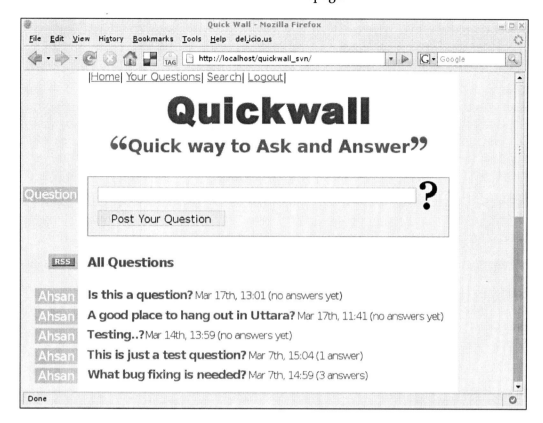

What Just Happened?

The first thing that we did was, add the line `Router::parseExtensions()` in the file `routes.php`. By adding this line, we indicate Cake to be extension sensitive to the incoming requests. So, the request `http://localhost/quickwall/questions/home` and `http://localhost/quickwall/questions/home.rss` are treated differently.

Next, we add the `RequestHandler` component to our `App` controller. The Request Handler component helps to obtain additional information about the HTTP requests that are made. It is used by the RSS helper (that is loaded automatically) to detect that an RSS feed is requested. When used in conjunction with `Router::parseExtension()`, `RequestHandler` will automatically switch the layout and view files to those that match the requested type.

In step 3, we created a new directory in `app/views/questions`. When a request is made to a controller action with an extension, Cake checks if a directory with the same name as the extension exists. If so, view files are rendered from that directory. In this case, our extension is `.rss`, so we created a directory named `rss`. We will store the view files for rss requests inside this directory.

Next, we create the view file for the `home()` action, if an rss request is made. The line `echo $rss->items($questions, 'transformRSS');` uses the `items()` function of the RSS Helper, and passes the `$questions` array to it. The second argument is the name of the function that is used to map the data array to the RSS elements. We declare the mapping function `transformRSS()` in the view file. In this function, we map the RSS elements like title, link, description etc. to the data passed to the view.

In the next step, we just make a single line change to the controller action. We send a variable named `channel` and assign in an array. The array contains a single element named `title`. This is used to set the title of the RSS channel.

In step 6, we add an image file to the directory `/app/webroot/img`, for the RSS link.

Lastly, in step 7, we use the image added in the last step to create a link in the view file of the `home()` action. This link points to the `home()` action of the `Questions` controller, but with a `.rss` extension. So, when this link is accessed, it returns a RSS document.

Summary

This chapter continued the enhancement to Quickwall that we saw through out this section. We started this chapter by showing how to use the Time Helper of CakePHP. Using the Time Helper, we presented nicely formatted dates.

Next, we moved to making a User page. The user page showed information about a particular user, along with all the questions that the user posted. From technical aspect, we saw how we can make the Auth Component differentiate between same action names from different controllers. We went on to link the user page with the search page.

Next, we saw the usage of pagination, and saw how easy it is to use the built-in pagination feature in CakePHP. We used it to paginate the questions in the homepage.

We ended the chapter by showing how to implement RSS Feed for Quickwall. Like almost everything in Cake, implementing RSS Feed was a piece of cake!

Index

Thank you for buying
CakePHP Application Development

Packt Open Source Project Royalties

When we sell a book written on an Open Source project, we pay a royalty directly to that project. Therefore by purchasing CakePHP Application Development, Packt will have given some of the money received to the CakePHP Project.

In the long term, we see ourselves and you—customers and readers of our books—as part of the Open Source ecosystem, providing sustainable revenue for the projects we publish on. Our aim at Packt is to establish publishing royalties as an essential part of the service and support a business model that sustains Open Source.

If you're working with an Open Source project that you would like us to publish on, and subsequently pay royalties to, please get in touch with us.

Writing for Packt

We welcome all inquiries from people who are interested in authoring. Book proposals should be sent to authors@packtpub.com. If your book idea is still at an early stage and you would like to discuss it first before writing a formal book proposal, contact us; one of our commissioning editors will get in touch with you.

We're not just looking for published authors; if you have strong technical skills but no writing experience, our experienced editors can help you develop a writing career, or simply get some additional reward for your expertise.

About Packt Publishing

Packt, pronounced 'packed', published its first book "Mastering phpMyAdmin for Effective MySQL Management" in April 2004 and subsequently continued to specialize in publishing highly focused books on specific technologies and solutions.

Our books and publications share the experiences of your fellow IT professionals in adapting and customizing today's systems, applications, and frameworks. Our solution-based books give you the knowledge and power to customize the software and technologies you're using to get the job done. Packt books are more specific and less general than the IT books you have seen in the past. Our unique business model allows us to bring you more focused information, giving you more of what you need to know, and less of what you don't.

Packt is a modern, yet unique publishing company, which focuses on producing quality, cutting-edge books for communities of developers, administrators, and newbies alike. For more information, please visit our website: www.PacktPub.com.

PACKT
PUBLISHING

Building powerful and robust websites with
Drupal 6

Build your own professional blog, forum, portal or community
website with Drupal 6

David Mercer

PACKT

Building Powerful and Robust Websites with Drupal 6

ISBN: 978-1-847192-97-4   Paperback: 330 pages

Build your own professional blog, forum, portal or
community website with Drupal 6

1. Set up, configure, and deploy Drupal 6

2. Harness Drupal's world-class Content
   Management System

3. Design and implement your website's look
   and feel

4. Easily add exciting and powerful features

5. Promote, manage, and maintain your live
   website

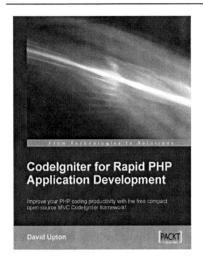

From Technologies to Solutions

**CodeIgniter for Rapid PHP
Application Development**

Improve your PHP coding productivity with the free compact
open source MVC CodeIgniter framework!

David Upton

PACKT

CodeIgniter for Rapid PHP Application Development

ISBN: 978-1-847191-74-8   Paperback: 220 pages

Improve your PHP coding productivity with the free
compact open-source MVC CodeIgniter framework!

1. Clear, structured tutorial on working with
   CodeIgniter

2. Careful explanation of the basic concepts of
   CodeIgniter and its MVC architecture

3. Using CodeIgniter with databases, HTML
   forms, files, images, sessions, and email

4. Building a dynamic website quickly and easily
   using CodeIgniter's prepared code

Please check **www.PacktPub.com** for information on our titles

PHP 5 CMS Framework Development

ISBN: 978-1-847193-57-5   Paperback: 328 pages

Expert insight and practical guidance to creating an efficient, flexible, and robust framework for a PHP 5-based content management system

1. Learn how to design, build, and implement a complete CMS framework for your custom requirements

2. Implement a solid architecture with object orientation, MVC

3. Build an infrastructure for custom menus, modules, components, sessions, user tracking, and more

4. Written by a seasoned developer of CMS applications

Mastering Joomla! 1.5 Extension and Framework Development

ISBN: 978-1-847192-82-0   Paperback: 380 pages

The Professional Guide to Programming Joomla!

1. In-depth guide to programming Joomla!

2. Design and build secure and robust components, modules and plugins

3. Includes a comprehensive reference to the major areas of the Joomla! framework

Please check **www.PacktPub.com** for information on our titles

Printed in the United States
141638LV00006B/33/P